ReFocus: The Films of Mary Harron

ReFocus: The American Directors Series

Series Editors: Robert Singer, Frances Smith, and Gary D. Rhodes

Editorial Board: Kelly Basilio, Donna Campbell, Claire Perkins, Christopher Sharrett, and Yannis Tzioumakis

ReFocus is a series of contemporary methodological and theoretical approaches to the interdisciplinary analyses and interpretations of neglected American directors, from the once-famous to the ignored, in direct relationship to American culture—its myths, values, and historical precepts.

Titles in the series include:

ReFocus: The Films of Preston Sturges
Edited by Jeff Jaeckle and Sarah Kozloff

ReFocus: The Films of Delmer Daves
Edited by Matthew Carter and Andrew Nelson

ReFocus: The Films of Amy Heckerling
Edited by Frances Smith and Timothy Shary

ReFocus: The Films of Budd Boetticher
Edited by Gary D. Rhodes and Robert Singer

ReFocus: The Films of Kelly Reichardt
E. Dawn Hall

ReFocus: The Films of William Castle
Edited by Murray Leeder

ReFocus: The Films of Barbara Kopple
Edited by Jeff Jaeckle and Susan Ryan

ReFocus: The Films of Elaine May
Edited by Alexandra Heller-Nicholas and Dean Brandum

ReFocus: The Films of Spike Jonze
Edited by Kim Wilkins and Wyatt Moss-Wellington

ReFocus: The Films of Paul Schrader
Edited by Michelle E. Moore and Brian Brems

ReFocus: The Films of John Hughes
Edited by Timothy Shary and Frances Smith

ReFocus: The Films of Doris Wishman
Edited by Alicia Kozma and Finley Freibert

ReFocus: The Films of Albert Brooks
Edited by Christian B. Long

ReFocus: The Films of William Friedkin
Steve Choe

ReFocus: The Later Films and Legacy of Robert Altman
Edited by Lisa Dombrowski and Justin Wyatt

ReFocus: The Films of Mary Harron
Edited by Kyle Barrett

edinburghuniversitypress.com/series/refoc

ReFocus:
The Films of Mary Harron

Edited by Kyle Barrett

EDINBURGH
University Press

Edinburgh University Press is one of the leading university presses in the UK. We publish academic books and journals in our selected subject areas across the humanities and social sciences, combining cutting-edge scholarship with high editorial and production values to produce academic works of lasting importance. For more information visit our website: edinburghuniversitypress.com

© editorial matter and organisation Kyle Barrett, 2022, 2023
© the chapters their several authors, 2022, 2023

Edinburgh University Press Ltd
The Tun—Holyrood Road
12 (2f) Jackson's Entry
Edinburgh EH8 8PJ

First published in hardback by Edinburgh University Press 2022

Typeset in 11/13 Ehrhardt MT by
IDSUK (DataConnection) Ltd

A CIP record for this book is available from the British Library

ISBN 978 1 4744 9441 0 (hardback)
ISBN 978 1 4744 9442 7 (paperback)
ISBN 978 1 4744 9443 4 (webready PDF)
ISBN 978 1 4744 9444 1 (epub)

The right of Kyle Barrett to be identified as editor of this work has been asserted in accordance with the Copyright, Designs and Patents Act 1988 and the Copyright and Related Rights Regulations 2003 (SI No. 2498).

Contents

List of Figures — vii
Acknowledgments — ix
Notes on Contributors — x

Introduction — 1
Kyle Barrett

Part I Biopics

1. *I Shot Andy Warhol*: Fame, Notoriety, and Mary Harron's Anti-biopics — 17
   Janice Loreck
2. On the Other Side of the Icon: Making Images and Restaging Celebrity Spectacle in *Anna Nicole* — 34
   Kimberly Lamm

Part II Feature Films and Production Contexts

3. Dream of the '90s: Mary Harron in Indiewood — 55
   Kyle Barrett
4. "I Like to Dissect Girls": Mary Harron's *American Psycho* as Gendered Metafiction — 74
   Coco d'Hont
5. "And Then I Met Lucy": Perfection, Same-sex Desire, and Social Control in Mary Harron's *The Moth Diaries* — 89
   Brittany Caroline Speller
6. Charismatic Breadwinner Killer: Gender Power Relations in *Charlie Says* — 105
   Gemma Piercy-Cameron

Part III Television and Short Film Production

7   Death to Disposal: Echoes of *American Psycho* in "The Rainbow
    of Her Reasons" (*Six Feet Under*)   125
    Gareth Schott
8   Sartorial Interventions: When Fashion and Film Collide   140
    Elena Caoduro

Filmography   157
Bibliography   159
Index   172

Figures

I.1	Mary Harron behind the scenes on *American Psycho*	6
I.2	Ernessa makes her presence known in *The Moth Diaries*	8
1.1	Valerie Solanas venting over her play	21
1.2	"Read my manifesto!" Solanas questioned as to why she shot Andy Warhol	23
1.3	Solanas in a psychiatric hospital	28
2.1	Anna Nicole introduces her home town	36
2.2	Anna Nicole's inspiration: Marilyn Monroe	42
2.3	Nicole gets images taken to attract *Playboy* magazine	47
3.1	Patrick Bateman pursues another victim	66
3.2	Bettie Page asking to be photographed at the beach	70
4.1	Opening credits reveal the highly expensive dish made for Patrick Bateman and friends	79
4.2	Patrick Bateman regales Paul Allen about Huey Lewis and the News before killing him	83
5.1	Lucy is drawn to Ernessa	91
5.2	Ernessa's "Other" gaze	92
5.3	Rebecca becomes more traumatized by the decay of her relationship with Lucy and her repression	101
6.1	A different path (tiny choice) where Leslie left the ranch with her biker rescuer	109
6.2	Leslie in charge of the conversation	113
6.3	Charles Manson as beta male	119
7.1	Patrick Bateman's morning routine	128

7.2	Claire Fisher describes the confinement of pantyhose through a musical number	136
8.1	Grace in Nancy Montgomery's pink dress after her murder	143
8.2	The couple meet for the first time in *Armani*	149
8.3	The couple meet again years on	152

Acknowledgments

This book would not be possible without the support and guidance of the *ReFocus* series editors Robert Singer, Gary Rhodes, and Frances Smith. Thank you for this amazing opportunity. I am indebted to Paula Blair for her help and wisdom to craft this collection in its earliest stages. My family have been nothing but supportive and encouraging throughout the whole process, so thank you Mum, Dad, Lee, Jen, and Forrest. Lilly, thanks for listening to my enthusiastic rants and your encouragement! My colleagues at the University of Waikato have been generous with their advice, so a massive thank you to Gareth Schott, Vanessa McLean, Lisa Perrott, Ann Hardy, Dean Ballinger, Wairehu Grant, Oliver Stewart, and Isabelle Delmotte. I would also like to express my gratitude to Bill Cochrane and Bevin Yeatman. Finally, I would like to say a huge thank you to all the authors in this book who have trusted me with their excellent work. It goes without saying that without their contributions we would not have this stellar collection on one of the best filmmakers working today.

Notes on Contributors

Kyle Barrett is a lecturer and filmmaker in Screen and Media Studies at the University of Waikato (NZ). His research focuses on digital technologies and its impact on creative practice. He also explores gender representation in a variety of media contexts. He has been published in *Approaching Twin Peaks: Critical Essays on the Original Series* (McFarland), *Iperstoria: Journal of American and English Studies*, *MeCCSA Journal*, *AMES: Media Education Journal*, *Directory of World Cinema: Scotland* (Intellect) and *European Journal of Communication*.

Elena Caoduro is lecturer in Media Arts at the University of Bedfordshire (UK) where she teaches film and media studies. She is the co-chair of the SCMS Transnational Cinemas SIG and her research on film and terrorism, globalization, nostalgia, and fashion films has been published in edited collections and journals such as *Alphaville: Journal of Film and Media*, *NECSUS: European Journal of Media Studies* and *CS: Journal of Media, Performing Arts and Cultural Studies*.

Coco d'Hont is an independent scholar who researches contemporary American fiction and popular culture. She holds a PhD from the University of East Anglia (UK). Recent projects include explorations of Marilyn Manson, published in the *European Journal of American Studies*, and Chuck Palahniuk's post-9/11 fiction.

Kimberly Lamm is Associate Professor of Gender, Sexuality, and Feminist Studies at Duke University (USA). She is the author of *Addressing the Other Woman: Textual Correspondences in Feminist Art and Writing*.

Janice Loreck is a teaching associate and researcher in Screen Arts at Curtin University in Perth, Australia. She is the author of *Violent Women in Contemporary Cinema* (Palgrave Macmillan) and Festival Coordinator for the Melbourne Women in Film Festival (MWFF).

Gemma Piercy-Cameron is a lecturer in Sociology and Social Policy at the University of Waikato (NZ) and completed her PhD in 2018. Gemma has a background in Labor Studies and an interest in gender at work, particularly the role of gender(s) in front-line service sector labor processes. A qualitative researcher, her PhD was an investigation into the work identity and learning of *baristas* and her current research extends this study to examine how masculinities are embedded into the categorization of *baristas* as skilled professionals.

Gareth Schott is an Associate Professor in Screen and Media Studies at the School of Arts, University of Waikato (NZ). His current research interests are focused on media representation of death and dying in the modern era. He is the author of *Violent Games: Rules, realism, effect* (Bloomsbury Press), and co-author of *Computer Games: Text, narrative and play* (Polity Press). His research has been funded by Royal Society of New Zealand Marsden Grant (NZ), Office of Film and Literature Classification (NZ), Arts and Humanities Research Council (UK), and University for Industry (UK).

Brittany Caroline Speller is completing her PhD in the Literature and Criticism program at Indiana University of Pennsylvania. Her research interests center around issues of gender and sexuality in film with a specific focus on the horror genre. She recently completed her second master's degree, this time in English from Auburn University, Alabama, while she also holds a prior MA in American history.

Introduction

Kyle Barrett

Twenty-first-century blockbuster cinema has been dominated by various superhero franchises. Relatively few of these comic book adaptations have been directed by women. To date, out of twenty-three released films, Marvel has only hired one female filmmaker, and even then, as a co-director for *Captain Marvel* (Walt Disney Studios Motion Pictures, Boden & Fleck, 2019). Subsequently, *Black Widow* (Walt Disney Studios Motion Pictures, Shortland, 2021) is the first film to be directed by a solo female filmmaker in the fifteen years since the Marvel cinematic universe began. DC's small oeuvre of superhero films over the past decade fare only marginally better, with *Wonder Woman*, its sequel *Wonder Woman 1984* (Warner Bros., Jenkins, 2017/2020), and *Birds of Prey* (Warner Bros., Yan, 2020). Katarzyna Paszkiewicz states in her book *Genre, Authorship and Contemporary Women Filmmakers* (2019) that within Hollywood and mainstream cinema, few women "have been able to produce a sufficiently extensive body of work, making it difficult to reflect on their authorship through examination of their 'recognizable style' or 'particular obsessions'."[1] Further to this, in 2021, Chloé Zhao was the second of only two female Academy Award winners for Best Director, for *Nomadland* (Searchlight Pictures, 2020), the first being Kathryn Bigelow for *The Hurt Locker* (Summit Entertainment, 2008) in 2009. According to Frances Smith and Timothy Shary, "the proportion of female directors working in Hollywood on the most successful films remains a lowly seven percent, a figure that has actually *declined* since 1998."[2] However, to contrast this decline in mainstream filmmaking, independent cinema appears to offer more opportunities: "statistics confirm that the number of women in this sector is proportionally higher than those who work in the film industry in Hollywood."[3] Filmmakers such as Kelly Reichardt, Sofia Coppola, Nicole Holofcener, Debra Granik, and Lisa Cholodenko all work at varying degrees of independence from Hollywood studios. Each filmmaker has developed a distinguished career in North American cinema despite, noted earlier by Paszkiewicz, not having an "extensive body of work." In the introduction to *Indie Reframed: Women's Filmmaking and Contemporary American Independent Cinema* (2015), there is recognition of the growth of independent American women filmmakers and that they are "for the first time, making their mark on cinematic storytelling as a very diverse and loosely unified group."[4] The increase of female filmmakers working within independent cinema employ a range of genres, aesthetic styles and diverse subject matter, from Reichardt's examination of radical environmentalism in *Night Moves* (Cinedigm, 2013) to Granik's observation of living off the grid in *Leave No Trace* (Bleecker Street, 2018). These filmmakers have a strong feminist perspective and often create narratives "in which differences of gender, ethnicity, race, class, sexual preference, etc. are key elements."[5] One filmmaker in particular has consistently explored these elements: Mary Harron. This volume in the *ReFocus* series aims to unearth the significance of the themes and practices that have emerged throughout the understudied career of one of the key filmmakers working in contemporary North American cinema. Harron has continuously examined gender, class, patriarchy and male control throughout her work in a variety of perspectives and has utilized a range of genres and experimented with various visual styles. Her filmography, which encompasses feature films, short films, advertisements and television, demands closer attention.

RADICAL OUTSIDERS

Harron was born in Bracebridge, Ontario, Canada in 1952.[6] Part of a creative family, her father, Don Harron, was an actor, comedian, writer, director and journalist, best known for his work with the Canadian Broadcasting Commission (CBC).[7] Harron was raised in London and later educated at Oxford University, receiving a BA in English literature in 1975.[8] Harron settled in New York, becoming part of the 1970s punk scene. She later wrote for *Punk* magazine and became the first person to interview the Sex Pistols for an American publication. Harron returned to London and became a critic for *The Observer*. She found work on *The South Bank Show* (ITV Studios/Sky Arts, 1978–present) and became a researcher for a BBC documentary on Andy Warhol. Harron returned to New York in the 1990s and worked for PBS, where she directed the documentary *The Winds of Change* (1994).

Harron, inspired from her research on the BBC Warhol project, was interested in directing a documentary focusing on Valerie Solanas, a writer infamously known for her assassination attempt on Warhol's life in 1968. Intrigued by Solanas' *SCUM* (Society for Cutting Up Men) *Manifesto*, which vehemently raged against male control and gender inequality, the filmmaker believed it had "a primal kick; it reached a core of anger I didn't know I possessed."[9] Harron struggled to get the documentary produced but met a figure who would become a key collaborator: producer Christine Vachon. Vachon had success with the LGBTQ+ classic *Go Fish* (Samuel Goldwyn Company, Troche, 1994) and established Killer Films in 1995, producing "low-budget, tawdry tales marked with the visual panache of new talent."[10] Vachon was also intrigued by Solanas' life and persuaded Harron to turn the documentary into a feature film.[11] The result was *I Shot Andy Warhol* (Samuel Goldwyn Company, 1996), one of the most subversive, complex feature debuts in US independent cinema. The film would cement Killer Films as a radical independent production company, as Patricia White discusses:

> With its dyke anti-hero, Warhol factory setting, and creative team—straight feminist director Harron; queer co-writer Dan Minahan; cast of indie icons including Lili Taylor, Jared Harris and Martha Plimpton; Ellen Kuras as cinematographer; plus Koffler, Vachon and Kalin—*I Shot Andy Warhol* epitomizes Killer Films' and New Queer Cinema's polymorphous appeal.[12]

Harron's depiction of Solanas (Lili Taylor) excels, according to Dana Heller, "beyond docudrama, lesbian chic and the much-beleaguered genre of feminist revenge narratives which generally portray avenging women as scorned lovers and/or soccer Moms gone postal."[13] The film also established the groundwork for many of Harron's recurring themes and practices, such as working within the biopic genre, blending various visual styles (black-and-white with color cinematography), and a protagonist who is a social outsider. The notion of fame and celebrity would also become part of Harron's oeuvre as well as the self-destructive nature of narcissism. Ken Dancyger observes that whether this makes Harron a satirist of celebrity, or merely a curious observer, the filmmaker is able to "take us into her character's inner need for celebrity and into the pathology generated by the clash of inner need and outer reality."[14] The need for fame and celebrity would later be explored in both *The Notorious Bettie Page* (Picturehouse, 2005) and *Anna Nicole* (Lifetime, 2013). *I Shot Andy Warhol* would also spark controversy, particularly from Factory-familiars, such as Lou Reed, who found the focus on Solanas to be unnerving.[15] However, the film earned Taylor a Special Jury Award at the Sundance Film Festival and Harron was nominated for an Independent Spirit Award.[16]

INDEPENDENT CINEMA

As highlighted at the start of this introduction, independent cinema appears to be ideally suited for filmmakers such as Harron that examine challenging content with complex, morally ambiguous protagonists. Independent filmmaking has been consistently debated as to what constitutes "independence" from mainstream, Hollywood studios. Michael Z. Newman reflects on independent cinema in *Indie: An American Film Culture* (2011) stating:

> The term *independent* has been used in the American film industry since before the establishment of the studio system in the 1910s and 1920s, and has undergone a series of shifts over the decades since then, though it has always referred to production, distribution, and exhibition outside of the Hollywood studios and mainstream theater chains.[17]

A remarkable shift in American independent filmmaking began in the late 1960s and early 1970s. This short era of filmmaking was dubbed the "Hollywood Renaissance" or "New Hollywood," where filmmakers adopted European art film sensibilities "to develop their own version of a new wave cinema."[18] Filmmakers such as Elaine May, Dennis Hopper, Martin Scorsese and Arthur Penn were provided studio support to craft personal, character-driven films with a somewhat abstract visual style. Their aesthetics incorporated jump cuts, filming on location and non-linear narrative structures. Films such as *Easy Rider* (Columbia Pictures, Hopper, 1969), *Taxi Driver* (Columbia Pictures, Scorsese, 1976), and *Bonnie and Clyde* (Warner Bros., Penn, 1967) broke new ground with audiences that were a stark contrast to the more traditional studio-financed films such as *The Sound of Music* (Twentieth Century Fox, Wise, 1965) and *Doctor Doolittle* (Twentieth Century Fox, Fleisher, 1967). The short-lived character-driven film era was soon replaced by B-movie concepts given substantial budgets from filmmakers Steven Spielberg and George Lucas, both with blockbuster hits *Jaws* (Universal Pictures, Spielberg, 1975) and *Star Wars* (Twentieth Century Fox, Lucas, 1977) respectively. The 1980s saw a surge of blockbusters and sequels that were box-office successes, and the personal, experimental films were soon abandoned by the studios after the critical and commercial failure of Michael Cimino's *Heaven's Gate* (United Artists, 1980). It would not be until the 1990s when there was a somewhat return to the personal style of filmmaking which received significant support from studios.

The 1990s saw mini-major studios, such as the Weinstein brothers' Miramax Films, become key producers in American cinema. In comparison to the true independent ethos of Vachon, the Weinsteins' approach was remarkably different (see Chapter Three). Miramax had success by supporting early works of both Steven Soderbergh and Quentin Tarantino. Soderbergh received commercial and critical acclaim for his understated drama *sex, lies, and videotape* (Miramax Films, 1989). Tarantino launched his career with crime drama *Reservoir Dogs* (Miramax Films, 1992), a relationship that would continue until Harvey Weinstein's arrest in 2018 for sexual assault and harassment allegations

(Weinstein was convicted and found guilty in February 2020). While the latter two films were not initial box-office hits, the filmmakers were recognized as *the* new talent in North American cinema.

Major studios, such as Twentieth Century Fox, Universal and Warner Bros., also saw the potential of this new talent and devised their own "independent" subdivisions. The result was coined "Indiewood," a term that Geoff King identifies as "an area in which Hollywood and the independent sector merge or overlap."[19] Indiewood further problematized the notion of independent cinema due to this intersection and studios were able to make "independence into a brand, a familiar idea that evokes in consumers a range of emotional and symbolic associations."[20] In terms of launching careers of new talent, this "branding" was somewhat successful. For the remainder of the 1990s and early 2000s a new generation of filmmakers such as Alexander Payne, Spike Jonze, and Paul Thomas Anderson found critical and commercial acclaim. They all, to varying degrees, paid homage to their New Hollywood predecessors as well as explored similar themes to one another, establishing a "smart cinema" that Jeffrey Sconce perceives "should be seen as a shared set of stylistic, narrative and thematic elements deployed in differing configurations by individual films."[21] While the above filmmakers received acclaim for their studies on complex, often male "loser" protagonists, other independent filmmakers were somewhat overlooked during this period, including Harron.

CHALLENGING THE PATRIARCHY: HARRON AS A FEMINIST FILMMAKER

After *I Shot Andy Warhol,* Harron established a partnership with writer/actor Guinevere Turner, who previously co-wrote and starred in *Go Fish.* Both Harron and Turner embarked on an adaptation of Brett Easton Ellis' infamous 1991 novel *American Psycho* (Lions Gate Films, 2000). The film was criticized as much as the novel for its depiction of violence and its hyper-masculine, misogynistic main character Patrick Bateman, played by the perfectly cast Christian Bale.[22] However, Harron and Turner focused more on the satiric edge of the novel and its attack on yuppie consumer culture, twisting Ellis' misogynistic tome into a feminist horror-satire that "finds humor in the emotional nihilism of these characters."[23] Both the film and the novel's horrific effect is, according to Martin Rogers, "not through the depiction of morally reprehensible acts but through their embodiment in what amounts to a cultural ideal; not by endorsing or displaying sexual, economic, and physical violence but by forcing the reader to identify with it."[24] The film has since received a re-evaluation, with the late film critic Roger Ebert describing it as "the most loathed film at Sundance" to "giving it his thumbs up," and has achieved cult status.[25]

Figure 1.1 Mary Harron behind the scenes on *American Psycho* (2000)

The film is also noted for its tongue-in-cheek approach to the horror genre. Horror maintained its popularity in the 1990s, with self-referential texts such as Wes Craven's *New Nightmare* (New Line Cinema, 1994) and *Scream* (Dimension Films, 1996) revisiting the slasher film with a postmodern twist. Though most of the violence occurs off-screen, *American Psycho* would cite and even incorporate footage of other classic horror films, such as *The Texas Chainsaw Massacre* (Bryanston Distribution Company, Hooper, 1974). *American Psycho* has remained Harron's most popular film, yet it would not compartmentalize her into the horror genre. One of Harron's strengths has been to adopt the structures of numerous genres, both in film and television, with relative ease.

MOONLIGHTING: WORKING IN THE SMALL SCREEN

In between feature film projects, Harron has worked as a director-for-hire for many prestigious television series. Before helming *American Psycho*, Harron directed an episode of the acclaimed television show *Homicide: Life on the Street* (NBC, 1993–1999) as well as the equally praised *Oz* (HBO, 1997–2003). Before embarking on *The Notorious Bettie Page*, Harron directed episodes on *Pasadena* (Fox, 2001), *The L Word* (Showtime, 2004–2009) and *Six Feet Under* (HBO, 2001–2005). Despite the cult of *American Psycho*, and the growth of Indiewood, many filmmakers found themselves with fewer opportunities to develop their own projects and, rather than accept more mainstream feature projects, would seek work elsewhere. Linda Badley, Claire Perkins, and Michele Schreiber comment:

> Many resist the crossover and choose to stay in the independent realm of production, waiting and thus using the lengthy amount of time it takes to secure financing for a film to remain close to their artistic vision. And, others continue to make films independently but move over into the commercial realm by directing for television.[26]

Harron has continuously returned to television throughout her career, most recently with the mini-series *Alias Grace* (CBC, 2017), which was distributed internationally by Netflix. As Schreiber notes, television is a highly collaborative medium and the director is often overlooked in terms of receiving the primary attention, meaning if "credit is often bestowed on a single individual in contemporary television series production, it is generally the writer-showrunner who is often also the show's creator and serves as an executive producer."[27] However, directing television is more common today for established filmmakers, for example David Fincher's involvement with both *House of Cards* (Netflix, 2013–2018) and *Mindhunter* (Netflix, 2017–present). Harron's work for these various series often would have familiar themes found throughout her work. *Alias Grace*, for instance, draws parallels to both *I Shot Andy Warhol* and *The Notorious Bettie Page* through its examination of patriarchy and the male gaze. These episodes should not be discounted as lesser than Harron's feature film work. On the contrary, they reinforce Harron as a filmmaker able to take on the challenge of directing single episodes in television shows that have been ongoing before her arrival and she still maintains her key interests.

STARING AT THE OUTSIDER: PIN-UPS AND VAMPIRES

The Notorious Bettie Page marked Harron's return to the biopic. It also reunited the filmmaker with Vachon and Turner. *The Notorious Bettie Page* extends Harron's fascination with social outsiders. Bettie Page became an underground bondage fetish pin-up icon in the 1950s and sparked outrage within conservative society. Page, played by Gretchen Mol, is depicted as an optimistic, naïve figure that, ultimately, remains an enigma. Page had a deeply religious upbringing and eventually retired from being a pin-up and became involved in evangelical Christianity. Harron took a deft approach to examine Page, one which "explores the complexity of her characters' infamy through visual experimentation—usually through employing different aesthetic registers to investigate the sometimes disparate but often confluent subjective and objective/historical perspectives."[28] This visual experimentation was established in *I Shot Andy Warhol*, blending black-and-white with color cinematography, and was expanded further by utilizing various panning and static shots that act as the male gaze. The film received mixed reviews and would be Harron's last biopic until *Anna Nicole*. Harron returned to directing for television and it would be six years before she made another feature film.

Harron ventured into the horror genre once more with an adaptation of Rachel Klein's *The Moth Diaries* (IFC Films, 2011). The film depicts the relationship between three boarding school students Rebecca (Sarah Bolger), Ernessa (Lily Cole), and Lucy (Sarah Gadon). As Lucy falls under Ernessa's influence, it weakens her relationship with Rebecca, who in turn begins to suspect that Ernessa may in fact be a vampire. Vampires became popular with teenagers once again largely due to the *Twilight* franchise (Summit Entertainment, 2008–2012), based on the young adult novels by Stephanie Meyer. *The Moth Diaries* was released prior to the final part in the franchise, *The Twilight Saga—Breaking Dawn: Part 2* (Condon, 2012), and was overlooked and criticized by some as an attempt to cash-in on *Twilight*'s success.[29] However, the film's atmosphere and its examination of a crisis of identity in teenagers make it one of Harron's most surreal films. Without the reliance on conventional vampire mythology, or ramping up the scares, the film is a contrast to the *Twilight* franchise. Its predominantly female cast and absence of significant heterosexual relationships may be some of the reasons why it was disregarded or failed to attract the same *Twilight* audience. Harron also further explores the nature of the outsider with the character of Ernessa and the complex nature of young female relationships. The film, in reflection, remains one of Harron's most underrated projects that deserves re-evaluation.

Figure I.2 Ernessa (Lily Cole) makes her presence known in *The Moth Diaries* (2011)

OBSERVER OF CELEBRITY: ANOTHER NOTORIOUS BIOPIC

Harron, again, delved into the corrupting nature of fame and celebrity in the 2013 Lifetime television movie *Anna Nicole*. Anna Nicole Smith (Agnes Bruckner), known for her work with *Playboy* magazine, her destructive party lifestyle and her marriage to eighty-nine-year-old businessman J. Howard Marshall (Martin Landau), made her a perfect, infamous figure for Harron to examine. Nicole's life would be further exploited in the reality television series *The Anna Nicole Show* (E!, 2002–2004), which maintained her celebrity up until her death in 2007 from a drug overdose. With regard to its visual aesthetics, the film is slightly more conventional than Harron's previous biopics, working within the Lifetime in-house style (see Chapter Two). However, it is still a challenging work that examines not only fame but how it "relates to women who push our collective buttons and whose actions fall outside the boundaries of 'acceptable' behavior."[30] Harron refuses to place any judgment on Smith. Instead, the filmmaker remains an observer through the key moments of her life, from Smith's early days as a stripper to her later marriage that drew conflict and ire from Marshall's family as well as derision from the public. Harron employs familiar biopic tropes such as voice-over narration. Yet, similar to *American Psycho*, the narration has a deadpan, tongue-in-cheek approach that brings a parodic edge with regard to the conventions of the biopic as well as Lifetime television films themselves.

Harron's next feature film, *Charlie Says* (IFC Films, 2018), returns to the themes of patriarchy and male control over women. Exploring Charles Manson's (Matt Smith) influence, impact, and brainwashing of several young women who became instrumental in the murders he ordered, Harron crafts a biopic that is, arguably, the summation of the dangerous effect of patriarchy that she has explored continuously throughout her career. *Charlie Says* was released amid other films examining the Manson family murders: *Once Upon a Time In . . . Hollywood* (Sony Pictures Releasing, Tarantino, 2019) and *The Haunting of Sharon Tate* (Saban Films, Farrands, 2019). *Charlie Says* is a complex film that adopts a non-linear narrative structure and places an emphasis of the Manson Family atrocities from a female perspective. The film reflects the viewpoint of former member, Lulu (Hannah Murray), as she recollects Charles' teachings during her incarceration on Death Row. Harron, as with her previous films, places no judgments on the characters and instead raises questions to the audience. The film received mixed reviews, a stark contrast to the acclaimed, male-dominated *Once Upon a Time In . . . Hollywood*. However, *Charlie Says* is subtler than the aforementioned titles that feature Manson (as will be argued in Chapter Six) and deserves a wider audience.

CHAPTERS

The following chapters have been organized into three sections: 1) Biopics, 2) Feature Films and Production Contexts, and 3) Television and Short Film Production. The first chapter, written by Janice Loreck, examines *I Shot Andy Warhol* and discusses Harron's enchantment with female figures that often receive negative attention. Loreck contextualizes Harron's film in the biopic, exploring the filmmaker's techniques that both embrace and challenge the parameters of the genre and, ultimately, reviews its strengths as an "anti" biopic.

In Chapter Two Kimberly Lamm analyzes *Anna Nicole* and discusses Harron's approach to Lifetime's house-style. Lamm explores how the filmmaker embraces the challenges and restrictions of directing a television movie. Building on Loreck's examination of fame in Harron's feature debut, Lamm argues that *Anna Nicole* is ostensibly a reflection on the convergence of mass culture and femininity that produce problematic images of female celebrities. Finally, the chapter regards the film as a significant work in Harron's oeuvre that challenges the sexist practices of the film industry.

The second section focuses on Harron's other feature films from a variety of perspectives. In Chapter Three Kyle Barrett studies *I Shot Andy Warhol*, *American Psycho*, and *The Notorious Bettie Page* within the context of Indiewood. Barrett reflects on Harron's aesthetics and use of satire, comparing Harron's work to that of her contemporaries. *I Shot Andy Warhol* is analyzed alongside Julian Schnabel's biopic *Basquiat* (Miramax Films, 1996). *American Psycho* is examined together with David Fincher's *Fight Club* (Twentieth Century Fox, 1999), both films noted for their deconstruction of toxic masculinity. Finally, Barrett examines *The Notorious Bettie Page* alongside Sofia Coppola's *Marie Antoinette* (Sony Pictures, 2006) in comparison to their respective visual styles.

Chapter Four, "'I Like to Dissect Girls': Mary Harron's *American Psycho* as Gendered Metafiction" provides an in-depth analysis of the filmmaker's most (in)famous film. Coco d'Hont contextualizes *American Psycho* within gendered metafiction, a concept that interrogates the boundary of fact and fiction in its representation of violent masculinity in popular culture. D'Hont argues the film was part of a trend in cinema that explored the crisis of masculinity at the end of the twentieth century. With comparison to *Silence of the Lambs* (Orion Pictures, Demme, 1991) and *Pulp Fiction* (Miramax Films, Tarantino, 1994), d'Hont contends Harron's adaptation is a subversive text as a depiction of masculine violence.

Chapter Five, by Caroline Speller, discusses *The Moth Diaries*, highlighting key themes that have appeared throughout Harron's career, such as notions of surveillance, censorship, and social control. Speller also reflects on the depiction of repressed female sexuality found in *I Shot Andy Warhol* and *The Notorious*

Bettie Page that continues in *The Moth Diaries*. Speller utilizes Michel Foucault's "Panopticism" to explore the film's use of surveillance and punishment within the context of the girls' boarding school. Speller also argues the film is somewhat a departure in style for Harron, particularly its use of the supernatural.

Gemma Piercy-Cameron concludes this section in Chapter Six by exploring *Charlie Says* and the conceptualization of masculinities. Piercy-Cameron argues that Harron incorporates several hypermasculinities within the character of Charlie to convey the severe impact of patriarchy on the young, female characters. The chapter posits that Charlie adopts various masculine gender roles throughout the film, from "breadwinner" to "rescuer/protector" in his efforts to brainwash his followers.

The final section discusses Harron's television and short film work. Gareth Schott's Chapter Seven, "Death to Disposal: Echoes of *American Psycho* in 'The Rainbow of Her Reasons' (*Six Feet Under*)" draws attention to the thematic associations between Harron's *Six Feet Under* episode "The Rainbow of Her Reasons" to *American Psycho*. Schott gives detailed analysis of the funeral cosmetics industry and its parallels to the lifestyle of Patrick Bateman, arguing that Harron's recurring thematic obsessions and visual style made her one of the strongest directors employed during the series' run.

In Chapter Eight Elena Caoduro's "Sartorial Interventions: When Fashion and Film Collide in *Armani* (2012)" reflects upon Harron's use of costume design in *American Psycho*, *Alias Grace*, and the short film *Armani*, a promotional work for the fashion designer Giorgio Armani. Caoduro argues fashion has been integral to Harron's work, detailing the significance of costume design with regard to the actor's body, character, and facilitating the development of the story. Caoduro ultimately problematizes the notion of "authored fashion film," arguing that Harron's collaboration with the designer challenges sole-authorship within filmmaking.

Finally, this *ReFocus* volume aims to analyze and critique one of North America's most challenging and intriguing filmmakers. Despite few feature films to date, Harron's collective filmography of shorts, features, adverts, and television episodes demonstrates a determined and creative filmmaker. This book will, ultimately, argue that Harron is a filmmaker worthy of further attention.

NOTES

1. Katarzyna Paszkiewicz, *Genre, Authorship and Contemporary Women Filmmakers* (Edinburgh: Edinburgh University Press, 2019), 35.
2. Frances Smith and Timothy Shary, "Introduction," in *ReFocus: The Films of Amy Heckerling*, edited by Frances Smith and Timothy Shary (Edinburgh: Edinburgh University Press, 2016), 3.

3. Paszkiewicz, *Genre, Authorship and Contemporary Women Filmmakers*, 139
4. Linda Badley, Claire Perkins, and Michele Schreiber,"Introduction," in *Indie Reframed: Women's Filmmaking and Contemporary American Independent Cinema*, edited by Linda Badley, Claire Perkins, and Michele Schreiber (Edinburgh: Edinburgh University Press, 2016), 9.
5. Veronica Pravadelli, "US Independent Women's Cinema, Sundance Girls, and Identity Politics," in *Feminisms: Diversity, Difference and Multiplicity in Contemporary Film Cultures*, edited by Laura Mulvey and Anna Backman Rogers (Amsterdam: Amsterdam University Press, 2015), 149.
6. Jennie Punter, "The Monday Q&A: Mary Harron," *The Globe and Mail*, 2011. Accessed May 25, 2018, https://www.theglobeandmail.com/arts/the-monday-qa-mary-harron/article600379/
7. Alison Lang, "Mary Harron," *Cutthroat Women: A Database of Women who Make Horror*, Accessed April 2, 2019, https://www.cutthroatwomen.org/harron 2018
8. Mary G. Hurd, *Women Directors and their Films* (Westport: Praeger Publishers, 2007), 63.
9. Mary Harron, "Introduction," in *I Shot Andy Warhol* (screenplay), Mary Harron and Daniel Minahan (New York: Grove Press, 1996), ix.
10. Patricia White, "Killer Feminism," in *Indie Reframed: Women's Filmmaking and Contemporary American Independent Cinema*, edited by Linda Badley, Claire Perkins, and Michele Schreiber (Edinburgh: Edinburgh University Press, 2016), 39.
11. Hurd, *Women Directors and their Films*, 63.
12. White, "Killer Feminism," 43.
13. Dana Heller, "Shooting Solanas: Radical Feminist History and the Technology of Failure," in *Feminist Time against Nation Time: Gender, Politics, and the Nation-State in an Age of Permanent War*, edited by Victoria Hesford and Lisa Diedrich (Lanham, MD: Lexington Books, 2008), 151.
14. Ken Dancyger, *The Director's Idea: The Path to Great Directing* (Burlington: Focal Press, 2006), 302.
15. Heller, "Shooting Solanas: Radical Feminist History and the Technology of Failure," 152.
16. Hurd, *Women Directors and their Films*, 63.
17. Michael Z. Newman, *Indie: An American Film Culture* (New York: Columbia University Press, 2011), 3.
18. Janet Staiger, "Independent of What? Sorting out difference from Hollywood," in *American Independent Cinema: Indie, Indiewood and Beyond*, edited by Geoff King, Claire Molloy, and Yannis Tzioumakis (Abingdon: Routledge, 2013), 18).
19. Geoff King, *Indiewood, USA: Where Hollywood Meets Independent Cinema* (London and New York: I. B. Tauris, 2009), 1.
20. Newman, *Indie: An American Film Culture*, 4
21. Jeffrey Sconce, "Irony, nihilism and the new American 'smart' film," in *Screen* (Vol. 4, No. 43, 2002), 349–69.
22. Mary Harron, "The Risky Territory of *American Psycho*," New York Times. Accessed April 9, 2000. https://www.nytimes.com/2000/04/09/movies/film-the-risky-territory-of-american-psycho.html
23. Angelica Jade Bastion, "The Female Gaze of 'American Psycho': How Mary Harron Made Fantasy Into Timeless Satire," *The Village Voice*. Accessed April 9, 2016. https://www.villagevoice.com/2016/06/07/the-female-gaze-of-american-psycho-how-mary-harron-made-fantasy-into-timeless-satire/
24. Martin Rogers, "Video Nasties and the Monstrous Bodies of *American Psycho*," *Literature-Film Quarterly* (Vol. 39, No. 3, 2011), 231–44.

25. Kate Bussmann, "Interview: Cutting Edge," *The Guardian*, 2009. Accessed May 23, 2018. https://www.theguardian.com/lifeandstyle/2009/mar/06/mary-harron-film
26. Badley et al., "Introduction," 9.
27. Michele Schreiber, "'I'm Absolutely the Right Person for this Job': Allison Anders and Mary Harron on Lifetime Television," in *Indie Reframed: Women's Filmmaking and Contemporary American Independent Cinema*, edited by Linda Badley, Claire Perkins, and Michele Schreiber (Edinburgh: Edinburgh University Press, 2016), 89.
28. Michele Schreiber, "Their Own Personal Velocity," in *American Independent Cinema: Indie, Indiewood and Beyond*, edited by Geoff King, Claire Molloy, and Yannis Tzioumakis (Abingdon: Routledge, 2013), 103.
29. Neil Young, "The Moth Diaries: Venice Film Review," *The Hollywood Reporter*, 2011. Accessed May 23, 2018. https://www.hollywoodreporter.com/review/moth-diaries-venice-film-review-231656
30. Schreiber, "'I'm Absolutely the Right Person for this Job': Allison Anders and Mary Harron on Lifetime Television," 97.

PART I
Biopics

CHAPTER I

I Shot Andy Warhol: Fame, Notoriety, and Mary Harron's Anti-biopics

Janice Loreck

INTRODUCTION

On 3 June 1968 Valerie Solanas shot and wounded artist Andy Warhol in his studio, an act for which she was found guilty and committed for three years to a psychiatric hospital. The shooting and its perpetrator are the focal points of Mary Harron's first feature, *I Shot Andy Warhol*. Harron's film is notable for the recognition it garnered the director and her lead actress, Lili Taylor, upon its premiere at the Sundance Film Festival, where it won Special Recognition for Outstanding Performance for Taylor. *I Shot Andy Warhol* also marks the beginning of the director's interest in dramatizing the lives of controversial women. In 2005, Harron returned to the biopic genre to document the career of 1950s pin-up model Bettie Page in *The Notorious Bettie Page*; in 2013, Harron filmed the life of former Playboy model Anna Nicole Smith in the Lifetime television movie *Anna Nicole*. In these films, Harron foregrounds the lives of women who achieve notoriety—or a form of "negative fame" or infamy for subversive acts—with *I Shot Andy Warhol* as the first entry in Harron's unofficial trilogy of biopics.

Like *The Notorious Bettie Page* and *Anna Nicole*, *I Shot Andy Warhol* focuses on a woman who achieved fame for the "wrong" reasons. As the title of the film implies, Solanas is best known for attacking Warhol, thereby achieving fame for an act of violence. However, the story of *I Shot Andy Warhol* also asserts that Solanas has another, more positive claim to fame. The film depicts Solanas as a witty and observant feminist writer who presaged the women's rights movement of the 1960s and 1970s through her *SCUM Manifesto*. Published in 1967, Solanas' manifesto speaks on behalf of the "Society for Cutting Up Men" (of which she was sole member and founder). It offers an account of women's existence under patriarchy and advocates—satirically, according to some interpretations—for the elimination of the male sex. The manifesto begins with the premise that men are inherently inferior to women and thus prone to self-hatred and victimization. This is because "the Y (male) gene is an incomplete X (female) gene," Solanas reasons. The manifesto then calls upon women to rebel against society, "take over the airwaves," "bust up" heterosexual couples, kill resistant men, and create a world of automation and anarchy. In an interview with *The Guardian*, Harron expresses admiration of Solanas' controversial document:

> I thought it was really funny, in a black way [. . .] And I could tell that she was an intelligent writer, with a very prophetic quality. She had an analysis of the patheticness of female behavior, how women were propping up the male ego, colluding in their own oppression by embracing this idea that men are so powerful and smart—but somehow so weak that they had to support them with every fiber of their being. She laid out these contradictions more clearly than anyone, at such an early stage.[1]

In keeping with this sentiment, the title card at the end of *I Shot Andy Warhol* refers to the *SCUM Manifesto* as a "feminist classic." Yet the film makes clear that Solanas did not achieve fame for her manifesto. Rather, as the title suggests, her violence is the primary source of her notoriety.

This chapter frames Harron as a maker of biographical films, a chronicler of notoriety and a director interested in women's negative fame. First, there will be an account of Harron as a proponent of a parodic form of biography: the "anti-biopic," or films about people who do not "deserve" one.[2] *I Shot Andy Warhol* provides an exemplary case study for how Harron's work conforms to the anti-biopic trend of the 1990s and 2000s in American filmmaking. Harron's specific contribution to this trend insofar as the "anti-celebrity" of her anti-biopics is premised upon women's notoriety, rather than, for example, cult celebrity or eccentricity, which is found in unconventional biopics such as *Ed Wood* (Touchstone Pictures, Burton, 1994) or *Man on the Moon* (Universal Pictures, Forman, 1999). Following this, the chapter will discuss Harron's approach to women's negative fame in *I Shot Andy Warhol*, *The Notorious Bettie Page*, and *Anna Nicole*. I consider how each film conveys Harron's interest in women's ability (or inability) to control their public persona, as well as the dual registers of irony and sympathy in Harron's work.

I SHOT ANDY WARHOL AND THE ANTI-BIOPIC

When asked why she chose to make a film about Valerie Solanas, Harron recalls seeing the *SCUM Manifesto* for the first time in a bookshop in South London in the late 1980s. Having worked on documentaries about The Velvet Underground and Andy Warhol, Harron recognized Solanas' name:

> I knew all about the *SCUM Manifesto*, or thought I did. Valerie Solanas, this crazy woman who shot Warhol, was the leader and sole member of a revolutionary organization called the Society for Cutting up Men (SCUM). She used to sell the yet unpublished "SCUM Manifesto" on street corners to indifferent passersby: it was, it had to be, a deranged rant, whose blurry mimeographed pages had been lost in the gutters of the 1960s.[3]

After purchasing a copy, Harron realized her assumptions about the manifesto were not correct. As stated above, Harron was struck by Solanas' humor and insight, as well as the idea that an impoverished, unacknowledged person might be a genius, noting that the tone of the manifesto is "deadpan, icily logical, elegantly comic; a strange juxtaposition."[4] In a later interview, Harron says she decided to undertake a "reverse-engineering documentary" about the Factory scene, "focusing on the least important person."[5] The proposed documentary evolved into a biopic project, with *I Shot Andy Warhol* as the eventual result.

Harron's choice of words, "reverse engineering," provide insight into the relationship that *I Shot Andy Warhol* has to fame and history. In dramatizing the life of a woman who achieved criminal notoriety rather than acclaim, *I Shot Andy Warhol* inverts the normative approach to film biography by focusing on a less-than-reputable person. Specifically, Harron undermines the "great man" biopic tradition established in Hollywood's classical era. According to Dennis Bingham, foundational biopics of the 1930s focus on laudable male individuals, a tendency epitomized by the Warner Bros.-produced "great man" films such as *The Story of Louis Pasteur* (1936), *The Life of Emile Zola* (1937) and *Juarez* (1939), all directed by William Dieterle. In this context, the biopic functions as a paean to their protagonists, celebrating their talent, strength of will and persistence. Great man biopics are hagiographic in nature, asserting "the 'deserving' virtues of their subjects."[6] Indeed, hagiography remains central to the biopic's intelligibility to this day; the specter of the great man haunts contemporary biographies, functioning as the norm that is upheld or subverted by filmmakers.

In making *I Shot Andy Warhol*, Harron becomes a proponent of what screenwriters Scott Alexander and Larry Karaszewski call the anti-biopic: "a movie about somebody who doesn't deserve one."[7] Anti-biopics appear as part of the parodic phase of the biopic cycle, a trend that gathered momentum in American cinema in the 1990s and saw the release of films such as

Ed Wood, *The People vs. Larry Flynt* (Columbia Pictures, Forman, 1996) and *Man on the Moon*. According to Bingham, the parodic phase is defined chiefly by its "choice of biographical subject," namely "undeserving" people who do not possess the usual talent or renown common to protagonists of the classic mode. The "great men" of classical biopics are defined by pro-social accomplishments, such as political success, artistic excellence or ingenuity, and personal qualities of talent, hard work, and strength of will. The subjects of anti-biopics, in contrast, are ignominious, talentless or simply obscure: the eponymous Ed Wood directed Hollywood's "worst ever film" *Plan 9 from Outer Space* (Valiant Pictures, 1959), Larry Flynt of *The People vs. Larry Flynt* was a pornographer, and the *Man on the Moon* refers to the late, unconventional comedian Andy Kaufman. Anti-biopics involve "mocking the very notions of heroes and fame" upon which traditional biography depends.[8] They also expand the dramatic possibilities of the biopic: they provide ironic dramatizations of persistence achieving ignoble rather than noble ends, of fame being accidentally bestowed rather than earned, of celebrity stemming from vice instead of virtue.

I Shot Andy Warhol conforms to the anti-biopic mode insofar as its protagonist commits an act of anti-social violence. The film's opening scene begins with a flash-forward to the titular deed; Solanas appears on-screen shooting at someone outside the frame. When her gun jams, the unidentified victim implores Solanas to leave, and she does. Later, after she has been arrested and is surrounded by throngs of reporters, Solanas instructs the crowd to read the *SCUM Manifesto*: "it'll tell you what I am," she declares. The scene establishes Solanas primarily as the woman who shot Andy Warhol, as well as a radical. As such, she is immediately constructed in terms of her difference from the subjects of classical biopics, such as Louis Pasteur, Émile Zola, and Benito Juárez. Indeed, Bingham goes so far as to group *I Shot Andy Warhol* with *The Assassination of Richard Nixon* (ThinkFilm, Mueller, 2004) and *Color Me Kubrick* (Magnolia Pictures, Cook, 2005); these "curios," as Bingham describes them, are about "marginal figures who settle like fleas on the coats of famous personalities."[9,10]

Harron is indeed a proponent of biographies about "undeserving" people who do not fit the model of the "great man." By focusing on a figure who gained notoriety, *I Shot Andy Warhol* challenges the biopic's naturalization of the connection between celebrity and "greatness." Although Solanas is publicly renowned, Harron's film acknowledges that her violent act against Warhol had negative repercussions. As the end title cards explain, Warhol never fully recovered, physically or mentally, from Solanas' attack. As an anti-biopic, however, *I Shot Andy Warhol* also celebrates Solanas' qualities, casting her as a neglected, transgressive provocateur.

Figure 1.1 Valerie Solanas (Lili Taylor) venting over her play

HARRON AS AN ANTI-BIOGRAPHER

Although Harron's anti-biopics follow the trend of celebrating the undeserving, her contribution to the cycle can be specified in two ways: the gender of her subjects and her directorial interest in the idea of notoriety. Firstly, Harron is a biographer of women. This is significant because fewer biopics have historically been made about women. Carolyn Anderson's survey of biographical films from 1929 to 1986 found that only twenty-eight percent of these texts feature female protagonists.[11] Similarly, George Custen calculates that thirty-five percent of biopics produced in Hollywood during the studio era (1927–1960) focused on the lives of women.[12] Notable exceptions include films about the Swedish monarch *Queen Christina* (Metro-Goldwyn-Mayer, Mamoulian, 1933), Catherine the Great in *The Scarlet Empress* (Paramount Pictures, Sternberg, 1934), the physicist *Madame Curie* (Metro-Goldwyn-Mayer, LeRoy, 1943), and Florence Nightingale in *The Lady with a Lamp* (British Lion Films, Wilcox, 1951). This reveals that fame has, at least historically, been an unusual position for women to occupy. Except in particular circumstances, such as queens who ascend to power through the accident of birth, the persona of the famous woman is subversive in itself. As Bingham explains, "Biography requires a protagonist who has done something noteworthy in the public world. Women historically have not been encouraged to become the subjects of discourse, at least not of any discourse that is taken seriously by a patriarchal society."[13] As such, biopics that focus on women resist established ideas about whose lives are important. Although Harron does not consider herself an "ideological filmmaker," she does recognize the significance of this act: "I do think I do women's histories," she says.[14] Such comments acknowledge the political significance of telling women's stories when the public record has for so long been a masculine space.

Harron's other authorial stamp on the anti-biopic is her focus on the phenomenon of celebrity—or, more accurately, notoriety—that women acquire through socially transgressive acts. Graeme Turner contends that the phenomenon of celebrity "is largely confirmatory of dominant values" and is bestowed upon those who embody these values.[15] However, some individuals do acquire renown for antisocial, and even criminal, behavior. Jack the Ripper, Ted Kaczynski ("the Unabomber"), Charles Manson, and the now-exonerated Amanda Knox are all examples of such individuals. This trend of negative celebrity has not gone unnoticed by filmmakers: directors interested in the lives of convicted criminals include Nicolas Winding Refn, who filmed a biography of Michael Gordon Peterson, *Bronson* (Magnet Releasing, 2008), Steven Spielberg, who told the story of Frank Abagnale in *Catch Me If You Can* (DreamWorks Pictures, 2002), and Ted Demme, who directed a biopic about cocaine smuggler George Jung, *Blow* (New Line Cinema, 2001). However, such biographies are still a minor grouping within the biopic genre. According to Bingham, anti-biopics of the 1990s and early 2000s tend to focus on cult or kitsch creative types rather than criminals, with films such as *Ed Wood* and *American Splendor* (Fine Line Features & HBO Films, Springer Berman & Pulcini, 2003) offered as parodies of "great artist" films like *Rembrandt* (United Artists, Korda, 1936) and *Chaplin* (TriStar Pictures, Attenborough, 1992).[16] *I Shot Andy Warhol* is therefore set apart by its interest in the concept of criminal renown. Indeed, transgressive fame and criminal violence is centralized in its title, *I Shot Andy Warhol*. Harron's interest in negative fame also continues in her later work; for instance, Bettie Page's notoriety is established from the opening scene of *The Notorious Bettie Page*, in which a police officer busts a shop owner for selling bondage photos of Page. *Anna Nicole* similarly begins by foregrounding Smith's unedifying claim to fame. The story opens with a montage of Smith at red carpet events, followed by an image of her dead body laid out in a morgue: "I'll be buried as international celebrity and balls-to-the-wall party girl, Anna Nicole Smith," she says in voice-over. Each of these women possess celebrity for qualities that contradict dominant values. In Solanas' case, it is criminal violence; for Page, it is her position as the object of sadomasochistic pornography; for Smith, it is her hedonism and sexual exposure as a model.

In keeping with the anti-biopic's interest in the nature of fame itself, *I Shot Andy Warhol* also investigates how Solanas' crime is motivated by her desire for recognition and celebrity. Harron speculates in the introduction to her and Daniel Minahan's screenplay that the greatest hardship in Solanas' life "was the obscurity, the lack of any sense of importance or respect or influence. It wasn't an easy life for an ambitious young woman who must have been looking for a way, any way, to crawl out of the shadows into the light."[17] Harron's observations on Solanas' life intersect with Chris Rojek's work on criminal celebrity. According to Rojek, criminal behavior is not always attributable to social disadvantage, mental illness or need. It can also be motivated by a desire to be recognized by society. Crime can emerge from an "overwhelming compulsion to be different, to possess fame, to break boundaries, 'to be a star—something literally, distinctively transcendent'."[18] The plot of *I Shot Andy Warhol* follows this logic to a significant degree. As the film progresses, Solanas grows increasingly angry and paranoid when Andy Warhol fails to return a precious copy of her play, *Up Your Ass*, which she gave him in the hope that he would produce it as a film. Solanas believes that Warhol has deliberately stolen her work; however, the painful truth is that Warhol misplaced the manuscript, showing that he did not value the document enough to ensure its safe keeping. This set of events aggravates Solanas. At the conclusion of the film, she justifies attacking Warhol by claiming "he is trying to steal all my work" and that he has "too much control over my life." Once Solanas is arrested and approached by reporters, she refuses to clearly explain why she shot Warhol. Instead, she diverts attention away from her act of violence and instructs the crowd: "read my manifesto!" In this moment, Solanas uses the media frenzy to promote her work. Negative publicity, in this instance, lifts her from obscurity.

In structuring the events of Solanas' life in this way, Harron's film dramatizes the motivation for Solanas' acts as originating from a desire for her work to be noticed. Providing such causal reasons for a person's deeds is a convention

Figure 1.2 "Read my manifesto!" Solanas questioned as to why she shot Andy Warhol

of biopics. As Linda Wagner-Martin summarizes, "it is a given that biography attempts to find explanations for a subject's acts."[19] This is usually accomplished by establishing character motivation in the plot, particularly by depicting formative events in the subject's childhood, such as Chaplin's upbringing as the son of a music hall actress in *Chaplin*, or Howard Hughes's impoverished childhood in *The Aviator* (Miramax Films, Scorsese, 2004). What is less conventional in *I Shot Andy Warhol* is that the film emphasizes Solanas' need for recognition more strongly than it does her childhood traumas, locating her crime in her desire for visibility. As Rojek argues: "If the desire to 'be someone' is not achieved by 'normal' means, some individuals will have a compelling propensity to use violence as a means of acquiring fame through notoriety."[20] Ignored and unrecognized, Solanas attracts the world's attention by shooting a man who possesses the recognition she desires. Indeed, once Solanas has been arrested, she appears outside the police headquarters surrounded by throngs of reporters. The scene is filled with the signifiers of twentieth-century fame: flashing lightbulbs, television cameras, and journalists vying for interviews.

Through its emphasis on negative fame, *I Shot Andy Warhol* is not only notable as a contribution to the anti-biopic trend of the 1990s. The film also establishes Harron's directorial interest in women's notoriety. *I Shot Andy Warhol* sets the trend, flagging a continuing authorial reluctance to explain a subject's notorious acts in ways typical of the genre's classic mode. When discussing *The Notorious Bettie Page*, for example, Harron repeatedly emphasizes that she did not wish to be reductive in her approach to Page's life: "So many biopics try to explain everything complex and mysterious about their character in terms of childhood trauma. I didn't want to be so reductive, to reduce Bettie's life to pop psychology."[21] This is a pertinent remark, as Solanas, Page and Smith each experienced traumatic events in their childhood. In *I Shot Andy Warhol* a psychiatrist explains that Solanas endured molestation at home; in *The Notorious Bettie Page* an early scene insinuates that Page was abused by her father; *Anna Nicole* shows a young Smith (known then as Vickie Lynn Hogan) witnessing her aunt's sexual assault. However, while these events are not unimportant, they do not go on to have much prominence in any of the films' plots. Other factors arise instead: Solanas' desire for recognition, Page's ease and enjoyment in posing for photographs, and Smith's need to make something of her life. *I Shot Andy Warhol* therefore not only shows the beginning of Harron's interest in the anti-biopic; it marks the beginning of an exploration of the unconventional and unexpected routes women take to public renown. Indeed, Solanas' notoriety has endured long after her demise: her manifesto has been reprinted ten times in English, she is the subject of a biography published in 2014 by Breanne Fahs, and a fictionalized version of Solanas appeared in the seventh season of television series *American Horror Story* (FX, 2011–present), where she was played by Lena Dunham.[22]

IRONY AND THE NOTORIOUS PERSONA

I Shot Andy Warhol also marks the beginning of Harron's interest in women's negative fame, as well as what Harron calls the "disconnect between the real woman and her public image."[23] *I Shot Andy Warhol*, *The Notorious Bettie Page* and *Anna Nicole* focus on women who perceive themselves differently to the way that outsiders do. Solanas sees herself as an overlooked writer, Page considers herself an ordinary woman (or, at least, it never occurs to her to think of herself as extraordinary), and Smith models herself upon the old Hollywood glamor of Marilyn Monroe. In each of Harron's films, the disparity between these women's notorious personae and their self-perception creates situational irony, a mode that is now characteristic of her biopics. In *I Shot Andy Warhol*, Harron makes it clear that Solanas' public identity is ultimately decided by forces beyond her own agency. This is the case even when Solanas actively attempts to establish a public persona as the author of her play *Up Your Ass* and then the *SCUM Manifesto*. The plot makes clear that Solanas' eventual notoriety occurs due to the broader culture's response to her actions, which emphasize her act of violence rather than her humor or prescience as a writer.

I Shot Andy Warhol highlights the mismatch between Solanas' desired and eventual fame on several occasions. It shows Solanas as she represents herself, Solanas as she is perceived externally by the media, and Solanas as she "truly" is (or, that is to say, as she is portrayed in the diegetic reality of the film). The film gives considerable attention to Solanas' writings and how they construct an authorial persona that is at odds with that of the violent radical. At one point in the film, Solanas reads aloud from her article "A Young Girl's Primer, or How to Attain the Leisure Class":

> Being fresh out of college, I found myself in a typically feminine dilemma of carving out for myself, in a male world, a way of life appropriate to a young woman of taste, cultivation and sensitivity. There must be nothing crass like work, however, a girl must survive. So, after a cool appraisal of the social scene, I finally hit upon an excellent paying occupation.[24]

The scene that plays out on-screen reveals that the "excellent paying occupation" is panhandling, selling dirty words for loose change, and, on occasion, sex work. On one hand, Solanas' voice-over is sincere; panhandling and sex work may indeed be a means by which a woman can earn a living. The article is also darkly funny; the genteel language contrasts with the suggestion that begging for money is "a way of life appropriate to a young woman of taste." However, irony is also a dominant feature of the sequence. Solanas' obvious poverty undermines the idea that panhandling and sex work will ever meaningfully empower her in 1960s New York City. As Harron explains: "The persona

Valerie adopts here—confident, cool, swinging, in charge—is an idealized self, the version of herself she most wanted to be [. . .] the reality included sordid rooms, inadequate food, and performing blow jobs to pay the rent."[25] Moreover, while the film shows that Solanas does indeed find the time to write, publishing her work proves more difficult. Warhol loses her manuscript and the Factory clique eventually excludes her from their group. The woman who shot Andy Warhol is therefore both victimized and a victim, and the film shows the disparities between the authorial Solanas, the "real" Solanas, and the Solanas who eventually becomes famous.

Harron returns to the mismatch of women's notoriety in *The Notorious Bettie Page* and *Anna Nicole*, two stories in which women's actions signify something different to their audiences than to the women themselves. In *The Notorious Bettie Page* this distinction is a key feature of the narrative. The film's screenplay was co-authored with Harron's frequent collaborator Guinevere Turner, who has worked on Harron's other films about outsiders and misfits, *American Psycho* and the Charles Manson biopic *Charlie Says*. The screenplay avoids depicting the world of sadomasochistic pornography as sleazy and deviant. Instead, Harron and Turner show events chiefly from the protagonist's (Gretchen Mol) perspective. Pin-up modeling is fun and freeing for Page; she laughs in between stern poses, chats with other models, and takes direction from pornographer Paula Klaw (Lili Taylor), who is warm and polite. These scenes contrast jarringly with a later moment depicting Senator Estes Kefauver's (David Strathairn) 1955 anti-pornography hearings, in which one of Page's photo shoots is recreated as a 16-milimeter movie. Contrasted with the clarity of the diegetic cinematography, the grainy image of Page bound and crawling across a studio floor appears seedy and debased. The moment shows how others see Page's world; as frightening, perverse, and alien. Indeed, Harron herself notes the mismatch between these internal and external perceptions, saying of Page: "I don't think she really understood the nature of those photographs."[26] In conjunction, Michele Schreiber also notes that the film explores "the arbitrary relationship between [women's] reality and how that reality is perceived by others."[27]

Indeed, Schreiber's comments apply equally well to *Anna Nicole* and *I Shot Andy Warhol*, pinpointing a trend in Harron's biopics. Each film emphasizes how the presentation of one's identity clashes with the wider, societal interpretations of the self. Like *The Notorious Bettie Page*, *Anna Nicole* privileges Smith's point of view until particular moments of scandal intervene, illuminating the transgressiveness of her behavior when intoxicated by alcohol or drugs. The climax of the film reenacts the filming of the infamous "clown video," a home movie made in 2006 that shows Smith, heavily pregnant and intoxicated on camera, wearing garish clown make-up. As in *I Shot Andy Warhol*, Harron's focus is on contrasts: a happy model versus a deviant pornographer, a glamor icon versus an addict, and a revolutionary versus a struggling woman.

SYMPATHY AND IRONY

I Shot Andy Warhol highlights the irony of Solanas' notoriety largely through the emotional relationship that the film establishes with the spectator. The film positions viewers to feel sympathy for Solanas and her circumstances. However, it does not invite empathetic identification with Solanas per se. This distinction is significant. Empathy would invite spectators to adopt Solanas' perspective and emotions. It would, hypothetically, involve inserting the spectator directly into an experience of her fear and paranoia. Harron does not adopt this approach in *I Shot Andy Warhol*. For example, while the film certainly characterizes The Factory cohort as cliquey, they are not controlling or dangerous in the manner that Solanas imagines. Warhol himself is characterized as an absent-minded and socially awkward individual—hardly a conspiring mastermind intent on exploiting Solanas for professional gain. Instead, sympathy rather than empathy is the dominant emotional response invited of spectators in relation to Solanas' situation; a feeling of pity that is premised on an understanding of the individual as distinct from oneself. This sympathetic distance allows the spectator to occupy several different positions in relation to the events depicted, including pity for Solanas as well as condemnation of her actions.

I Shot Andy Warhol chiefly evokes sympathy through moments that emphasize Solanas' hardships; a position that accommodates viewers' compassion but also makes room for irony regarding the mismatch between Solanas' desired and eventual fame. This occurs particularly at moments when the film contrasts Solanas' imagined persona with the truth of her experiences. When Solanas experiences rough sex with a john in an alleyway, for example, the scene cross-cuts to show her reading from the *SCUM Manifesto* direct to camera: "you've got to go through a lot of sex to get to anti-sex, and SCUM's been through it all. And they're now ready for a new show; they want to crawl out from under the dock, move, take off, sink out." The bravado of Solanas' authorial voice contrasts with the scene in the alleyway. She is cornered, an expression of rage and disgust on her face.

Near the film's conclusion, the narrative shows Solanas' self-perception growing increasingly divorced from reality as her mental health deteriorates. Her delusions become a particularly strong source of irony and pathos in the film's closing sequences. In one scene, a psychiatrist relays Solanas' response to her own crime in voice-over:

> In regard to the incident on June 3rd, the patient says "I shot Andy Warhol. He is trying to steal all my work." She says that she is glad that he is in the hospital and hopes he dies. She also complained that "if Andy has really forgiven me, why hasn't he been to see me?"[28]

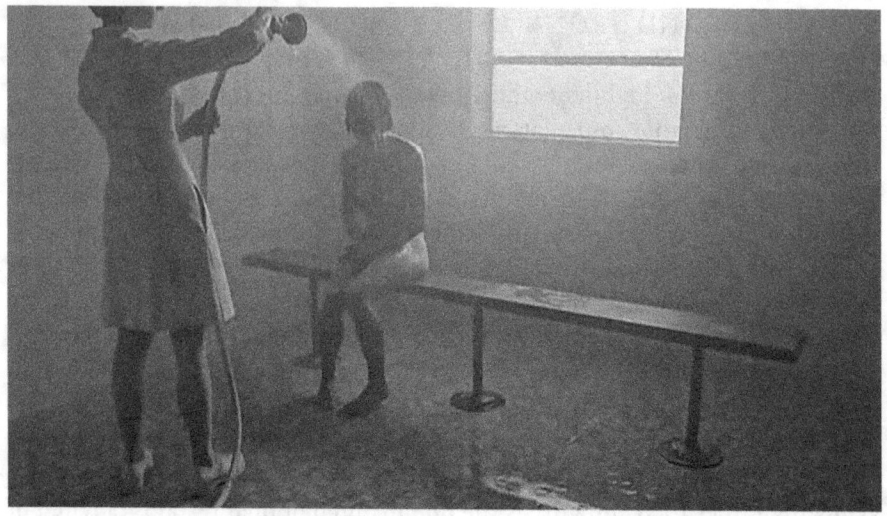

Figure 1.3 Solanas in a psychiatric hospital

As this dialogue plays out, the scene shows a lifeless Solanas being admitted to psychiatric care. She sits naked in a large bathroom, looking frail as a nurse showers her body. The bravura of Solanas' authorial persona is gone and there is nothing of the dangerous, defiant radical in the on-screen image. By showing her vulnerability, the scene invites feelings of compassion for Solanas. The irony evoked in the juxtaposition of voice-over and image bolsters this emotional positioning; the obvious reason why Warhol has not been to see Solanas is because he is injured and afraid, but she, too, is vulnerable. This irony highlights that notoriety is imposed from without. Solanas may have indeed shot Andy Warhol, but her ultimate fame is the "wrong" fame, a disempowered notoriety.

In the story that it wishes to tell about the nature of negative fame, *I Shot Andy Warhol* stages what Tarja Laine describes as "triadic" identification. Such identification describes the moment when spectators identify with an imagined "third gaze," often at the same time that they inhabit their own point of view and those of an on-screen character. This gaze can take the form of a policing gaze belonging to the wider society. Such identification occurs because spectators bring knowledge of societal norms to the processes of spectatorship, and such norms can manifest as an imagined look at various points in the film.[29] The social look is a very present dynamic in *Anna Nicole* and *The Notorious Bettie Page*, which repeatedly emphasize Smith's and Page's vulnerability to judgment. During an audition for an acting role, for example, a director says to Bettie: "it's quite a treat to meet the notorious Bettie Page." The moment is a rude awakening for the young woman, who is surprised to be exposed in such a way. This moment stages the intervention of the policing social gaze of conservative 1950s America; a look that the film has cued contemporary viewers to anticipate will eventually catch up with Page. The threat of social judgment looms heavily when Page asks Paula Klaw why she must pose in eight-inch heeled stilettos. Klaw does not admit the subversive nature of the pornography they are producing. Instead, she replies: "Customers who want this stuff, they're very respectable, very high-quality people. Doctors, lawyers, diplomats, even a judge!" Klaw's protestations reveal the truth all too clearly. In mainstream 1950s America, bondage fetishes are not at all considered respectable, and Page will eventually be judged for her involvement in the scene.

In *I Shot Andy Warhol*, the broader, social gaze intervenes several times—for instance, when Solanas appears garish in lipstick and eyeshadow as she goes to meet her publisher, or when she poses dramatically with a gun and bandolier, performing the role of the violent revolutionary that she never truly becomes. However, the social look intrudes most dramatically in a scene in which Solanas appears on *The Alan Burke Show* (WNEW, 1966–1970). The conservative social commentator begins his interview by asking, "I understand you're a lesbian, and a somewhat mannish one at that: what's the matter, didn't anyone ever take you to the prom?" The scene cross-cuts to the studio audience laughing, gasping and tittering in response to Burke's insults. In this moment, society's gaze (albeit of an arch-conservative kind) scrutinizes and dismisses Solanas. The moment suggests that the public recognition needed for celebrity can also shame and denigrate. The scene also enables a mode of spectatorship that invites sympathy for Solanas but not total identification per se. Just as spectators condemn Burke's victimization of Solanas, they must also inhabit an awareness of the studio audience's prejudice in order for the scene to be intelligible. In moments like these, *I Shot Andy Warhol* invites spectators to understand Solanas and adopt her point of view, but it also ensures a degree of distance from the biographical subject, a sympathy for Solanas *as well as* knowledge of how she is perceived.

This privileging of sympathy instead of empathy is an authorial signature in Harron's anti-biopics more generally. Although it is a made-for-television movie, *Anna Nicole* follows very similar structures to Harron's feature film biographies insofar as the plot provides motivations for the protagonist's behavior. *Anna Nicole* explains Smith's addictions, as well as invites sympathy for her predicament, depicting drugs as Smith's escape from the stress of her career (Smith herself often spoke of the difficulties she had posing naked for *Playboy* magazine, which she described as "really scary").[30] Performing the role of sexual object empowers Smith, but the accompanying glare of celebrity is also shown to be exhausting. In an interview following the release of *Anna Nicole*, Harron argues that the film suits the Lifetime television network precisely because the female-dominated audience is more likely to feel sympathy for Smith. As Harron explains, Lifetime is a "female-centric" network, and, as such, it was possible to "do a sympathetic take on Anna" in the vein of earlier movies such as *Liz & Dick* (Lifetime, Kramer, 2012), a biography of Elizabeth Taylor and Richard Burton, and *Amanda Knox: Murder on Trial in Italy* (Lifetime, Dornhelm, 2011). [31] Likewise, spectators are strongly invited to understand Bettie Page's enjoyment of her pin-up modeling career in *The Notorious Bettie Page*. As the film repeatedly shows, Page is completely at ease while posing but experiences difficulty in her acting class. Her performance instructor is condescending, whereas pornographers Irving (Chris Bauer) and Paula Klaw are supportive. By engaging viewers to adopt a sympathetic rather than empathetic stance, Harron's films frame the protagonists' actions as understandable to the spectator. Sympathy provides reasons for a woman's actions without offering moral or ethical justifications—a useful strategy for an anti-biographer dealing with controversial subject matter.

CONCLUSION

I Shot Andy Warhol is a key film in Harron's body of work that illuminates her approach to the biopic genre. It signals Harron's ongoing, anti-biographical interest in "undeserving" subjects; people like Solanas, Page, and Smith, whose behaviors contradict dominant cultural values. Further to this, *I Shot Andy Warhol* signals the beginning of her interest in women's negative fame. In *I Shot Andy Warhol*, Harron focuses on Solanas' desire for recognition as a motivator for her criminal behavior. Solanas seeks fame as a form of validation, visibility, and enfranchisement as an artist and political agitator. *The Notorious Bettie Page and Anna Nicole* take a similar interest in women's unexpected routes to fame. Page achieves notoriety accidentally as a consequence of her modeling career, whereas Smith deliberately (and fatally) pursues celebrity to transcend her origins as an impoverished girl. Harron's anti-biopics are also characterized by dual tones of irony and sympathy in relation to their controversial subjects. The films position spectators to take a stance of sympathy yet distance from Solanas, Page, and Smith.

Harron's work does raise some questions about how she contributes, as a filmmaker and biographer, to the public construction of women's lives. As a film about a woman who mostly failed to achieve her ambitions, *I Shot Andy Warhol* could be identified as participating in what Bingham calls the "victimology" tendency in female biopics. As Bingham explains regarding classical biographies of women:

> [. . .] female biopics overall found conflict and tragedy in a woman's success. A victim, whatever her profession, made a better subject than a survivor with a durable career and a nontraumatic personal life [. . .]

Female biopics frequently depicted their subjects as certainly or possibly insane, made so by the cruelties of a victimizing world, or by the subject's insistence on having her own way in the world.[32]

Such "victim" biopics include *I'll Cry Tomorrow* (Metro-Goldwyn-Mayer, Mann, 1955), *Lady Sings the Blues* (Paramount Pictures, Furie, 1972) and *Frances* (Universal Pictures, Clifford, 1982), which retell the lives of Lillian Roth, Billie Holiday and Frances Farmer respectively. These films contrast with the great man narrative, which portrays the male protagonist as an achiever. As an ideological construction, the great man naturalizes the relationship between masculinity, talent and the will to succeed. In contrast, fame's treacherousness for women, as well as the ease with which celebrity transforms into notoriety, is a continuing theme in Harron's work. The tragic permeates *I Shot Andy Warhol* and *Anna Nicole* in particular; the latter is bookended by Smith's early death due to drug abuse, whereas the former ends with Solanas' institutionalization. While *The Notorious Bettie Page* does not conclude sadly, it shows Page ending her modeling career and reaffirming her religious faith. Fame is thus a difficult position for women to occupy in Harron's films—only Page has a future, and only once she gives up her career.

However, Harron's anti-biopics circumvent the problem of great men and victimized women by taking an ironic position on fame more generally. The problem is not with women and their "non-greatness." Rather, it is the absurdity of fame itself that matters most—its capacity to make celebrities of fools and fools of celebrities. In parodic anti-biopics like *The People vs. Larry Flynt* and *Ed Wood*, fame is a product of others' perception of the individual, even an accident of history or the luck of cult infamy, rather than a consequence of individual greatness. In Harron's anti-biopics, fame is similarly volatile. While Harron describes Solanas in interviews as a neglected genius, the plot events in *I Shot Andy Warhol* problematize such statements. In spite of her humor and insight, Solanas' work is widely ridiculed until she decides to shoot Warhol. Solanas' talents may be legitimate, but recognition only emerges as a by-product of her notorious violence.

Harron's anti-biopics therefore demonstrate a truism of celebrity: that it is a social phenomenon rather than personal quality. As Turner explains, celebrity is not "a property of specific individuals" but consists of "the way in which the individual is represented," perceived and remembered.[33] Indeed, the statement at the heart of Harron's film, "I shot Andy Warhol," encapsulates this precept. Although uttered by Solanas as her "claim to fame," the infamy of the statement must nevertheless be produced: by media, by biographers, and through the act of narrative. Harron undertakes this as a filmmaker and biographer. Both ironic and sympathetic, her films show the complex ways that women's lives are lived and created.

NOTES

1. Kate Bussmann, "Cutting Edge: Celebrated Filmmaker Mary Harron Talks about Sex, Violence and Satire," *Guardian*, March 6, 2009, https://www.theguardian.com/lifeandstyle/2009/mar/06/mary-harron-film.
2. Scott Alexander and Larry Karaszewski, *Man on the Moon: The Shooting Script* (New York: Newmarket Press, 1999), vii.
3. Mary Harron, "Introduction: On Valerie Solanas," in *I Shot Andy Warhol*, by Mary Harron and Daniel Minahan (London: Bloomsbury, 1996), vii.
4. Ibid., viii.
5. Anisse Gross, "Interview with Mary Harron," *Believer*, April 2014, https://believermag.com/an-interview-with-mary-harron/.
6. Dennis Bingham, *Whose Lives Are They Anyway?: The Biopic as Contemporary Film Genre* (New Brunswick, NJ: Rutgers University Press, 2010), 149.
7. Alexander and Karaszewski, *Man on the Moon: The Shooting Script*, vii.
8. Bingham, *Whose Lives Are They Anyway?: The Biopic as Contemporary Film Genre.*, 18.
9. Ibid., 148.
10. Bingham's use of the term "fleas" signals the subjects' abject status as "other."
11. Carolyn Anderson, "Biographical Film," in *Handbook of American Film Genres*, edited by Wes D. Gehring (Westport: Greenwood, 1988), 336.
12. George F Custen, *Bio/Pics: How Hollywood Constructed Public History* (New Brunswick, NJ: Rutgers University Press, 1992), 144.
13. Bingham, *Whose Lives Are They Anyway?: The Biopic as Contemporary Film Genre*, 213.
14. Gross, "Interview with Mary Harron."
15. Graeme Turner, *Understanding Celebrity*, Second Edition (Los Angeles: SAGE, 2014), 25.
16. Bingham, *Whose Lives Are They Anyway?: The Biopic as Contemporary Film Genre*, 147–8.
17. Harron, "Introduction: On Valerie Solanas," xvii.
18. Chris Rojek, *Celebrity* (London: Reaktion Books, 2001), 151.
19. Linda Wagner-Martin, *Telling Women's Lives: The New Biography* (New Brunswick, NJ: Rutgers University Press, 1994), 7.
20. Ibid., 146.
21. "Production Notes: *The Notorious Bettie Page*" (Dendy Films, March 8, 2007), 5.
22. Nancy A. Hewitt, "Solanas, Valerie," in *Notable American Women: A Biographical Dictionary Completing the Twentieth Century, Volume 5*, edited by Susan Ware (Cambridge, MA: Harvard University Press, 2004), 603.
23. B. Alan Orange, "Anna Nicole: Exclusive Interview with Director Mary Harron," *MovieWeb*. Accessed December 6, 2016, http://movieweb.com/anna-nicole-exclusive-interview-with-director-mary-harron/.
24. Valerie Solanas, "A Young Girl's Primer, or How to Attain the Leisure Class," *Cavalier*, July 1966, 38.
25. Harron, "Introduction: On Valerie Solanas," xvii.
26. Mary Harron, "Mary Harron and 'The Notorious Bettie Page'," interview by Madeleine Brand, April 14, 2006, http://www.npr.org/templates/story/story.php?storyId=5342546.
27. Michele Schreiber, "'I'm Absolutely the Right Person for This Job': Allison Anders and Mary Harron on Lifetime Television, Michele Schreiber," in *Indie Reframed: Women's Filmmaking and Contemporary American Independent Cinema*, edited by Linda Badley, Claire Perkins, and Michele Schreiber (Edinburgh: Edinburgh University Press, 2016), 97.
28. Mary Harron, director *I Shot Andy Warhol* (1996, Samuel Goldwyn Company, MGM), DVD.
29. Tarja Laine, *Shame and Desire: Emotion, Intersubjectivity, Cinema* (Brussels: P.I.E. Peter Lang, 2007), 9.

30. Larry King, "Interview with Anna Nicole Smith," *Larry King Live* (CNN), May 29, 2002, http://edition.cnn.com/TRANSCRIPTS/0205/29/lkl.00.html/.
31. Todd Gilchrist, "*American Psycho* Director Mary Harron Talks *Anna Nicole*," *Hitflix*, February 20, 2014, http://uproxx.com/hitfix/american-psycho-director-mary-harron-talks-anna-nicole/.
32. Bingham, *Whose Lives Are They Anyway?: The Biopic as Contemporary Film Genre*, 217.
33. Turner, *Understanding Celebrity*, 11.

CHAPTER 2

On the Other Side of the Icon: Making Images and Restaging Celebrity Spectacle in *Anna Nicole*

Kimberly Lamm

"Images have to be made." Richard Dyer[1]

INTRODUCTION

Whether focused on mainstream or independent cinema, feminist film scholarship of late has foregrounded the durability of impediments that limit the aspirations of women directors.[2] Certainly global trends in women's film production pose significant challenges to the entrenched sexism of the film industry, but it is still difficult to refute that sexism is built into its institutional machinery.[3] The consistently small number of women behind the camera proves this, as does the recent revelations that sexual harassment is constitutive norm for women working in film. This norm likely effects all the jobs and professions encompassed by the film industry, but the actresses associated with the recent iteration of the #MeToo movement, and the photographs that accompanied reports of their claims, suggested that the industry's reliance on images of women for its profitable seductions is part of the problem. Despite all the interventions into this equation, film still teaches us to read images of women's sexualized display as expressions of availability and vulnerability. Writing about the "endless photo spreads of [Harvey Weinstein's] female targets," Jacqueline Rose observes that the "voyeuristic pleasure" these images provoke—even when they are presented in the context of "outrage or a cry for justice"—is "of course is the pleasure on which the cinema industry thrives and which made these women vulnerable in the first place."[4]

Many of Harron's films explore this vulnerability, and critics' inability to recognize the feminism animating this exploration attests to the stubborn force of the patriarchal criteria of choice: a standard of taste that instinctively confirms the value of the aesthetic qualities and narrative forms that mirror a masculine identified subjectivity and sees those associated with femininity as inferior. Though Harron has achieved a rare level of success as a woman director, her work is frequently bashed and maligned. Often working with the genre of the biopic—a "low" film genre that has, because of the value it places on the individual, a significant (if only partially acknowledged) place in feminist film history— much of Harron's work confronts the conditions that make this bashing possible.[5] She attends to the fact that women's lives, and things associated with women's lives, are often considered lower and less valuable, not worthy of the edifying identifications viewers expect from film. Reading negative reviews of her films—many of which are, as she puts it, "horrible"—it is clear that neither film critics nor viewers consider the possibility that Harron might be trying to question the gendered hierarchy of film genres or is highlighting how American mass culture and historical iterations of women and femininity are conflated and dismissed.[6]

In this chapter I analyze Harron's made-for-television film *Anna Nicole*. "Cruelly lampoon[ed]" in the press, *Anna Nicole* tells the story of model Anna Nicole Smith (Agnes Bruckner): her rise in the 1990s from a waitress and pole dancer to a *Guess* and *Playboy* model and reality television star, her infamous marriage to oil tycoon J. Howard Marshall II (Martin Landau), and her death in 2007 from a drug overdose.[7] Drawn from a script based loosely on a 2011 *New York Magazine* article "Paw Paw & Lady Love," *Anna Nicole* tracks how Smith became an icon of white female celebrity in American culture who enacted its promises, dangers, pleasures, and disasters.[8] *Anna Nicole* is also a playful meditation on how mass culture and femininity are conflated and then dismissed through images of female celebrities. Mirroring her own work as a director, Harron composes scenes that focus on Smith producing images with her body and making herself into an icon of the sexual display expected of white heterosexual women in American culture. This crucial aspect of *Anna Nicole* is connected to Harron's choice to highlight—rather than downplay— the tacky, silly, and clichéd feminine display Smith perfected and make it part of her film's visual landscape. The slightly campy aesthetic of *Anna Nicole* helps to denaturalize the connection between white women's bodies and feminine display; it also functions as a lever that allows us to see femininity as a specific form of visual work.

At the opening of *Anna Nicole*, Smith narrates the story of her humble origins in Texas. In these initial scenes, Harron directs viewers' attention to Smith, but also the processes by which images of Smith were created: she leaves the white lines of the video frame and the red recording light visible, and when the shot widens, viewers can see the lights, a director, and a sound technician holding a microphone. This meta-commentary on the production

Figure 2.1 Anna Nicole (Agnes Bruckner) introduces her home town

of an image—a consistent dimension of *Anna Nicole*—allows Harron to ironically play up Smith's performativity without making her the target of ridicule. Performing her ditzy small-town Southern charm, wearing a big smile and a light blue floral sun dress with spaghetti straps and a revealing neckline, Smith stands with her hand on her hip and gestures up to the sign for her home town in Texas: Mexia. "Welcome to my home town," she says as though she is a tour guide or a hostess. Viewers will later see that this video segment was produced for a 1993 appearance on *Larry King Live*, which confirmed her celebrity status; she had just become the newest model for *Guess* jeans and had been named *Playboy*'s "Playmate of the Year."

In the next shot, Smith stands in front of "Crispy Carl's Fried Chicken" where she once worked and met her first husband. But mentioning him was a mistake: "Shoot but I don't want to talk about him... Cut...cut." Smith playfully waves her hands in front of the camera to occlude her face. With this lighthearted dismissal of Smith's first husband, Harron hints that *Anna Nicole* will tug toward the men in her life, but the primary focus will be on Smith's perspective of her own life story. This is a simple but significant choice, as Smith became a celebrity by producing an image of her body that hyperbolically embodies fantasies of a white American femininity that gives itself over the familiar scripts of masculinized desire.

Staging an affinity between making images and working as a hostess or a waitress, the fact that *Anna Nicole* is a film made for television is important. In the last twenty years, more women directors have started working in television, not only to circumvent the sexist restrictions of the film industry or pay the bills, but to direct in a medium that has, through the genre of "quality television," moved closer to the prestige of film. As many feminist scholars of television have argued, the "quality" of quality television becomes salient the more shows mark their distance from television's link to the feminization of mass culture.[9] Television has long been associated with the domestic spaces of the suburban home—think of the soap opera—and reflects capitalism's entrenched reliance upon the sexual division of labor to decide who and what are productive are valuable.[10] By paying attention to the connection between the work of posing for images and domestic labor (which extends into restaurant work) and letting that connection run subtly through *Anna Nicole*, Harron suggests that the devaluation built into perceptions of the work typically assigned to women inflects assumptions about female celebrities that make them mass culture's most obvious targets. If women are implicitly associated with and tied to domestic reproduction—the work that is so often given freely in the name of love—then they can be punished for bringing the skills associated with that work to the marketplace. This logic explains the feminist argument of *Anna Nicole*, but also helps us understand the negative reception of Harron's work.

ANNA NICOLE AND HARRON AT *LIFETIME*

Anna Nicole did not just appear on television, it appeared on Lifetime: Television for Women, a cable channel started in 1984 and designed to cultivate an audience of women viewers with shows and films that feature female leads. Lifetime is not considered a channel for "quality television"; the insult of feminization clings stubbornly to it. This is particularly the case with Lifetime's made-for-television films, which, as Caitlin Benson-Allott points out, are "widely ridiculed for their melodramatic focus on women's crises" and are "scorned even by other woman-oriented television shows, including HBO's *Sex and the City*."[11] I think Harron challenges the ideas that make it easy to dismiss Lifetime (and other visual commodities designed for women), which makes it interesting that when Harron was approached with the script for *Anna Nicole*, she was skeptical about directing a film for the channel. Harron admits she had "a bit of that bias," the bias that comes from the entrenched assumption that visual media made to address women is trivial and sappy.[12] There are certainly valid feminist criticisms of Lifetime: presuming to address all women, the channel "recycles stereotypes of normative white femininity," and in so doing, occludes differences among women.[13] It can easily be read as a commodification and co-optation of liberal feminism.[14] However, I am more interested in connecting *Anna Nicole* to Lifetime's premise that women should have access to virtual spaces that value their aspirations and do not ignore the specific impediments they face as women.

In the case of Smith, the imperative to appear as an appealing image was both an aspiration and an impediment. After the opening sequence in which Smith welcomes viewers to Mexia, *Anna Nicole* shifts to a montage of Smith posing on the red carpet. Set to catchy but vacuous club music, this sequence of images shows Smith waving and blowing kisses to fans and the paparazzi. Her poses are campy citations of old Hollywood glamor. The cameras flash across the screen and her body and Smith seems to absorb the light as a kind of touch that she responds to with wide smiles and exaggerated gestures. Every pose is a campy pin-up.

As if to prove that there was an actual body and person animating these images, this montage ends with an image of Smith's corpse on a hospital gurney. Her hair is yellow, and her face is as white as the sheet that covers her. The camera approaches her body slowly from above until the image of Smith's face begins to blur and fade. In the voice-over Smith states, "I'll be buried as international celebrity and balls-to-the-wall party girl Anna Nicole Smith, but I was born Vicki Lynn Hogan." The voice-over—a staple of the biopic—foregrounds Smith's capacity to tell her own story and place the girl she once was, "Vicki Lynn Hogan," at its center. Smith's voice marks a distinction between Harron's portrayal of her dead body and the spectacle of Smith's death that took place in the media. In her analysis of how celebrity corpses are criminalized, Jacque Lynn Foltyn describes the chorus of voices that placed themselves before the problem of Smith's life and death: "Night after night, day after day, radio and television commentators and a motley assortment of family members, lovers, hangers-on and lawyers speculated about the cause of Smith's demise and the condition of her decomposing criminalized body."[15] Much of the speculation reinforced a "moral discourse" that allowed people to discuss Smith's "character and personality flaws."[16] Harron's portrayal rejects this impulse to make the corpse evidence of a crime the celebrity inflicted upon herself. This reflection challenges the logic of disposability that shapes perceptions of the "white trash" female celebrity: there is hardly anything more deserving of disdain than the story of a white lower-class woman who made a career of sexualized display. It can be easily thrown away.

DANGEROUS CELEBRITY

The misogyny directed at female celebrities online highlights the fact that western culture has a ravenous appetite for devouring images of women who are in the media spotlight. Often a celebrity's fall from grace will bring the misogyny animating this appetite and its cruel satisfactions into sharp relief. In her analysis of the media "feeding frenzy" that took place in response to the case against Martha Stewart, Carole A Stabile observes, "like all women in a sexist culture,

[Stewart] had somehow 'asked for it'—she had turned herself into a brand, she had sold out the domestic sphere, she was too confident, too 'brash,' too much."[17] Though her class position was different, Stabile's description of the pervasive sense that Stewart had exceeded the acceptable bounds of womanhood also applies to Smith. In their work examining the gender discrepancies of twenty-first-century celebrity, Su Holmes and Diane Negra draw attention to the fact that male celebrities are far less likely to be on the receiving end of public disdain.[18] They cite a *New York Times* article, "Boys Will Be Boys, Girls Will be Hounded by the Media," in which Alex Williams writes that "Men who fall from grace are treated with gravity and distance, while women in similar circumstances are objects of derision, titillation, and black comedy."[19] In his reading of Smith through the category of "white trash," Jeffrey Brown argues that Smith's lower class and white Southern origins gave people even more license to transform her into an object of derision. Commenting on the fact that Smith "mugged for the imagegraphers" even though her body was no longer streamlined and polished, Brown writes that she "committed perhaps the most significant class transgression imaginable: she made a spectacle of herself."[20]

Questioning the cultural impulse to denigrate female celebrities who make spectacles of themselves, Harron's portrayal of Smith draws from a reparative sympathy and a subtle but discernible feminist perspective.[21] The result is more than a fair account of Smith's story; Harron highlights the commodity feminism implicitly animating Smith's career ambitions and places her work in a tradition in which women have represented themselves within the visual genres of sexual display as "self-aware, assertive, strong, and independent," as Maria Elena Buszek puts it in her study of the feminist pin-up.[22] *Anna Nicole* also offers a thoughtful analysis of the circumscribed forms of visibility available to women in American culture, and is highly cognizant of the fact that images of women's sexual assertion can be made into or perceived as "silly caricatures" that "construct [women's] humiliation and passivity as turn-ons."[23] Indeed, I read Harron's film as a feminist meta-commentary on the expectation that women make pleasing images of their bodies, as it reveals the punishments wielded against women for attempting to survive, benefit from, and even make a career out of their own capacities to produce pleasing images with their bodies.

In this sense, *Anna Nicole* is a feminist argument about the production of an iconic image of a white woman "making a spectacle of herself." But rather than relishing in the "trainwreck" that Smith's life became, the film attends to the life story, psychic history, and the multiple forms of affective and reproductive labor that the most recognizable icons of Smith occlude. Harron creates this attention by showing Smith at work making images: photographers, camera equipment, sets, and flashing lights are displayed consistently in *Anna Nicole*. Portraying the machinery and mediums for producing images, Harron deconstructs Smith's iconic visuality and breaks it down into their various parts.

This gives viewers the opportunity to see her images as products of the affective and reproductive labor that has traditionally been assigned to women.[24] Indeed, these scenes of image-making are the foundations of Harron's investigation into the ways in which women's lives are shaped by the expectation that they transform themselves into idealized visual images. But rather than its seamless, ready-to-consume surface, in *Anna Nicole*, Harron depicts the working side of the icon and marks the differences between the life, desire, and labor Smith put into her images and the purposes those images were made to serve. The working side of the icon identifies a theme many of Harron's films pursue—*The Notorious Bettie Page* most explicitly—but also reflexively denotes the work of the woman filmmaker who produces images of women in the service of feminist arguments.

VISUALIZING A CELEBRITY: HARRON'S AESTHETICS

The visual genres, mediums, and styles through which Harron tells her story highlights the thorough and precise research she brings to her filmmaking practice. In *Anna Nicole*, Harron recreates the warm, airbrushed glow of *Playboy* covers, pin ups, and centerfolds and the soft haziness of Lifetime made-for-television movies to show Smith working as a pole dancer, posing for soft porn photographs, and appearing on reality television. Harron denaturalizes these image-making practices and unhinges them from the exploitations with which they are habitually connected. Harron certainly depicts Smith crashing into the reality of a female celebrity and making a spectacle of herself, but she also resists the logic of denigration that shape responses to images of women by carefully depicting the labor Smith put into her primary form of work: crafting images of her body.

Anna Nicole can obviously be understood as a reflection on a woman embodying a particularly white definition of American femininity. There is no doubt that whiteness gave Smith access to a place in the American cultural spotlight that, while circumscribed, has been systemically closed to women of color. Many photographs of Smith exemplify what Richard Dyer identifies as the "glow of white women."[25] It is the images she produced for *Guess*—black-and-white photographs that allude to Marilyn Monroe, Jayne Mansfield, and the repertoire of erotic poses that defined 1950s Hollywood glamor—that illustrate the capacity of visual technologies to create the "white woman as the idealized creature of light."[26] The idealization of whiteness illuminating these photographs is the ground of Smith's hyper-sexualization but also grants her sexual display a transcendent quality. Noting that the concept of a "star" is located in "idealized forms of whiteness," Sean Redmond argues that the "idealized white female star floats between being the ultimate object of desire and a subject who nonetheless remains above and beyond sexual desirability."[27] Access to this space "above and beyond sexual desirability" is connected to the idea that white women are, inherently, "innocent" and therefore far from sexual commodification, which gives them more license to performatively embody an exaggerated iteration of feminine sexuality. In these ways and more, images of white women reinforce white dominance; they circulate as visual commodities that extend the power and reach of western visual culture, making substantial (if unnoticed) contributions to the visual economy of racial difference.[28]

While women gain access to power if they align themselves with familiar images of white femininity—a power Smith quite effectively capitalized upon by making herself into a celebrity icon—they are also hinged precariously between racial privilege and the oppressions of gender and class. This means white women are often unable to wield the power that white skin can often give them to defend themselves against the denigrations that lurk on the other side of idealization. As Camilla Griggers argues, while white women are positioned "inside the American family and its 'values'," they are also "the battered, the raped, the incested, and the murdered."[29] In other words, white women are "icon[s] of social privilege" but also "its sacrificial victim[s]."[30] *Anna Nicole* explores this paradox. It demonstrates how Smith relied upon white femininity to become a celebrity icon but also shows how her story aligned with a script of a woman sacrificed on the bright, harsh stage of celebrity.

For women, celebrity exposure translates into vulnerability, and Harron makes it clear that from the beginning Smith's life was shaped by the threat of sexual violence. Recall that at the scene of her corpse, Smith tells viewers she was born "Vicki Lynn Hogan." With the soft announcement of her given name, the film shifts to a pastoral scene of a little white girl (Julia Walters), small and mousy, riding her bike against a background of autumn foliage. This image sets up the muted brown palette that contrasts sharply with the film's title, which appears in lavender pink cursive letters at the top of the screen. This pink hints that much of *Anna Nicole*'s style will mirror the hyper-femininity of Smith's display. By playfully taking up this display and replicating the visual images and genres through which Smith built her image, Harron opens spaces for viewers to question the ease with which American culture judges a woman. By exaggerating the "femininity" of image-making, Harron makes visible its process of construction—nothing is innate or natural to the image, to the white girl, to femininity. And if everything is constructed, it follows that it is also deconstruct-able. Both Harron and Vicki Lynn Hogan's skill lies in the purposeful mastery of image-making. And both master the form of female image-making so well that their execution raises questions about how perfect, dangerous, or reflexive the image-making truly is, offering sharp insights about the malleability of white femininity as a formal structure.

As the scene progresses, Vicki Lynn approaches her home (a humble ranch-style house) as her mother (Virginia Madsen) leaves for work as a sheriff deputy. Before getting into the car, Vicki Lynn's mother remarks on the messiness of her brown hair: it looks like "something has been nesting in it." A subsequent scene portrays the adolescent Vicki Lynn brushing her hair at a dressing table. Along with putting on make-up and stuffing her bra, brushing her hair is part of preparing herself to go to the bowling alley to meet boys. Her mother disapproves of this scene and its implications, and locks Vicki Lynn in the bedroom. Outside the locked door, her mother heatedly explains that she is protecting her and laments the burdens of having a child too young. With these two opening scenes, Harron has exposed a double-bind particular to girls: they have to be well-groomed and "pretty," but when the investment in their own image becomes eroticized as an expression of their own sexuality, it is perceived with punitive suspicion. Vicki Lynn's image becomes a site of pleasure, punishment, danger, and moral reprimand, but also a line of escape.

The next scene depicts Vicki Lynn putting away socks in her mother's bedroom. She drops one, and sees a stack of magazines under the bed. She reaches for the inaugural edition of *Playboy* with Marilyn Monroe on the cover. This is the photograph of Monroe from the Miss America contest in Atlantic City in 1952. Wearing a black dress with a narrow white collar and deep V-neck that extends to her waist, Monroe's arm is stretched high into a crowd-pleasing wave. Her wide, lipstick-drawn smile invites viewers into the magazine's more titillating pages, where one could indulge in the sexualization of visual consumption and see Monroe's iconic *Golden Dreams* pin-up.

Figure 2.2 Anna Nicole's inspiration: Marilyn Monroe

Harron suggests a connection between the sexual availability of Monroe's image and sexual violence. Vicki Lynn's stepfather (William Day) enters the bedroom unaware of this little girl under the bed. He lights a cigarette, aggressively drinks a bottle of beer. When a teenage girl (her mother's younger sister) enters the house, she sees Vicki Lynn's stepfather with fear and quickly walks away. Off screen viewers can hear the man try to force himself into the girl's room, and it is clear he has been sexually abusing her. Vicki Lynn closes her eyes and covers her ears to block out the sounds of a struggle. She picks up *Playboy* magazine again and lovingly touches the image of Monroe's face and the outline of her body.

SPECTER OF GLAMOR: SMITH AND MONROE

Soon after her mother kicks the man out, Vicki Lynn hears a woman's voice sweetly calling her name. As she looks up, she sees Anna Nicole waving in the mirror. Her platinum blonde hair is sculpted into a short bouffant; she wears a bright fuchsia-red deep-cut dress, and sparkly diamonds that hang from her ears and over the tops of her large round breasts. Exaggerated and schlocky, this is the mythical celebrity image Anna Nicole, a star with a look heavily indebted to Monroe. In the voice-over, Smith says that she "always felt that if she hadn't become aware of Marilyn, she never would have become Anna."

Set against hyper-masculinity and domestic iterations of sexual violence, the movement from the image of Monroe on the cover of *Playboy* to the apparition of Anna Nicole demonstrates that for Smith, Monroe was a lot more than a sexy image to emulate. The icon of Monroe was a promise that the sexual display of white women can be a form of protection and a path to success. She embodied the possibility of succeeding within the culture's insistence that women live and represent exploitation. This fantasy sequence could easily be dismissed as an example of the silly melodrama associated with the Lifetime channel and even worse, a girl's stargazing and dreams of fame, which are often read, as Kim Allen explains, as "deluded fantasies in need of correction."[31] But given Harron's emphasis on the work Smith put into becoming a model and a celebrity, this portrayal of Vicki Lynn's intense identification with Monroe can be understood as a reflection of the way class inflects the celebrity ambitions of girls. As Allen argues, girls' attraction to and emulation of celebrities are far more productive than people assume, which is particularly true for girls of the working class, for whom "*becoming* a celebrity may be seen as a more attainable aspiration" since they have been "traditionally excluded from accessing 'high status' professional careers."[32]

Behind the aura of this fantasy image is the reality that women are often punished for attempting to capitalize on the forms of visibility presented to them in American visual culture. While Monroe foresees Smith's ascendancy as a celebrity icon, she also emblematizes the overexposure and hyperconsumption to which Smith will be subjected. Indeed, the *Playboy* Vicki Lynn finds under her mother's bed was just one of many images of Monroe to appear in 1953. From that year forward, Monroe became one of the world's most recognizable icons of white American femininity, standing for, temporarily benefiting from, and getting destroyed by the insatiable appetite for consuming images of women's bodies.

Monroe crystallizes what historian Joanne Meyerowitz identifies as "the proliferation in the mass media of sexual representations of women" in the twentieth century, a major shift in the history of sexuality, women, and popular culture.[33] As Meyerowitz explains, whereas "illustrations and photographs of scantily clad and nude women" were "once considered disreputable," in the twentieth century such images could be seen everywhere, "grac[ing] billboards, calendars, television, movies, and magazines."[34] The "exposed female body" became "ubiquitous" and American culture's "primary public symbol of eroticism."[35] Monroe is an icon of this public eroticism, as a meta-image that stands for the proliferation of images. Though this is far less obvious, she also represents a specific form and dimension of women's work—appearing as a pleasing image—and its exploitation. It is precisely this work that Dyer highlights in his analysis of Monroe in *Heavenly Bodies* (1986). Dyer explains that he chose to focus on Monroe because she spoke out against the alienation of her labor, and her images address that exploitation. Dyer writes, "Unthreatening, vulnerable, Monroe always seemed to be available, on offer."[36]

The scenes of *Anna Nicole* that feature Smith's identification with Monroe suggest that it is not just *images* but *icons* that Harron takes as her subject. Icons are typically understood as highly recognizable, affectively charged images dense with symbolic meanings. Icons function like cultural mirrors; they reflect the values and ideals through which collectivities see themselves. Though they are considered positive forms of visibility, as is the case with beloved celebrities, politicians, or individuals, there is often a punitive underside to the affirmation the icon materializes.[37] This is easy to see with sexualized images of women, which are, as Abigail Solomon-Godeau argues in "The Other Side of Venus: The Visual Economy of Sexual Display" (1996), "icons" of "modern mass consumer culture."[38] A celebrity icon such as Smith exemplifies the equation between images of women's sexual availability and the consumption Solomon-Godeau highlights. In turn, Solomon-Godeau's argument helps to explain why female celebrities like Smith are perceived to be disposable "trash." She argues that ubiquitous icons of women putting their heterosexuality on display transmit a "banal possessability" that allows masculinized viewers to imagine themselves mastering commodification and capitalism's alienating effects through acts of consuming, and then disposing of, these images.³⁹ This is the "other side" of the celebrity icon that Harron explores with such precision in *Anna Nicole*.

HARRON'S SOCIETY OF SPECTACLE

Anna Nicole shows that Smith's image followed the script of spectacle. It became more available, consumable, and disposable. Spectacle was the word Guy Debord used to identify the thick accumulation of images that is capitalism's most banal and explicit sign. Debord famously defined the spectacle as "capital accumulated to the point where it becomes an image," by which he means that the circulation of commodities is so extensive and thorough, capital now congeals in vision itself.⁴⁰ In spectacle culture, Susan Willis writes, "we consume with our eyes," and images of women putting their bodies on display become figures for the sexualized ease of that consumption.⁴¹ By highlighting the work Smith put into crafting her image, Anna Nicole restages the spectacle of Smith and halts the unreflective ease with which her image was consumed.

As Harron portrays it, Vicki Lynn transformed into Anna Nicole not just because she identified with Monroe, but because she acquired and deployed the skills of feminine sexual display that Monroe exemplifies. Living out the story her mother warned against—dropping out of high school, having a child as a teenager—Vicki Lynn begins to transform into Smith when she starts working as a pole dancer. Harron portrays Smith applying for a waitressing job as a young single mother without a job or a place to live. After a shot of the Houston skyline, Smith is in her car looking at a neon sign for a strip club. The focus on the neon image of a woman wearing a cowboy hat and cowboy boots foresees what will become Smith's primary occupation: not waitressing, but another kind of service, the visual display of her body. Indeed, inside the strip club, the manager (David Dwyer) tells Smith that they don't have any waitressing positions available, but offers her the possibility of working on the "pole dancing side." She looks at a woman in a turquoise bikini circling a pole and asks about the pay. The manager says that "even without too much on top" she could make ten times as much—"the sky's the limit."

Though Smith takes up the manager's offer to try pole dancing, she is more scared than enthused. Harron portrays her in the dressing room alone wearing a cotton gray bra looking in the mirror with fear. An African-American woman (Carla Fisher) wearing a silver lamé dress comes into the room. She highlights to Smith's whiteness as naiveté, and suggests that black women do not have the luxury of not knowing about the demand to make themselves into sexualized images. After describing her as "pitiful," the black woman throws her a hot pink outfit and then gives her a Xanax and a glass of champagne. This is a theme that Harron will return to over the course of *Anna Nicole*. Smith actually wasn't comfortable posing topless, but the demand for topless images provoked her to drugs and drinking; the more the public wanted to see her nude the more drugs and alcohol she consumed. Her name is called out softly. She looks up, and there, in the mirror, is the mirage of Anna Nicole again. Harron frames her appearance with a wide-angle shot that shows Smith and this mythical image of Anna Nicole on two sides of the mirror. Smith's cotton bra and underwear, white ankle socks, and tennis shoes contrast sharply with the highly exaggerated "Anna Nicole" in her hot-pink dress—all image. The outfit Smith holds (also hot pink) is a link between them. Anna Nicole blows Smith a kiss and winks at her as she fades into the bright lights of celebrity spectacle.

After an awkward and embarrassing start, Smith becomes a skilled pole dancer. With every revealing dip and turn of her body, she puckers her lips into a seductive look as if she is posing for the camera. While she gets a lot of attention at the strip club—the DJ announces her as the club's new "dancilicious" star—another woman attracts all the men to her pole. It is her enormous breasts that steal the show: her royal blue bikini top barely covers them, and her garter belt is teeming with cash. Smith is visibly dismayed at all the attention this woman receives, and in the next scene she is telling a plastic surgeon that she wants her breasts to be the size of "whatever lives in this bag." When the surgeon expresses disbelief, Smith turns the bowling bag upside down so dollar bills spill out on her desk. This exaggerated image literalizes Smith's body as a site of monetary investment.

Smith's huge breasts are the perfect supplement to her pole dancing skills and she becomes the strip club's star. But as Jeffrey A. Brown argues, Smith's breasts, which "carried [her] curvaceousness to an almost cartoonish extreme" made her a site for scrutiny and ridicule.[42] Her breasts became "objects not just of male fascination but public speculation."[43] Speculation here means a form of guessing premised on intrusive looking and the demand to know, but speculation also suggests financial risk—the bet Smith placed on her breasts when she made them her assets. No one assumes they are real; they are the exaggerated response to an impossible demand to create an image of femininity that reflects male heterosexual desire.

Setting her sights beyond a comfortable life for herself and her son, Smith hears that *Playboy* is searching for talent and arranges for a photo shoot that will produce images she can submit to the magazine. In a humble studio, wearing a leopard-print bikini, Smith is intent on arranging her body into languid poses and sensuous expressions. She leans into the lens with her pouting lips and postures that suggest the pleasures of sexual submission. Harron makes it clear that posing for photographs demands a particular set of skills that Smith possessed and translated into polished, profitable images.

Figure 2.3 Nicole gets images taken to attract *Playboy* magazine

In her study of modeling and what she identifies as "glamor labor," Elizabeth A. Wissinger demonstrates that while the photo shoot had been a "highly scripted performance elicited by tight control of the model" in the late twentieth century it became a "free-form exchange prompting the model to bring the unexpected to the transaction."[44] The development of this spontaneous "transaction" emerged out of the increased commodification of visual imagery and the historical moment in which "models became workers who sold their likenesses for profit."[45] Harron's scenes highlight the sexualization at work in these transactions. After one shot with his 35mm camera, the photographer (Al Vicente) tells Smith that "his time is free" but raises a faux concern about the cost of the "film stock, development, and printing." Producing photographs "ain't cheap," he explains, and asks "How are you going to pay for this?" The scene then switches to a club where Smith is giving the photographer a lap dance to cover the cost of "film stock, development, and printing." Harron switches back and forth between the images of Smith in the club (backlit for a hazy sensuous aura) and images of Smith in the studio (brightly lit from the side to highlight the sharp lines of Smith's perfected body) to suggest the connections between them. More than a form of payment, the lap dance highlights the intense and sexual physicality Smith brought to the act of being photographed and transmitted through her images.

These scenes of Smith posing and dancing for a photographer draw attention to Harron's engagement with the aesthetic of *Playboy* images—their slick, airbrushed gloss—as well as the premise and argument of the magazine—naturalizing white women's sexual availability. Smith graced the cover of

Playboy five times over the course of her career, and in 1993 she was Playmate of the Year. Harron composes two scenes that stage the production of two *Playboy* covers: her first cover in March 1992 (a relatively demure shot of Smith in a formal gown); another cover that appeared in February 1994 (Smith is photographed against a red background loosely wearing a red robe she holds up over her breasts). In these scenes, Harron focuses on the abundance and technological sophistication of the camera equipment. These depictions of professionals producing images announce Smith's celebrity status, but also signal that she is more exposed to scrutiny, judgment, and the hostilities directed at women who attempt to capitalize upon their own sexual display. Just after depicting the production of the *Playboy* covers, Harron shows Smith on the set of her famous advertisement for *Guess*. The CEO of *Guess* asks his assistant where the new girl is. She responds by pointing to Smith and asking "the fat one?"

CONCLUSION: SMITH'S NEW REALITY

While *Playboy* masks its scrutiny of women's bodies under a soft, airbrushed gloss, the magazine functions as a pivot between Smith's work acquiring the skills to produce images of sexual display and "making a spectacle of herself." The theme of judgment explicitly announces itself when Harron reproduces segments from Smith's reality television show *The Anna Nicole Show*, which appeared on the E! (Entertainment Network) channel from 2002 to 2004. Derided by critics, but popular with audiences—its debut was the most watched show in E!'s history—Harron makes the production of the show a cruel continuation of the visibility Smith had been pursuing since she identified with the icon of Monroe. Leaving the white lines of the video frame and the red recording light visible, the scenes of Smith's reality television show harken back to the video sequence that opens Harron's film in which Smith introduces the viewers of *Larry King Live* to her home town of Mexia. However, rather than playfully and humbly staging her ascension from her status as a white woman from a poor background who has suddenly become a nationally recognized star, Harron's representation of Smith's reality TV show suggests that it became a tool for putting Smith back where she belongs.

True to reality TV's overlaps with celebrity culture and its "technology of intense visualization," *The Anna Nicole Show* not only documents, but enacts the overexposed ruin—the "trainwreck"—of Smith's celebrity status. By staging the production of *The Anna Nicole Show*, Harron suggests that Smith gave herself over to the narrative of celebrity denigration—overexposed, out of control, overweight, a spectacle for others to visually consume.[46] As Brown argues, audiences watched it for "the freak show nature of the series" and "Smith's apparent failings."[47] Smith's weight gain, her overeating, and her garish image made a spectacle of those failings. However, whereas audiences assumed they were laughing at her, Smith's skill constructing her image suggests that, in fact, she knew she was giving audiences the other side of Anna Nicole—the icon of white hyper feminine and sexualized display.

One scene from Harron's restaging of the reality show takes place in the kitchen, resituating Smith within the frame of domestic labor and its connection to television's low status. She wears bright blue eye shadow, pink lipstick, and a bright orange and pink sweat suit. While absent-mindedly eating popcorn, she tries to talk her son into cooperating with the producers. Deepening her exploration of celebrity culture and its effects on women's lives, Harron is condensing the tabloid surveillance of Smith's body into these scenes, making them extensions of what Brown identifies as the "merciless criticism" of the press, who called her "a blimp, a pig, a cow, an embarrassment, even an obscenity."[48] The self-presentations that provoked these judgments became the material of the show and Harron depicts her attorney and the producers encouraging her weight gain and goofy dumb-blonde antics that provoked the public's ravenous desire to consume her image and spit it out with sexist epithets. By focusing on the work Smith put into the production of her image, Harron's *Anna Nicole* deepens her fascinated engagement with celebrity culture and opens up the possibility of restaging the familiar spectacle of the sacrificed female celebrity by thoughtfully exposing the vulnerability, violence, and work that its icons so easily occlude.

NOTES

1. Richard Dyer, *Heavenly Bodies: Film Stars and Society*, Second Edition (London: Routledge, 1986/2004), 4.
2. In *Women's Cinema, World Cinema* Patricia White cites the work of Martha M. Lauzen, "who puts the proportion of female directors at nine percent in 2008, the same percentage she had measured ten years earlier" (1). See also Katarzyna Paszkiewicz, *Genre, Authorship, and Contemporary Women Filmmakers* (Edinburgh: Edinburgh University Press, 2018); Linda Hadley, Claire Perkins, and Michele Schreiber, *Indie Reframed: Women's Filmmaking and Contemporary American Independent Cinema* (Edinburgh: Edinburgh University Press, 2017).
3. https://womenintvfilm.sdsu.edu/wp content/uploads/2018/01/2017_Celluloid_Ceiling_Report.pdf Patricia White's book is devoted to studying the work of women directors around the globe in order to examine the "cultural work the concepts and institutions of women's cinema and world cinema perform and project" (2). *Women's Cinema, World Cinema: Projecting Contemporary Feminisms* (Durham, NC: Duke University Press, 2015).
4. Jacqueline Rose, "I am a knife," *London Review of Books* (Vol. 40, No. 4, February 22, 2018). https://www.lrb.co.uk/v40/n04/jacqueline-rose/i-am-a-knife. Accessed March 25, 2018.
5. Near the opening of Denis Bingham's study of the biopic, he claims that the "term 'biopic' is frequently used as a pejorative not much different from 'oater' for westerns and 'weepie'

for women's films." *Whose Lives Are They Anyway? The Biopic as Contemporary Film Genre* (New Brunswick, NJ: Rutgers University Press, 2010), 11.

6. Harron is referring to a review of *I Shot Andy Warhol* in the *Hollywood Reporter*. "Mary Harron Interviewed by Anisse Gross." *The Believer* (Vol.12, No. 3, March/April 2014). https://www.believermag.com/issues/201403/ Accessed November 2017. This formulation about the patriarchal criteria of choice is indebted to Andreas Huyssen, "Mass Culture as Woman: Modernism's Other," in *After the Great Divide: Modernism, Mass Culture, Post-Modernism* (Bloomington: Indiana University Press, 1986). Patricia White writes about something akin to the patriarchal criteria of choice when she discusses Kathryn Bigelow's engagement with the genre of the action film, which some argue "unfairly elevate her standing over that of women directors who make films about women" (3). She cites Virginia Woolf's *A Room of One's Own*, in which she discusses the importance attributed to sport and the trivialization of an aesthetic practice such as fashion, which is associated with women.
7. Caetlin Benson-Allott, "'Made for Quality Television?' *Behind the Candelabra* (Steven Soderbergh, 2013), *Anna Nicole* (Mary Harron, 2013)," *Film Quarterly* (Vol. 66, No. 4, Summer 2013), 5.
8. Dan P. Lee, "Paw Paw & Lady Love," *New York Magazine* (June 5, 2011). http://nymag.com/news/features/anna-nicole-smith-2011-6/ Accessed February 10, 2018.
9. See Charlotte Brunsdon, "Problems with Quality," *Screen* (Vol. 31, No. 1, 1990), 67–90. Janet McCabe and Kim Akass, "Introduction: Debating Quality," in *Quality Television: Contemporary American Television and Beyond*, edited by Janet McCabe and Kim Akass (London: I. B. Tauris, 2007), 1–12. Anikó Imre, "Gender and Quality Television," *Feminist Media Studies* (Vol. 9, No. 4, 2009), 391–407.
10. Lynn Spigel, "The Suburban Home Companion: Television and the Neighborhood Ideal in Postwar America," in *Welcome to the Dreamhouse: Popular Media and Postwar Suburbs* (Durham, NC: Duke University Press, 2001), 31–59. Lynne Joyrich, "All That Television Allows: TV, Melodrama, Postmodernism, and Consumer Culture, " in *Private Screenings: Television and the Female Consumer*, edited by Lynn Spigel and Denise Mann (Minneapolis: Minnesota University Press, 1992), 227–52.
11. Benson-Allott, "'Made for Quality Television?'", 5.
12. "Mary Harron Interviewed by Anisse Gross." *The Believer*.
13. Julie D'Acci, "Introduction," Special Issue on Lifetime: A Cable Network "For Women," *Camera Obscura: Feminism, Culture, and Media Studies* (Vols. 11–12, May 1994), 7.
14. Eileen R. Meehan and Jackie Bryars, "Telefeminism: How Lifetime Got Its Groove 1984–1987," *Television and New Media* (Vol. 1, No. 1, 2000), 33–51.
15. Jacque Lynn Foltyn, "Bodies of Evidence: Criminalizing the Celebrity Corpse," *Mortality* (Vol. 21, No. 3, 2016), 246–62,
16. Ibid.
17. Carol A. Stabile, "Getting What She Deserved: The News Media, Martha Stewart, and Masculine Domination," *Feminist Media Studies* (Vol. 4, No. 3, 2004), 318, 328.
18. Sue Holmes and Diane Negra, "Introduction," in *In the Limelight and Under the Microscope: Forms and Functions of Female Celebrity*, edited by Sue Holmes and Diane Negra (New York: Continuum, 2011), 1–16.
19. Cited in Holmes and Negra, "Introduction," in *In the Limelight and Under the Microscope*, 2.
20. Jeffrey A. Brown, "Class and Feminine Excess: The Strange Case of Anna Nicole Smith," *Feminist Review* (Vol. 81, 2015), 91.
21. In the interview with Anisse Gross, Harron does not dismiss her work's affinity with feminism outright, but does see it as a limitation, "Mary Harron Interviewed by Anisse Gross," *The Believer*. Steven S. Kapica connects Harron's *The Notorious Bettie Page* to

"current feminist discourse" and argues that it "appropriate[s] and recover[s] Bettie Page for a third wave feminist audience." Steven S. Kapica, "Multivalent Feminism of *The Notorious Bettie Page*," *Jump Cut: A Review of Contemporary Media*, (No. 55, Fall 2013).
22. Robert Goldman, Deborah Heath, and Sharon L. Smith, "Commodity Feminism," *Critical Studies in Communication* (Vol. 8, 1991), 333–51. Maria Elena Buszek, *Pin-Up Grrls: Feminism, Sexuality, and Popular Culture* (Durham, NC: Duke University Press, 2006), 8.
23. Ibid.
24. For a classic account of deconstruction in feminist film practice see Annette Kuhn, "Textual Politics," in *Women's Pictures: Feminism and Cinema* (London: Pandora, 1982), 160.
25. Richard Dyer, *White* (London: Routledge, 1997), 122.
26. Dyer, *White*, 140.
27. Sean Redmond, "The Whiteness of Stars: Looking at Kate Winslet's Unruly White Body," in *Stardom and Celebrity: A Reader* (London: Sage, 2007), 263–74.
28. These ideas are indebted to Eva Cherniavsky's *Incorporations: Race, Nation, and the Body Politics of Capital* (Minneapolis: Minnesota University Press, 2006), 71–99, 100–30.
29. Camilla Griggers, *Becoming-Woman* (Minneapolis: Minnesota Press University Press, 1997), xii.
30. Griggers, 10.
31. Kim Allen, "Girls Imagining Careers in the Limelight: Social Class, Gender, and Fantasies of 'Success'," in *In the Limelight and Under the Microscope: Forms and Functions of Female Celebrity*, edited by Sue Holmes and Diane Negra (New York: Continuum, 2011), 149–73.
32. Ibid.
33. Joanne Meyerowtiz, "Women, Cheesecake, and Borderline Material: Responses to Girlie Pictures in the Mid-Twentieth-Century U.S," *Journal of Women's History* (Vol. 8, No. 3, Fall 1996), 9–35.
34. Ibid.
35. Ibid.
36. Dyer, *Heavenly Bodies*, 46.
37. These ideas are indebted to Nicole R. Fleetwood, *On Racial Icons: Blackness and the Public Imagination* (New Brunswick, NJ: Rutgers University Press, 2015), 9.
38. Abigail Solomon-Godeau, "The Other Side of Venus: The Visual Economy of Sexual Display," in *The Sex of Things: Gender and Consumption in Historical Perspective*, edited by Victoria de Grazia (Berkeley: University of California Press, 1996), 113–50.
39. Ibid., 123.
40. Guy Debord, *The Society of the Spectacle*, translated by Donald Nicholson-Smith. (New York: Zone Books, 1967/1994), 25.
41. Susan Willis, *A Primer for Daily Life* (New York: Routledge, 1991), 31.
42. Jeffrey A. Brown, "Class and Feminine Excess: The Strange Case of Anna Nicole Smith," *Feminist Review* (Vol. 81, 2015), 91.
43. Ibid, 80.
44. Elizabeth A. Wissinger, *This Year's Model: Fashion, Media, and the Making of Glamor* (New York: NY University Press, 2015), 80.
45. Ibid, 85.
46. Misha Kavka, *Reality TV* (Edinburgh: Edinburgh University Press, 2012), 163. See also Holmes and Negra on the "trainwreck," "Introduction," 2–3.
47. Brown, 92, 93.
48. Brown, 81.

PART II

Feature Films and Production Contexts

CHAPTER 3

Dream of the '90s: Mary Harron in Indiewood

Kyle Barrett

The Hollywood system, that began in the 1920s, started to decline in the mid-1960s as both television and shifting cultural attitudes drew the attention of audiences away from cinemas. A new strategy was fashioned wherein young filmmakers were provided studio support to craft personal stories that reflected the tumultuous times of 1960s America. The result was the "Hollywood Renaissance," or, "New Hollywood," which Geoff King notes was, "the outcome of a conjunction of forces: social, industrial and stylistic."[1] Filmmakers such as Martin Scorsese, Elaine May, Francis Ford Coppola, Arthur Penn, and Paul Schrader emerged during this period and crafted films "in which they tell the stories they want to tell in the ways they want to tell them."[2] Collectively, they revitalized Hollywood cinema, which has had a lasting impact on filmmakers around the world. This crossover of independent filmmakers into the studio system was a substantial move away from conventional practices. Robert Kolker comments:

> The small group of filmmakers who emerged in the late 1960s and early 1970s were able to take brief advantage of the transitional state of the studios, using their talents in critical, self-conscious ways, examining the assumptions and forms of commercial narrative cinema [. . .][3]

Yet, the aforementioned filmmakers' personal style of filmmaking was short lived. The blockbuster launched initially with *The Exorcist* (Warner Bros., Friedkin, 1973), followed by *Jaws* (1975). The extraordinary success of both films meant that the high concept B-movie would establish a new studio system at the tail end of the 1970s. The blockbuster proliferated in the 1980s, with high-budget, mass-appeal films that have maintained control of the box office ever since. However, the 1990s saw a new wave of filmmakers establish a cinema that, according to Claire Perkins, "evokes the Hollywood renaissance era of 1967–1975."[4] This would, once again, challenge, subvert but ultimately become part of the Hollywood system.

This adventurous form of Hollywood cinema in the 1990s to mid-2000s was coined "Indiewood," where independent cinema and studio production became blurred. Filmmakers such as Paul Thomas Anderson, Steven Soderbergh, and Quentin Tarantino were given support of studios through subsidiary "independent" branches to create projects. These films were a stark contrast to the studio-financed blockbusters, which Emmanuel Levy states, "steer clear of controversial issues and employ stories based on the lowest common denominators" and were being challenged by new filmmakers who dealt with darker and more controversial subject matter.[5]

There was also a rise of production companies that became mini-majors, which Michael Z. Newman defines as "divisions of Hollywood studios owned by media conglomerates and thus are not independent of Hollywood companies."[6] Miramax Films, established in 1979 by the now disgraced Harvey and Bob Weinstein—Harvey was convicted of several sexual assaults and is now incarcerated for up to twenty-three years—is the most well known company during this period, distorting studio and independent filmmaking further. Miramax Films was, at first, a small distribution company that eventually became, according to Yannis Tzioumakis, "the leader of the 'indies' in the 1990s."[7] The company was purchased by Disney in 1993 and elevated the Weinsteins further as powerhouse producers.

Miramax Films set their sights on riskier material and sought to acquire a variety of independently produced films. John Pierson notes that the Weinsteins' "modus operandi is more like a throwback—the 'mogul operandi.' Miramax is filmmaker-friendly in name, but a much more deadly minefield in practice."[8] Soderbergh and Tarantino received support from the Weinsteins in the early stage of their careers. Soderbergh's feature debut *sex, lies, and videotape* (1989) and Tarantino's *Pulp Fiction* were distributed by Miramax. These films ignited the filmmakers' careers, and "a new benchmark was set and the reach of indie/specialty films into the wider marketplace was increased."[9] Though these films (and filmmakers) were critically acclaimed, other directors within the independent sector were overshadowed.

Indiewood can be considered a male-dominated environment, where the above filmmakers, alongside Alexander Payne, Spike Jonze, David O. Russell, and Wes Anderson, received accolades and media attention from film critics and audiences alike. These filmmakers would, ultimately, "offer an attractive blend of creativity and commerce, a source of some of the more innovative and interesting work produced in close proximity to the commercial mainstream."[10] This chapter will place Mary Harron within the context of Indiewood and will examine her first three feature films, *I Shot Andy Warhol*, *American Psycho*, and *The Notorious Bettie Page*, with comparison to projects from some of her contemporaries. Prior to this examination will be a discussion on the development of Indiewood and the difficulty of defining "independent" filmmaking. Harron's debut is discussed in conjunction with Julian Schnabel's biopic *Basquiat*, a film that also features Andy Warhol as a central character. *American Psycho* is analyzed alongside David Fincher's testosterone satire *Fight Club*, highlighting their common themes and contrasting visual styles. Finally, *The Notorious Bettie Page* will be examined with Sofia Coppola's extravagant biopic *Marie Antoinette*, focusing on visual aesthetics and the re-appropriation of the gaze in both films. I will argue that Harron crafts her films through specific visual techniques, satire, genre, and tongue-in-cheek humor, in subtler and more creative ways than her contemporaries.

WHAT IS INDEPENDENT CINEMA?

There has been consistent debate about the definition of "independent cinema" and what constitutes an "independent film." Levy notes that a conventional definition of an "independent film" is, ideally, a "fresh, low-budget movie with a gritty style and offbeat subject matter that express the filmmaker's personal vision."[11] Being "independent" has become increasingly difficult to categorize as it "currently encompasses different movements, forms and expressions, such as black independent film, exploitation filmmaking, new queer cinema or smart cinema, among others."[12] Despite the complexity of a clear definition, attributes of an independent film are transparent: a low-budget, relatively unknown cast with established actors occasionally in supporting/cameo roles, minimal emphasis on plot, and complex, often morally compromised, protagonists. However, as noted above, independent films encompass "different movements," and distinguish themselves from other forms of cinema, mainly the "mainstream," which Newman defines, as "a category niche cultures or subcultures construct to have something against which to define themselves and generate their cultural or subcultural capital."[13] Effectively, big budget Hollywood productions are independent cinema's counterpoint. Indeed, as Newman continues, independent film "profits from its alterity, which sustains it and has the potential to be politically progressive and counter-hegemonic." Harron's approach to filmmaking fits within this mold, having worked consistently with other "independents" such as producer Christine Vachon and actor/writer Genevieve Turner. Their collaborations have resulted in films that have been counter-hegemonic to both Hollywood and Indiewood films (this will be discussed in detail below). For the purposes of this chapter, Harron's status as an "in-between" independent filmmaker will be analyzed through Linda Badley, Claire Perkins, and Michelle

Schreiber's description of independence as, "the realm of financing, production and artistic intent that exists in between avant-garde and experimental films and studio-financed Hollywood production."[4] Before examining Harron's early career, there will be a discussion of the aforementioned New Hollywood, the precursor to Indiewood.

A NEW HOLLYWOOD

The proliferation of television resulted in the weakening of the studio system during the late 1950s and 1960s and created a panic within the majors, including Warner Bros., Paramount and Twentieth Century Fox. Prior to this decline, each major studio "was a self-contained filmmaking factory with its own labor pool of producers, directors, writers, players, and technicians, turning out many films a month during the years of peak production."[5] Parallel to this deterioration saw the rise of European cinema, particularly in France with the "Nouvelle Vague," or the "French New Wave." French directors such as François Truffaut and Jean-Luc Godard pursued "authorship" within their work in an attempt to "make their films more 'personal'."[6] American filmmakers, such as Scorsese and Penn, were particularly inspired by this new, experimental style, utilizing techniques such as: handheld cinematography, shooting on location, jump-cuts in editing, and revisionist tendencies with regard to genre, especially gangster films.

The release of both *The Graduate* (United Artists, Nichols, 1967) and *Bonnie and Clyde* (Warner Bros., Penn, 1967) established the New Hollywood of the 1960s. Both films were thematically different but "mature" in their approach to their respective subject matter. *Bonnie and Clyde*, an homage to the Warner Bros. gangster films of the 1930s and 1940s, utilized a somewhat postmodern aesthetic, employing some of the above noted Godard/Truffaut techniques. The film depicts the titular characters as young anti-heroes, terrorizing conservative society, subtly commenting on the counterculture of the 1960s. The film's explicitly violent ending, where both characters are savagely gunned down in slow motion, firmly established a new direction in 1960s American cinema. *The Graduate* examines the isolation of youth in the 1960s, where many felt adrift following the baby boomers successes in the 1950s. Its protagonist, Ben (Dustin Hoffman), enters into an affair with the older, married Mrs. Robinson (Anne Bancroft), who is also in a lifeless existence. He later breaks off the affair when he falls in love with her daughter Elaine (Katharine Ross). The film's success at the box office arguably lies in its critique of the previous generation, despite the questionable protagonist. *The Graduate* paved the way for further "rebellious" films.

New Hollywood hit its stride with Dennis Hopper's *Easy Rider* (Columbia Pictures, 1969). The film was made on an estimated budget of $400,000, which

Janet Staiger notes, "produces a visible image of the potential financial success of such independently produced films."[17] The film portrays two hippies on a road trip across America, coming into conflict with conservative society. The film ends with the lead characters being killed by two "rednecks." *Easy Rider* connected with its youth-orientated audience and generated a worldwide box office gross of $60,000,000.[18] However, these successes would be short lived. The smaller, personal films were profitable for a few years before audiences began to drift away.

The mid-to-late 1970s saw the birth of the blockbuster. The release of *The Exorcist*, *Jaws*, and *Star Wars* "fueled Hollywood's commercial recovery in the later 1970s after three decades of steep decline."[19] As the blockbuster was reinvigorating the studios, the low-budget personal films dwindled. Michael Cimino's *Heaven's Gate* has been noted as the final product of New Hollywood. Its infamous troubles during production were reported in the press, particularly when the film's budget "ballooned from an original $7.8 million to $40 million, not to mention the cost of promotion, and it died at the box office."[20] The commercial and critical disaster of the film resulted in the production company, United Artists, being sold to Metro-Goldwyn-Mayer. The blockbuster took over the box office, still to this day maintaining its stronghold. It took over another decade before independent filmmakers were able to revitalize American cinema.

INDIEWOOD AND THE INDEPENDENTS

As noted at the beginning of this chapter, Indiewood was seen as a blurring of studio and independent production. King defines Indiewood as "a kind of cinema that draws on elements of each, combining some qualities associated with the independent sector, although perhaps understood as softened or watered-down, with other qualities and industrial practices more characteristic of the output of the major studios."[21] If New Hollywood presented the possibility of independent filmmakers working with studio support, Indiewood would be the next evolution of this notion. Tzioumakis notes, from the mid-1990s Fox, Paramount, Universal, and Warner Bros. established "specialty film divisions with a view to produce and distribute their own brand of American independent film."[22] These "specialty film divisions" provided the opportunity for filmmakers to create work that challenged the studio system, and push boundaries further by incorporating more so-called "art" cinema practices, meaning a personal, authorial style.[23] As the studios were both establishing and acquiring independent companies, such as Fox Searchlight, Sony Pictures Classics and New Line Cinema (owned by Twentieth Century Fox, Sony, and Warner Bros. respectively), this meant that, as observed by Thomas Schatz, "the true independents were left to compete on the narrowest of margins."[24] However, this did not diminish the verve of independent filmmakers working beyond both the mainstream and Indiewood. It provided momentum to push boundaries further.

Indiewood films were neither too experimental nor too conventional that blockbuster-orientated audiences would shy away or those more inclined toward independent productions would not feel unchallenged. They are "generally designed to be difficult to access but also offer some more distinctive features, implying an audience role that can differ in some respects from that associated with 'the mainstream,' or that can include particular kinds of viewer appropriations [. . .]."[25]

Indiewood films can be considered, as noted by Jeffrey Sconce, a form of "Smart Cinema" which "might thus be described as dark comedy and disturbing drama born of ironic distance; all that is not positive and 'dumb'."[26] Films such as *American Beauty* (DreamWorks Pictures, Mendes, 1999), *Magnolia* (New Line Cinema, Anderson, 1999), and *About Schmidt* (New Line Cinema, Payne, 2002) certainly take an ironic approach to their subject matter, exploring themes of repressed homosexuality/midlife crisis, illness, misogyny, and interconnectedness, and life as a widower respectively.

Other notable films made during this period utilized somewhat unconventional storytelling practices. Fragmented non-linear narratives and "hypothetical futures," for example, became synonymous with Indiewood cinema.[27] With narrative experimentation, filmmakers are able to take old formulas and transform them into something slightly more complex yet adhering to the conventions found in classic genres. Films such as *Pulp Fiction*, *The Limey* (Artisan Entertainment, Soderbergh, 1999) and *Memento* (Newmarket, Nolan, 2000) explore the crime/thriller genre but utilize scrambled narratives where the viewer would have to piece the film together themselves.

Indiewood films also feature many references to popular culture that "mobilize techniques of irony and blankness to position themselves knowingly in relation to film historical discourses of authorship, genre, narrative, and style."[28] Tarantino is probably the most obvious postmodernist filmmaker of the 1990s, prevailing in referencing 1960/70s exploitation cinema, establishing a cinema that revisits "the traditions of classical genre filmmaking by crossing them with the stylistic innovations of art cinema, as well as an intense self-consciousness and the use of allusion and quotation."[29] However, it is argued that films made in such a manner are created with style over substance and, as a result, are devoid of any sense of authenticity.[30] Despite this accusation, it cannot be denied that Indiewood films challenged the status quo with regard to Hollywood practices.

In the independent sector, a producer was investing in filmmakers creating projects that were reminiscent of underground filmmaking of the 1950s/1960s. Christine Vachon is recognized as a central figure of the New York independent film scene.[31] Vachon helped launch the career of Todd Haynes, collaborating on all of his films since his debut, *Poison* (Zeitgeist Films, 1991) and has "made a career out of producing distinctive features without making the kind of compromises that afflict other well-intentioned indie outfits."³² Vachon has continuously championed subversive, low-budget LGBTQ+ films, in particular Rose Troche's *Go Fish*, a landmark in New Queer Cinema. Unlike other independent producers who have moved into more commercial filmmaking, Vachon "has remained true to her gay and lesbian, often experimental calling."³³ In 1995, Vachon established Killer Films with producing partner Pamela Koffler when they "decided it was time to keep the production company's shingle out fulltime and start developing projects."³⁴ Vachon's approach to producing was radically different to her contemporaries, particularly the Weinsteins. Patricia White comments:

> while Harvey Weinstein earned notoriety and the nickname Harvey Scissorhands for wresting creative control away from filmmakers in his awards-driven vision of independent film commerce, Vachon represented his antithesis: fidelity to the directors' visions—often those of first-timers with correspondingly low budget projects—was the central plank of Killer's platform.³⁵

Killer Films support of low-budget, up-and-coming filmmakers created an environment of experimentation that would appeal to audiences that were looking beyond both mainstream blockbusters and Indiewood, retaining a traditional independent filmmaking ethos. One of the first films to be produced by Killer Films was *I Shot Andy Warhol*, continuing Vachon's penchant for examining societal outsiders which was a perfect project for a first-time filmmaker with the same obsessions: Mary Harron.

SHOOTING THE POSTMODERNIST: *I SHOT ANDY WARHOL* AND *BASQUIAT*

I Shot Andy Warhol focuses on Valerie Solanas (Lili Taylor), the writer known for creating the infamous *SCUM* (Society for Cutting Up Men) *Manifesto*. In Harron's own words, the power of the *Manifesto* "isn't just the attack on men but also the attack on the way women behave with men; it investigates the psychic damage done to both sexes."³⁶ Harron explores Solanas' troubled life, from her history of child abuse at the hands of men in her family, to working as a prostitute in the 1960s to support her writing. Through her friend Candy Darling (Stephen Dorff), Solanas becomes, for a brief period, part of Andy Warhol's (Jared Harris) circle of creatives at his Factory. Solanas' erratic behavior begins isolating her from the Factory and she eventually sinks into paranoia, believing that Warhol has stolen her play, *Up Your Ass*. This finally leads her to attempt to assassinate the artist in his Factory. The attempt is a failure but Solanas receives fifteen minutes of fame. After being sent for psychiatric evaluation, Solanas is given a sentence of three years in prison. This brief summary of the film's "plot" highlights the themes that would continue throughout Harron's career, that of the social outsider and poisonous attainment of fame/celebrity. At the film's core is Solanas' relationship with Warhol and the perceived control he had over her and, by extension, her creativity.

I Shot Andy Warhol was part of a small group of films in the 1990s that featured Warhol as a supporting character. Warhol was portrayed by Crispin Glover in *The Doors* (TriStar Pictures, Stone, 1991) and David Bowie in *Basquiat*. Released in the same year, *I Shot Andy Warhol* and *Basquiat* explored Warhol's relationship with the protagonists of both films, Solanas and Jean-Michel Basquiat (Jeffrey Wright) respectively. While both *Basquiat* and *I Shot Andy Warhol* fall within the biopic genre, the filmmakers' visual approaches were drastically different. Julian Schnabel's direction is typical of a standard biopic. Framed in a linear narrative, and conventional visual style, the film depicts Basquiat's troubled life as he rises and falls from grace due to his heroin addiction. Harron's approach, however, utilizes a fragmented style that incorporates black-and-white cinematography, Super-8 home movies, and a non-linear narrative. Harron depicts Solanas "sympathetically, but makes no attempt to hide her disturbing, abrasive behavior in the process."[37] The film opens post-assassination attempt, with Solanas storming the Factory. Harron abandons conventional establishing shots of the location and introductions to the characters. For instance, Warhol is only glimpsed via shots of his arm and feet as he lies on the floor wounded, and Solanas is introduced with a gun in her hand trying to fire the jammed gun to finish him off. The directness of the opening scene creates a jarring effect on the viewer and becomes "a scene of consequences of actions rather than the actions themselves."[38] Harron employs this directness throughout the film, with Solanas reading from her *SCUM Manifesto* directly to the camera. By having the character "perform" the *Manifesto*, Harron attempts to visualize the protagonist's anger and portray Solanas as a "visionary whose tragedy stemmed from a lack of self-awareness; she possessed little understanding of her actions."[39] Though Schnabel does not refrain from the darker side of Basquiat through his addiction and change of personality with newfound fame, the film shies from delving deeper into the character's actions. However, both films can be noted for their use of New York locations. *I Shot Andy Warhol*, obviously, spends a lot of time in Warhol's Factory, examining the environment Warhol created for himself and his "hanger-on" cohorts. Harron depicts this atmosphere as somewhat toxic as Warhol both embraces and pulls away from the (non-)creatives in his life, sparking Solanas' fury when he continually postpones reading her play then claiming he lost it. In *Basquiat*,

Schnabel portrays his relationship with the title character as genuine and kind. Yet it is commented upon by secondary characters throughout the film that Warhol was once again using another artist for his own purposes. While Harron explores this in slightly more depth with Warhol's attitude toward Solanas, Schnabel avoids delving deeper into Warhol's intentions.

Harron's somewhat non-judgmental depiction of Solanas can also be seen in relation to her own experience of working in a male-dominated industry. Harron's period at the BBC saw her "surrounded by 'boy geniuses' who were expected to go off and make movies, but she had to have 'a lot more drive to push herself'."[40] The film itself was, as noted above, released during the emergence of predominately male-centered Indiewood, where other "boy geniuses" were touted as radically changing American cinema. The film can, ultimately, be seen to suggest:

> that the grand narratives of radical feminism and the fifteen-minute micronarratives of postmodern fame continue each other, animate cultural possibilities for one another, and occasionally produce massive historical gaps which themselves – far more than the individual agents involved – become a legend most.[41]

These themes would resonate throughout Harron's career and her observations on masculinity were about to expand substantially. Harron's next project, her most (in)famous film, *American Psycho*, would prove that it would be difficult to pigeonhole Harron within one particular genre or style.

UNLEASHING THE BEAST: *AMERICAN PSYCHO* AND *FIGHT CLUB*

Bret Easton Ellis' controversial novel, *American Psycho* (1991), drew the attention of producer Edward R. Pressman, who acquired the film rights in 1992. Ellis' book can be read as "a satire of consumer culture and the hegemonizing and dehumanizing forces of global capital on language and identity."[42] His scathing attack on American Yuppie consumer culture was ripe for adaptation and fellow Canadian filmmaker David Cronenberg was attached to direct based on a script by Ellis himself. However, Cronenberg left the project, and during a visit to Cannes in 1996 to secure, unsuccessfully, pre-distribution rights, Pressman became aware of Harron's interest in directing the adaptation. Harron had been developing the project with actor-writer Guinevere Turner, who had success starring in Vachon-produced *Go Fish*. Canada-based studio Lions Gate eventually purchased the rights, with hopes of Leonardo DiCaprio, who expressed interest in the role of Patrick Bateman, to star.

However, Harron was determined to cast British actor, Christian Bale, in the lead role, which led to a strained relationship with the company. When Lions Gate announced DiCaprio's involvement in Cannes in 1998, it appeared Harron was dropped from the project as the actor demanded that the film be helmed by Oliver Stone. Stone himself "began to chip away at Harron's script, preparing to rewrite it altogether" and his approach seemed to steer away from the satire that Harron and Turner wanted to explore in great detail.[43] When Stone left the project due to disagreements with DiCaprio, who also departed to star in *The Beach* (Twentieth Century Fox, Boyle, 2000), Harron was back on board with the team she wanted.

Harron's approach to the adaptation of the novel was to focus on the satire rather than the excessive violence. The controversy of the book was found in its intentionally tedious descriptions of pop albums, cosmetics and high-end fashion balanced with meticulous accounts of the brutal murders carried out by Bateman. Thomas Heise comments:

> Though serialized violence in *American Psycho* is an extension of the deadening effects of serialized consumer exchanges in an economy where commodities and bodies become interchangeable and indistinguishable, this point largely escaped the notice of the novel's harshest critics.[44]

Oscillating between these two themes proved too much for readers, and publishers of the novel, which resulted in many countries around the world restricting access to the book. Australia, for instance, placed an R18 rating on the book, preventing anyone under the age of eighteen accessing the novel.[45] However, the overt postmodern satire, and, as Heise notes above, its interchangeable themes, meant the novel would make a perfect film adaptation, particularly as so many postmodernist films were produced in the era of Indiewood.

Several films were produced in the 1990s and early 2000s that examined forms of extreme masculinity, such as *Magnolia*, the male-centered *Three Kings* (Warner Bros., Russell, 1999) and, probably the most overt masculine film, David Fincher's adaptation of Chuck Palahnuik's novel *Fight Club*. Fincher's film, described by Thomas Schatz as "a brutal, nihilistic, seriocomic character study that slides into nightmare farce, and a film that was aggressively anti-Hollywood in its postmodern take on male-action tropes and celebrity culture that pervade contemporary cinema,"[46] is perhaps the most obvious film in which to compare to *American Psycho*. While somewhat thematically similar, the filmmakers' approaches were starkly different. Both films feature misogynistic characters prone to extreme violence. *Fight Club*'s central characters, The Narrator (Edward Norton) and Tyler Durden (Brad Pitt), present themselves as anti-establishment anarchists, against consumer society—Patrick Bateman would be their ideal target—yet they perpetuate an extreme form of masculinity. Mark Ramey comments that through an ersatz Nietzschean examination, the film can be seen as:

> an irresponsible, misogynistic and reactionary text. It is not a fraternal "call-to-arms" but rather a debased and dehumanizing spectacle: the fight club is just a gladiatorial arena for unreconstructed men who cannot adjust to the pluralism of the twenty-first century. *Fight Club* is a film for boys who want to be real men and think that means fighting each other.[47]

Indeed, the film can be seen as a crisis in male identity, and the actions of the characters, from setting up underground fights to militant terrorism against corporations and the upper class, makes them appear almost juvenile. Fincher depicts the violence as over-the-top, particularly in one sequence where Tyler is beaten up by the owner of the bar where the fight club takes place. Instead of fighting back, he takes every blow, with blood oozing out of his face. Tyler finally overpowers the owner and bleeds all over him by shaking himself like a dog just for "the sheer exhilaration and corporeal contact apparently missing in these modern men's lives."[48] The apparent void in these characters' lives, which cannot be filled with consumerism, makes them revert to primitive, juvenile but extremely violent behavior. Though both films play on the absurdity of this notion, their approaches to violence differ.

Harron has commented on her treatment of violence in the film, stating that "I felt that the only way to stop it from being really exploitative was [to affect] a kind of cool detachment [. . .] If we're seeing the murders from the killer's point of view, you would get into it."[49] Centering the viewer into Bateman's perspective creates an unnerving experience. To aid this approach, Harron employs further subjective techniques, similar to *Fight Club*. Both films feature a deadpan use of voice-over as the characters describe their lives: Bateman gives a detailed account of his morning routine, which becomes banal the more descriptive it gets; The Narrator in *Fight Club* highlights his tedious existence by explaining his need to purchase IKEA furniture. Harron's probe into Bateman and his world becomes more exaggerated and tongue-in-cheek as the film progresses. The scene in which Bateman hires two prostitutes becomes an un-erotic montage as he admires himself in the mirror more than enjoying sex. Although *Fight Club* fully displays its testosterone, Harron uses subtler scenarios to undermine Bateman, and the rest of his male Wall Street colleagues' masculinity during a scene where they compare their business cards. The scene is "full of exaggerated drama as they draw the business cards and the camera zooms in on the elegant fonts" and Bateman feels emasculated when his own card is upstaged by a colleague.[50]

American Psycho also defies the horror-slasher genre in which it is often categorized. Again, instead of relishing the most violent aspects of the novel, Harron uses the audiences' familiarity with the horror genre to fill in the gaps of Bateman's violent outbursts, which often happen off-screen. Well-known horror films are even incorporated into the *mise en scène*, when after one of the early murders, "Patrick compulsively exercises in his apartment, skipping rope and then performing a seemingly torturous amount of crunches in front of a television playing Tobe Hooper's 1974 *The Texas Chainsaw Massacre*."[51] The film only slightly verges into conventional horror in one sequence, however Harron turns this into an over-the-top chase sequence. With *The Texas Chainsaw Massacre* already referenced within the film, Harron has Bateman wield a chainsaw as he pursues one of the prostitutes through an apartment building. Wearing nothing but shorts and bright white trainers, the scene becomes a parody of a stalk-and-chase and "allows the movie to 'play' at being a slasher film for a few minutes, without ever committing itself to being a 'real' horror film."[52] Though there were popular, self-referential horror films produced in the 1990s, most notably *Scream* (Craven, 1996), which was produced by Miramax Films' subdivision Dimension, *American Psycho*'s "treatment of slasher films as internal objects is more than mere cheekiness. This is what makes [the film] more than another self-referential horror movie."[53]

Though Fincher's *Fight Club* has an innovative visual style, Harron's subtle direction, use of tongue-in-cheek humor and over-the-top performance by Christian Bale has endured, rightfully cementing *American Psycho*'s status as

Figure 3.1 Yuppie Chainsaw Massacre: Patrick Bateman (Christian Bale) pursues another victim

a cult favorite. Harron's approach to the adaptation makes it one of the best satires to emerge during the cycle of "men-in-crisis" films.

INFAMOUS PIN-UP: *THE NOTORIOUS BETTIE PAGE* AND *MARIE ANTOINETTE*

The Notorious Bettie Page marks Harron's return to the biopic. The film extended Harron's curiosity into social outsiders and deepened her exploration of male dominance, with a particular emphasis on the male gaze. The male gaze, as Laura Mulvey famously explored in her seminal essay "Visual Pleasure and Narrative Cinema" (1975), can be described as follows:

> The determining male gaze projects its phantasy on to the female figure which is styled accordingly. In their traditional exhibitionist role women are simultaneously looked at and displayed, with their appearance coded for strong visual and erotic impact so that they can be said to connote *to-be-looked-at-ness*.[54]

Harron's re-appropriation of the male gaze is consistently employed throughout the film, setting the tone in the opening scene, which, "insinuates that Bettie's femininity is officially seen as a threat that must be contained. The gaze implied in the tilt up her body evinces suspicion and investigation as much as it does lust."[55] The introduction of Bettie Page (Gretchen Mol) in the opening scene is purposefully mundane but provocatively shot. The film opens on the 1955 Senate investigation on the effects of pornography on minors. Page sits waiting to be called in to testify. The innocuousness of the scene is provocatively challenged as Harron utilizes the camera to objectify Page by slowly tilting up from her feet, exploring her body. The shot begins Harron's interrogation of "to-be-looked-at-ness," effectively challenging the viewer's own voyeurism. This is further reinforced as a young guard stands awkwardly looking at Page, clearly attracted to her. Page acknowledges his gaze with an awkward smile before looking away. In comparison to the opening of *I Shot Andy Warhol*, with its chaotic introduction to Valerie Solanas, *The Notorious Bettie Page*'s calm introduction to the character, though seemingly banal, subtly sets the tone for the rest of the film.

Similarly, Sofia Coppola's biopic *Marie Antoinette* opens on a shot of objectification. The title character, played by Kirsten Dunst, leisurely lies as she is pampered by a maid. Surrounded by pink pastry, she dips her fingers into the icing and licks her fingers. She flicks a look at the camera "as if to say, 'What are you looking at?' She then lies back as if the audience is not worth the bother."[56] The shot is static throughout, a contrast to Harron's moving, tilting camera, but objectifies the character in her decadence. The knowing look to the camera, again, challenges the viewer's voyeurism, a perfect introduction to the complex protagonist. The shot instantly encapsulates the character's status and attitude. However, Coppola throughout the film avoids delving into the complexities of societal structures with the aristocracy of late eighteenth-century France, eschewing historical accuracy to create a film wherein the audience is "aware of the degree to which the female protagonist is defined and constrained by the image—and with it identity—imposed upon her both by her society and the film itself."[57] The various contradictions within the character, both challenging the French upper-class status quo then embracing the life of luxury as queen create a polemical portrait.

The visual style of the film makes use of bright colors to emphasize both Marie Antoinette's indulgences as well as her naivety. Coppola's interests lie within expressing "an Impressionist painting of passive, clueless bewilderment, but also of innocent, impetuous pleasure."[58] The film is peppered throughout with brightly colored, extravagant costumes as well as vivid pinks, reds, and blues of cakes and shoes. As the audience is drawn further into Marie Antoinette's world, we are asked "to identify with the female protagonist, and, in several crucial scenes, our vantage point almost entirely merges with Marie Antoinette's as we, the audience, become the object of the narrative's gaze."[59] Again, this re-appropriation of the gaze reinforces Coppola's unwillingness to lay judgment on the character. There are no moments of simplistic condemnation or praise toward Marie Antoinette's actions. As the film draws to a close, the character's eventual demise is never seen on screen. The last shot depicts her once extravagant bedroom decimated by angry mob rioters during the French Revolution and we, the audience, are left to make our own judgments about the character.

Similarly, *The Notorious Bettie Page* utilizes a strong visual aesthetic that reinforces Harron's examination of a polemical figure in history. Harron makes use of some of the same techniques used in *I Shot Andy Warhol*, where the visual style provides a sense of place and period setting. The style also reinforces both Page's optimism and, at times, despair within patriarchy. Schreiber writes:

> For Harron, this visual exploration takes place primarily through the interplay between different film formats: archive footage, which is used to provide historical context; black-and-white cinematography, with which is the format in which most of the film is shot; and color cinematography [. . .] She also inserts color and black-and-white 8 and 16mm footage at key points in the narrative. When and why Harron uses these different formats speaks to the psychology of Bettie.[60]

The film acts as a contrast to *I Shot Andy Warhol*. Whereas Solanas actively challenged patriarchy, Page's life is engulfed by male control and objectification, even willingly to pose for her male audience. Yet, as with Harron's earlier film, there is no sense of judgment on Page for being involved in fetish pin-ups. The film, ultimately, follows "no argument about pornography or morality, emphasizing Page's sweetness and innocence in displaying the body God gave her."[61] In fact, Harron's exploration of the underground bondage world features eccentric characters that are livelier, and somewhat more appealing, than their conservative counterparts. The brother and sister team Irving and Paula Klaw (Chris Bauer and Lili Taylor) who take the bondage photographs of Page have a network of both employees and clients that reflect a similar dynamic to Warhol's Factory. Harron even continues this comparison by casting Jared Harris as photographer John Willie, playing a somewhat darker mirror image to his portrayal of Warhol as someone that fame eluded and has descended into alcoholism and creating pornography.

The dichotomy of Page's world, one within the reality of the conservative 1950s, the other with the Klaws, is highlighted in several scenes throughout the film. After Page's boyfriend Marvin (Jonathan M. Woodward) discovers her alternative career, he chastises her but she does not find anything wrong about her modeling. Page's positive attitude dismays him. Her comfort in both worlds, ultimately, kept her an outsider. Sarah Haight notes:

> Clad in black bustiers, often brandishing a whip, Page was both fierce and demure, a happy dominatrix whose appeal was in her ability to seem both utterly unattainable and girl-next-door sweet (if the girl-next-door wore six-inch stilettos and a sheer red chiffon bathrobe, as Page did in one infamous shot).[62]

Harron heightens this divide during the scenes set in Miami when the black-and-white cinematography switches to color. The beach scenes are amplified in color, and, as Schreiber notes above, attribute to the psychology of Page. The beach scenes depict the simplicity in which Page wanted to live her life. And though relaxing on the beach, Harron films Page as if she continues to pose, even when she's not in front of a camera. Finally, in the last scenes of the film, Page renounces her pin-up career and pursues a life in evangelical Christianity. Harron concludes the film with the two contrasting worlds, with Page handing out Bibles and then, as the credits roll, real-life footage of one of the Klaws' color films of her posing. The end-credits reinforce the notion of the gaze and Harron, again, refuses to make an overall statement about Page and we are simply left to stare at a complex figure.

Figure 3.2 Bettie Page (Gretchen Mol) asking to be photographed at the beach

CONCLUSION

Reflecting on Harron's films within the era of Indiewood has revealed her to be one of the most challenging and creative filmmakers to emerge during the 1990s. In comparison to her predominately male contemporaries, she has developed an approach to similar themes and concepts in their films with subtle visual aesthetics. Harron's willingness to explore and not judge even her most extreme characters allows for more complex and reflexive filmmaking. Both *Basquiat* and *I Shot Andy Warhol*, though sharing similar characters, are vastly different in their approaches to their real-life subjects. Harron seeks to develop the themes of masculine control, with Warhol's power over Solanas who is ultimately punished for undermining her. *Basquiat* is more concerned with a conventional rise-and-fall narrative without too much investigation of Warhol and Basquiat's power dynamic. *American Psycho*'s savage satire incorporates elements of the postmodern horror film to fully evoke the absurdity of extreme masculinity and consumer culture. In contrast to *Fight Club*, with its similar themes, *American Psycho*'s subtle, visual approach amplifies its parody to delve deeper into the world of its protagonist. *The Notorious Bettie Page* and *Marie Antoinette* are films that focus on "conflicts with individuals rather than with systems, and the eternal gaze."[63] Both are reinforced with visual styles that re-appropriate the notion of the gaze without, again, laying any judgment on their respective protagonists. Harron's career to date is highlighted by "opting for genres that have a distinct style and consequent aesthetic payoff in spite of troubled and troubling main characters," and her unconventionality and diversity reveals "a courage not often seen among film directors."[64] Finally, though Indiewood went into decline in the mid-2000s, and the blockbuster continues to encroach the box office via superhero franchises, it has never hindered the spirit of true independent filmmakers, such as Harron and her collaborators, who continue to make films with personal visions.

NOTES

1. Geoff King, *New Hollywood Cinema: An Introduction* (London: I. B. Tauris, 2002), 48.
2. Sherry B. Ortner, "Against Hollywood: American Independent Film as a Critical Cultural Movement," in *HAU: Journal of Ethnographic Theory* (Vol. 2, No. 2, 2012), 1–21, 6.
3. Robert Kolker, *A Cinema of Loneliness*, Fourth Edition (New York: Oxford University Press, 2011), 3.
4. Claire Perkins, "Beyond Indiewood: The Everyday Ethics of Nicole Holofcener," in *Camera Obscura* 85 (Vol. 29 No. 1, 2014), 137–59, 139.
5. Emmanuel Levy, *Cinema of Outsiders: The Rise of American Independent Cinema* (New York: New York University Press, 1999), 8.
6. Michael Newman, *Indie: An American Film Culture* (New York: Columbia University Press, 2011), 4.
7. Yannis Tzioumakis, "Between 'indiewood' and 'nowherewood': American independent cinema in the twenty-first century," in *International Journal of Media & Cultural Politics* (Vol. 10, No. 3, 2014), 285–300, 29.
8. John Pierson, *Spike Mike Reloaded: A Guided Tour Across a Decade of American Independent Cinema* (New York: Miramax Books, 2003), xviii.
9. Geoff King, *Indiewood, USA: Where Hollywood Meets Independent Cinema* (London and New York: I. B. Tauris, 2009), 93.
10. Ibid., 1.
11. Levy, *Cinema of Outsiders: The Rise of American Independent Cinema*, 2.
12. Katarzyna Paszkiewicz, *Genre, Authorship and Contemporary Women Filmmakers* (Edinburgh: Edinburgh University Press, 2019), 137.
13. Newman, *Indie: An American Film Culture*, 5.
14. Linda Badley, Claire Perkins, and Michele Schreiber, "Introduction," in *Indie Reframed: Women's Filmmaking and Contemporary American Independent Cinema*, edited by Linda Baldey, Claire Perkins, and Michele Schreiber (Edinburgh: Edinburgh University Press, 2016), 5.
15. Kolker, *A Cinema of Loneliness*, 3.
16. Todd Kennedy, "Off with Hollywood's Head: Sofia Coppola as Feminine Auteur," in *Film Criticism* 35 (Vol. 1, 2010), 37–59, 39.
17. Janet Staiger, "Independent of What? Sorting out difference from Hollywood," in *American Independent Cinema: Indie, Indiewood and Beyond*, edited by Geoff King, Claire Molloy, and Yannis Tzioumakis (Abingdon: Routledge, 2013), 18.
18. "Easy Rider Box Office" World Wide Box Office, Accessed April 4, 2018. http://www.worldwideboxoffice.com/movie.cgi?title=Easy%20Rider&year=1969
19. Thomas Schatz, "Conglomerate Hollywood and American Independent Film," in *American Independent Cinema: Indie, Indiewood and Beyond*, edited by Geoff King, Claire Molloy, and Yannis Tzioumakis. (Abingdon: Routledge, 2013), 128.
20. King, *New Hollywood Cinema: An Introduction*, 91.

21. King, *Indiewood, USA: Where Hollywood Meets Independent Cinema*, 1.
22. Tzioumakis, "Between 'indiewood' and 'nowherewood': American independent cinema in the twenty-first century," 292.
23. Sharon Waxman, *Rebels on the Backlot: Six Maverick Directors and How They Conquered the Studio System* (New York: HarperCollins Publishers 2005), x.
24. Thomas Schatz, "Going Mainstream: The Indie Film Movement in 1999," in *A Companion to American Indie Film*, edited by Geoff King (Chichester: John Wiley & Sons, Inc., 2017), 276.
25. King, *Indiewood, USA: Where Hollywood Meets Independent Cinema*, 33.
26. Jeffrey Sconce, "Irony, nihilism and the new American 'smart' film," in *Screen* 43 (Vol. 4, 2002), 349–69, 358.
27. David Bordwell, *The Way Hollywood Tells It: Story and Style in Modern Movies* (London: University of California Press, Ltd, 2006), 73.
28. Perkins, "Beyond Indiewood," 140.
29. Paszkiewicz, *Genre, Authorship, and Contemporary Women Filmmakers*, 140.
30. Levy, *Cinema of Outsiders: The Rise of American Independent Cinema*, 57.
31. King, *Indiewood, USA: Where Hollywood Meets Independent Cinema*, 260.
32. Levy, *Cinema of Outsiders: The Rise of American Independent Cinema*, 19.
33. Pierson, *Spike Mike Reloaded: A Guided Tour Across a Decade of American Independent Cinema*, 43.
34. Patricia White, "Killer Feminism," in *Indie Reframed: Women's Filmmaking and Contemporary American Independent Cinema*, edited by Linda Baldey, Claire Perkins, and Michele Schreiber (Edinburgh: Edinburgh University Press, 2016), 38.
35. Ibid., 39.
36. Mary Harron, "Introduction," In *I Shot Andy Warhol*, Mary Harron and Daniel Minahan (New York: Grove Press, 1996), ix.
37. Mary G. Hurd, *Women Directors and their Films* (Westport: Praeger Publishers, 2007), 64.
38. Ken Dancyger, *The Director's Idea: The Path to Great Directing* (Burlington: Focal Press, 2006), 313.
39. Levy, *Cinema of Outsiders: The Rise of American Independent Cinema*, 396.
40. Ibid., 397.
41. Dana Heller, "Shooting Solanas: Radical Feminist History and the Technology of Failure," in *Feminist Time against Nation Time: Gender, Politics, and the Nation-State in an Age of Permanent War*, edited by Victoria Hesford and Lisa Diedrich (Lanham, MD: Lexington Books, 2008), 185.
42. Martin Rogers, "Video Nasties and the Monstrous Bodies of *American Psycho*," in *Literature-Film Quarterly* (Vol. 39, No. 3, 2011), 231–44, 231.
43. Nisha Gopalan, "*American Psycho*: the story behind the film," *The Guardian* (2000). Accessed May 2, 2018. https://www.theguardian.com/film/2000/mar/24/fiction.breteastonellis
44. Thomas Heise, "*American Psycho*: Neoliberal Fantasies and the Death of Downtown," in *Arizona Quarterly: A Journal of American Literature, Culture, and Theory* (Vol. 67, No. 1, 2011), 135–60, 138.
45. Malcolm Sutton, "Police ask for new edition of *American Psycho* to be kept from Adelaide bookshelves," ABC News (2015). Accessed: May 2, 2018. http://www.abc.net.au/news/2015-07-17/american-psycho-removed-from-adelaide-bookshelves/6628846
46. Thomas Schatz, "Going Mainstream: The Indie Film Movement in 1999," in *A Companion to American Indie Film*, edited by Geoff King (Chichester: John Wiley & Sons, Inc., 2017), 265.
47. Mark Ramey, *Studying Fight Club* (Leighton Buzzard: Auteur, 2012), 9.

48. Melissa Iocco, "Addicted to Affliction: Masculinity and Perversity in *Crash* and *Fight Club*," in *Gothic Studies* 1 (Vol. 9, 2007), 46–56, 47.
49. Gopalan, "*American Psycho*: the story behind the film."
50. Svetlana Asanova, "Consumerism and Madness in Mary Harron's *American Psycho*," in *Gender Forum* 40, (2012), 1–13, 7.
51. Rogers, "Video Nasties and the Monstrous Bodies of *American Psycho*," 235.
52. Ibid., 236.
53. David Robinson, "The Unattainable Narrative: Identity, Consumerism and the Slasher Film in Mary Harron's *American Psycho*," in *CineAction* 68 (2006), 26–35, 30.
54. Laura Mulvey, "Visual Pleasure and Narrative Cinema," in *Screen* (Vol. 16, No. 3, 1975), 6–18, 11.
55. Dennis Bingham, *Whose Lives Are They Anyway? The Biopic as Contemporary Film Genre* (New Brunswick, NJ, and London: Rutgers University Press, 2010), 352.
56. Kennedy, "Off with Hollywood's Head: Sofia Coppola as Feminine Auteur," 48.
57. Ibid., 45.
58. Bingham, *Whose Lives Are They Anyway? The Biopic as Contemporary Film Genre*, 366.
59. Kennedy, "Off with Hollywood's Head: Sofia Coppola as Feminine Auteur," 48.
60. Schreiber, "Their Own Personal Velocity," 103.
61. Hurd, *Women Directors and their Films*, 65–6.
62. Sarah Haight, "WWD: Women's Wear Daily," in *Los Angeles* (Vol. 196, No. 125, 2008), 14.
63. Bingham, *Whose Lives Are They Anyway? The Biopic as Contemporary Film Genre*, 376.
64. Dancyger, *The Director's Idea: The Path to Great Directing*, 315.

CHAPTER 4

"I Like to Dissect Girls": Mary Harron's *American Psycho* as Gendered Metafiction

Coco d'Hont

INTRODUCTION

When Mary Harron agreed to direct the film adaptation of *American Psycho*, she took on a project that was controversial before it had even started. The chaotic publication history of Bret Easton Ellis' 1991 novel, which includes publisher withdrawals, sales restrictions in multiple countries, and damning reviews, suggested that the production of Harron's second feature film would be complex and challenging.[1] After the film's release, initial responses were mixed. During its first screening at the Sundance Festival in 2000, Harron noticed that "the audience didn't know if it was supposed to be funny or not."[2] While some critics praised the film for its acting and interpretation of the novel,[3] Ellis himself stated that he found the film superfluous and an unnecessary adaptation of his story.[4] This chapter makes the case for a different interpretation of the film, not simply as an adaptation of a novel, but as a critical interrogation of the use of violent masculinity as a pop-cultural metaphor. Instead of as a literal translation of a novel into a different medium, Harron's *American Psycho* should be read as a sophisticated cinematic commentary, not only on Ellis' novel and the controversy it inspired, but also on the culture from which it emerged.[5]

This chapter reads *American Psycho* as a form of gendered metafiction: a cinematic text which uses its metafictional exploration of the boundary between fiction and fact to interrogate how violent masculinity was constructed and represented in popular culture of its time. The film was released in 2000, at the end of a decade shaped by a heated debate about the supposed "crisis of masculinity."[6] For some American men, the 1990s were a period of decreasing patriarchal dominance and economic security. As Susan Faludi explains in *Stiffed*:

The Betrayal of the Modern Man, this caused the reduction of masculinity from action to ornament.[7] The sense of unease provoked by this reduction of masculinity to an ornamental illusion led to the creation of grassroots activist groups such as the Promise Keepers, and a search for "true" masculinity by authors such as Robert Bly.[8]

Despite this concern about the supposedly damaged status of masculinity, or possibly as a reaction to this sense of vulnerability, the definition of masculinity as "man controlling his environment," often through violence, became a central concern of American popular culture of the era.[9] Harron's adaptation of *American Psycho* emerged in, and challenged, this cultural climate. The cultural connection between violence and masculinity that characterized this period is illustrated by the success of filmmakers such as Jonathan Demme (*Silence of the Lambs*) and David Fincher (*Se7en*). While not portraying serial killers, similar depictions of violence were found in Quentin Tarantino's debut and sophomore efforts: *Reservoir Dogs* and *Pulp Fiction*. Within these films, masculinity is virtually synonymous with violence, some of which generated considerable controversy. For instance, *Silence of the Lambs* was perceived as transphobic due to its depiction of a serial killer who turns his female victims into a bodysuit; *Pulp Fiction* features problematic types of behavior such as drug abuse, racism, and homophobia.

Although the violent masculine films of the 1990s differed notably in terms of setting, they display a similar concern with violence as the only way in which men can assert and maintain their masculinity, frequently in contrast to female victims or "feminized" men. *Reservoir Dogs*, for example, features an almost exclusively male cast of characters who use vicious violence and torture to control and dominate each other. Many of these films feature a problematic contrast with a conceptualization of femininity as weakness and passivity.[10] Even though violent masculinity is a cultural construct with a long history, Tarantino's characters differ from those featured in earlier films such as *First Blood* (Orion Pictures, Kotcheff, 1982). While Rambo's (Sylvester Stallone) actions are legitimized—however problematically—by the fact that he is presented as the hero, filmmakers such as Tarantino offer no such consolation. Instead, they present the violent male as an out-of-control maniac who will do whatever it takes to maintain his dominant position. *American Psycho* consciously interacts with this conflicted socio-cultural context. Even though the film features an extremely violent male protagonist, Patrick Bateman (Christian Bale) is not a hero but an exaggerated representation of violent masculinity as a cultural metaphor in the context of 1980s yuppie culture.

American Psycho also differs from other films which were released during the same period, such as Ridley Scott's historical drama *Gladiator* (DreamWorks Pictures, 2000). In *Gladiator*, the main character Maximus (Russell Crowe) seeks to avenge his murdered family to reinstall his position as a Roman general. He uses the violence he is forced to commit as a gladiator to escape from his enslavement and reassert himself as a powerful man who is in control of his environment. The film positions him in opposition to the "feminized" emperor Commodus (Joaquin Phoenix), whom he eventually kills, reinforcing the connection between violence, masculinity, and power. Contrary to this film, which idealizes a traditional image of masculinity as a form of violent control, Harron situates *American Psycho* within existing feminist critiques of gender representation in film generally and horror film specifically, echoing their characterizations of popular culture as a phenomenon that both reflects and perpetuates gender stereotypes and sexism.[11,12]

American Psycho is part of Harron's "feminist project" that started with *I Shot Andy Warhol*, a fictionalized account of the life of radical feminist Valerie Solanas.[13] In *American Psycho*, Harron used its depictions of 1980s neoliberal yuppie culture to explore the evolution of violent masculinity in recent American cinema. In its framing of Bateman as a deeply problematic representation of violent masculinity, the film places him in a cinematic tradition that includes films such as *Reservoir Dogs* or *First Blood* but which is also influenced by genres such as the slasher film and film noir. The film does not take the idea of violent masculinity for granted but critically interrogates it as an artificial ideological construct. Harron cleverly uses the characteristics of film as an audio-visual medium to deconstruct Ellis' story, turning the film into a critical narrative which not only reflects, but also interrogates and contests its cultural context. The film asks important questions about the role of cultural products in the creation, communication, and perpetuation of violent masculinity as a highly problematic token of gendered inequality.

THE RULES OF DISSECTION: WHAT IS GENDERED METAFICTION?

Mary Harron's film adaptation of *American Psycho*, co-written with independent film icon Guinevere Turner, who also appeared in the film as the memorable character Elizabeth, is a form of metafiction: a type of fiction which "self-consciously and systematically draws attention to its status as an artefact in order to pose questions about the relationship between fiction and reality."[14] Traditionally, metafiction has been defined as a specifically literary phenomenon, which uses narrative devices to highlight its own artificiality. Adapting the notion of metafiction to film may initially appear too far a conceptual leap, which runs the risk of overlooking the differences between literary fiction as a written medium, and film as an audio-visual form of communication. However, metafiction has been described as "a function of reading" rather than a set characteristic of any given text.[15] This suggests that metafiction is a mode of interpretation, rather than a construct that only applies to literature. The concept of metafiction can therefore be adapted to facilitate the reading of *American Psycho* as a cinematic reinterpretation of a literary text (adding a new layer of meaning), rather than a straightforward translation of a literary text into a different medium (without making any changes to its message). Reading *American Psycho* as metafiction opens up significant lines of enquiry which are often obscured by other analytical approaches to film adaptation. Longstanding issues that affect the scholarly interpretation of film adaptations include the "fidelity problem," meaning the overtly strong focus on film as a mere cinematic translation of a supposedly superior literary text.[16] The main problem associated with this approach is its framing of film as an inherently inferior product, the merit of which depends on the faithfulness of its translation of the literary text into a new medium.

Other critical approaches stress the impossibility of comparing film adaptation and literary text and arrive at a description of film as "an inevitable abandonment of 'novelistic' elements."[17] This type of critical enquiry results in a view of film adaptations as cultural products that are, at best, simplified versions of the original text. While recent developments in the field have resulted in an increased emphasis on the film adaptation as a creative product in its own right, addressing the potential of the film adaptation as a creative commentary on the source text remains a complex critical undertaking.[18] Because this chapter reads *American Psycho* as a form of metafiction, it can explore the very nature of the film as fiction, resulting in a better understanding of the fictional story in its own right, as well as the socio-cultural context in which it emerged. The metafictional approach does not treat the film as appearing in a critical void, but situates it within a cultural framework, and allows for a critical dissection of the properties of that framework in return.

American Psycho functions as a specific type of metafiction, which uses the exploration of the boundary between fact and fiction to interrogate violent masculinity within the pop-cultural landscape of the 1990s. Harron draws connections between the film's setting in the hyper-masculine yuppie culture of the 1980s and violent masculinity in 1990s films to encourage viewers to consider the film's dynamics as a work of fiction, and invite a broader critical consideration of violent masculinity as an artificial ideology. The film appeared at the end of a decade in which the theory of gender as a social construction or performance gained wider currency,[19] supporting the conceptualization of masculinity as a construct that "does not exist except in contrast with 'femininity'."[20] This view of gender as a fluid social construction contrasts sharply with discussions of masculinity as a stable idea threatened by an unspecified crisis, which inspired calls for the replacement of the "soft male" with "Wild Man" fierceness in the film's social context.[21] Despite the problematic implications of the Wild Man ideal, it was explored, communicated, and promoted through a wide range of cultural products. Several commercially successful, in some cases even Oscar-winning films, such as *Silence of the Lambs*, featured male protagonists who used extreme violence to establish and increase their masculinity.[22] *American Psycho*, in contrast, critically investigates how masculinity exists as a cultural construct that is communicated and maintained through extreme violence. Its reinterpretation of a controversial novel is an opportunity to explore not only the gender relations discussed within its story, but also the extra-textual culture in which it emerged.

FROM DE- TO RE-CONSTRUCTION: *AMERICAN PSYCHO* AS GENDERED METAFICTION

Instead of regarding film adaptation as a cultural form that involves the inherent simplification of a literary story, the analysis in this chapter departs from a conceptualization of film adaptation as a reinterpretation of a literary text. In the process, the film becomes a new original work with its own critical potential, rather than a diluted translation of an earlier text. Due to the differences between film and literature—or, rather, what Linda Hutcheon and Siobhan O'Flynn consider to be the shifting from "the telling to showing mode" of adapting one medium to another[23]—Harron's interpretation of *American Psycho* is inherently different to Ellis' novel.[24] The most important differences appear in the three areas which, in the case of *American Psycho*, most significantly distinguish film from novel: vision, sound, and editing. The film does not merely work through the addition or removal of these dimensions, but transforms each dimension by changing perspective and focalization, mixing sound and vision, and reordering scenes to alter the plot. These specific aesthetic choices are not merely needed to adapt a novel (words on a page) into a film (an audio-visual work) but are actively used by Harron to reinterpret and evaluate the story. The result is a work of gendered metafiction that critically explores how violent masculinity functioned as a social metaphor within the popular culture of its time.

The most striking visual difference between novel and film is the difference between the novel as a sequence of words and the film as a sequence of images. Instead of taking this obvious contrast for granted, Harron actively uses the translation process from word to image to deconstruct the narrative. She develops the film's opening scene into a statement of intent which promises the dissection of violent masculinity as a cultural trope, by playing with the audience's expectations of violence and disrupting the possibility of straightforward interpretation. The film's opening credits show red drops of liquid against a white background. Because of the novel's controversial status as a serial killer narrative, the interpretation of the drops as blood clots is

Figure 4.1 Opening credits reveal the highly expensive dish made for Patrick Bateman and friends

immediately invoked, especially when subsequent shots show more dripping red liquid and knives. However, as the credits roll on, the red liquid is revealed to be a sauce that is poured over a meat dish, served in the restaurant where Bateman is having dinner with his friends. If viewers were expecting a serial killer narrative glorifying violent masculinity, based on their interpretation of the red liquid as blood, their expectations are firmly undermined by the ironic juxtaposition of the suggestion of serial killing with the "civilized" pursuit of fine dining.

This confusing opening positions the film as one in which expectations and conventions are scrutinized and disrupted. This is a film where nothing is quite what it seems and where nothing we see should be taken for granted. The film presents itself as a fictional construction aimed at confusing its viewers and inviting them to reconsider their responses to a stor they might think they already know.

Furthermore, the opening credits make a statement about the cultural representation of violent masculinity. Its highly stylized appearance, which almost resembles abstract art, suggests that its violence is heavily aestheticized and made into an artificial art form. The remainder of the film proceeds to explore these statements in much more detail, paradoxically by omitting most of the explicit violence that earned the novel its notoriety. Whereas the film does feature violent scenes, some of them bloody, they do not show violence in as much detail as the graphic descriptions in the novel, or as Demme or Fincher did in *Silence of the Lambs* and *Se7en*. Harron does not flinch from violence but uses it in a very different manner to almost ridicule the violence Ellis described in so much detail in the novel. The scene in which Bateman murders his colleague Paul Allen (Jared Leto), for example, shows Bateman in a bloodstained suit wielding an axe but omits shots of the weapon making contact with Allen's body. This directorial decision may be caused by the impossibility of showing such extreme violence on screen, but it also suggests that the violence all takes place in Bateman's head. It could also be a consequence of Harron's decision to frame the film as a feminist work that does not contribute yet more gendered violence to the collective unconscious. In any case, Harron uses the void the absence of this type of violence creates to address the subject of cultural representations of violent masculinity in depth.

The narrative is opened up to facilitate a more nuanced discussion of cultural representations of violent masculinity by shifting the focalization and narration from Bateman to a multiplicity of perspectives. Ellis' novel is written in a first-person perspective and narrated by Bateman, a stylistic choice which has inspired lengthy discussions about his unreliability as a narrator.[25] The only viewpoint offered by the novel is Bateman's, and there is no way to assert the validity of any of his claims, actions, and descriptions. The entire narrative universe, including Bateman's identity, his violent acts and the appearances of his female victims, are the result of a specifically masculine discourse that does not allow alternative voices. The result is a claustrophobic narrative universe that never allows the reader to see beyond the boundaries of Bateman's point of view. In the film, on the other hand, Bateman is portrayed by actor Christian Bale, which allows viewers to observe him from a more distant perspective. While Bateman's voice occasionally appears as a voice-over, the viewers do not experience the story through his eyes but observe him as a character among other characters. This metafictional shift in perspective invites the viewer to reconsider the novel as a masculine construction by a male author, dominated by a male narrator. The viewers are encouraged to step outside of the confined space of Bateman's complicated mind, and not only study his behavior from a distance, but also consider the other characters as fictional constructions. Bateman's narrative monopoly is destroyed, and other perspectives emerge from the void this destruction creates.

BATEMAN'S GAZE

As Bateman spends so much time observing himself and other people, the gaze acquires a crucial status as a token of power within the novel. In the film, observation becomes a central strategy for the communication and exercise of discipline and control. In itself, this focus on the gaze is not a new cinematic technique. Laura Mulvey's extensive analysis of scopophilia in mainstream film, for example, concludes that the effectiveness of the Hollywood film depends on "its skilled and satisfying manipulation of visual pleasure" and thus codes "the erotic into the language of the dominant patriarchal order."[26] This argument is illustrated by films such as *Silence of the Lambs*, in which the gaze of masculine characters is a sinister instrument of violent masculinity. From the male police officers who stare at main character Clarice Starling (Jodie Foster) when she interrupts a discussion about their hunt for serial killer Buffalo Bill (Ted Levine), to the scene in which Buffalo Bill watches her through night-vision goggles, the recurring moments of masculine observation of female characters turn the film into a disturbing depiction of the ways in which men control and discipline women. This association between the gaze and violent masculinity is even more apparent in horror subgenres such as the slasher film, in which virtually invisible murderers kill sexualized female victims in deeply disturbing ways.[27] These contemporary "folktales" not only reflect, but also perpetuate, the cultural image of masculinity as a construct that needs to be exercised and maintained through violent, and often sexualized, acts.[28]

American Psycho reverts this power balance. Harron and script writer Guinevere Turner "turn [the female gaze] on violence and the ugly underbelly of the male ego," using the female gaze as a deconstructive force that reveals the fragile basis of gendered inequality.[29] In doing this, the film nuances the conceptualization of the female gaze as either a "masochistic position" or a "masculinization of spectatorship" and instead explores the potential of the female gaze as a critical tool.[30] Bateman's seemingly coherent interpretation of violent masculinity as an ideological representation of power is destabilized and problematized by the critical looks of Bateman's female fellow characters. This mechanism is particularly apparent in the scene where Bateman invites two prostitutes, Christie (Cara Seymour) and Sabrina (Krista Sutton), to his apartment. While Bateman delivers a monologue about Phil Collins and tries to impress the women by telling them that he has a well-paid job at investment bank Pierce & Pierce, the film frequently cuts to shots of the women's faces. On many occasions, Christie and Sabrina make eye contact with each other, looking bored or even cynical. Even though Bateman seems oblivious to the women's gazes, the film uses these shots to deconstruct and ridicule his carefully constructed persona of a successful Wall Street trader. By not restricting itself to Bateman's perspective, and including the responses of female characters, the film invites a reconsideration of the violent masculine persona Bateman attempts to embody. This technique does not completely destroy Bateman's identity and its ideological significance, as both women are eventually viciously killed, and their views are obliterated. However, even though female characters die, their criticisms do not. As the film progresses Bateman's mental and social stability slowly begins to unravel, and his idealization of violent masculinity is increasingly called into question.

A second feature inherent to film as a medium, and absent from *American Psycho*'s novel version, is sound. Following the destabilization of Bateman's focal monopoly, Harron splits his character into a visual and an auditory component. Bateman's persona is divided in two, separating him into a voiceless body that can be freely observed, and a voice with limited agency that merely comments on the scenes. This cinematographic device undermines the dominance of Bateman that characterizes the novel and allows for a more distanced perspective on Bateman as a character and a narrator. In the novel, which is rendered completely through Bateman's voice, there is no way to establish whether the representations of speech are accurate reflections or narrative transformations, even though the story contains lengthy dialogues. The film, in contrast, reduces Bateman's voice to a voice-over that occasionally comments on the progression of events, and the voice of one character who communicates with other characters, rather than controlling the entire story. This split representation of Bateman allows for the critical dissection of him as a character, as well as the violent masculinity he tries to embody.

Instead of portraying Bateman as a representation of masculine control and neoliberal power, Harron reconstructs his character as a male incarnation of the generic female character in mainstream film, which functions as an "erotic object" with the sole purpose of providing visual pleasure.[31] The scene that most remarkably demonstrates the alienating effect of this transformation occurs early in the film, and depicts Bateman's morning routine and apartment. By giving Bateman's environment a sterile look Harron further reduces him as a character and reinforces the audience's gaze. Shots of Bateman's fashionable abode bleed into close-ups of his body, and his voice comments on his appearance while he exercises, showers, and applies a range of beauty products. Bateman becomes an object that can be observed and judged. The film shows him almost naked, then fully naked, inviting considerations of him as a sex object or blank slate upon which sexual fantasies can be projected. This visual component of Bateman's identity has little agency of its own; it has no voice and only exists in its observation. His voice, meanwhile, becomes nothing but background noise and acquires an almost ironic quality when he tells the viewer that "alcohol dries out the face and makes you look older." The scene's conclusion that "there is no real me" resolutely positions Bateman as a cipher, a fake construction, or a puppet that can be manipulated at will. Not only does this cinematic move undermine conceptualizations of masculinity as unrestricted power, it also turns Bateman into a figure through which a more nuanced analysis of gender can be communicated.

Bateman becomes a cultural cipher engaging in vicious sexualized violence in an attempt to maintain his masculine identity, communicating the film's suggestion that popular culture not only glorifies but actively promotes gendered violence. Harron further develops this critical suggestion by connecting *American Psycho* to similar cultural products produced during the same decade, such as the oeuvre of Tarantino. She does so, not only by including violent and gendered content, but more importantly by referencing and critically dissecting its aesthetic dimension. One of the most notorious scenes produced by Tarantino occurs in *Reservoir Dogs*, in which a man is tortured while Steelers Wheel's "Stuck in the Middle With You" is playing in the background. Pop music also plays a significant role in Bret Easton Ellis' novel, which contains detailed analyses of the oeuvres of pop artists such as Phil Collins, Whitney Houston, and Huey Lewis and the News. While these sections are easy to read and appear more comprehensible than some of the novel's more violent scenes, their function within the novel remains a topic of debate. Some scholars have suggested that, because these sections often appear close to scenes of extreme violence, they are somehow connected to them, and may be interpreted as a commentary or alienating mechanism.[32]

In the film version, however, pop music is merged with scenes rather than discussed in isolation. This leads to disturbing moments such as the murder of Bateman's colleague Allen, executed by a dancing Bateman, while Huey Lewis and the News's song "It's Hip to Be Square" blasts from the speakers of his expensive audio system. While this scene can be read as a nod to Tarantino's work, its disturbing effects work in a slightly different way. Whereas Tarantino lets the song play in the background, Harron lets Bateman deliver a lengthy review of Huey Lewis and the News's album just before killing Paul. This directorial choice acts as a metafictional comment on the scene's violence, and highlights Bateman's actions as fictional enactments of violent masculinity. As he discusses the music, Bateman's tone of voice

Figure 4.2 Patrick Bateman (Christian Bale) regales Paul Allen (Jared Leto) about Huey Lewis and the News before killing him

and movements gradually become artificial and unreal, as if he is an inhuman puppet performing a lethal act of violence. Music and violence become inextricably intertwined, which further cements the statement made during the opening credits that popular culture involves the development of violence into an aesthetic symbol. By including the Huey Lewis speech, rather than omitting this part of the novel from the screenplay, Harron and Turner developed it into a comment on the film's status as a form of pop culture, rather than merely using the music as a soundtrack to a violent scene.

A third difference between film and novel is the use of editing techniques. The film transforms and adapts horror clichés into critical mechanisms that dissect and criticize existing representations of violent masculinity in popular culture. It does this by borrowing aesthetic elements of the novel, which consists of many short chapters that vaguely resemble diary entries and lack any obvious chronological connection to each other. Superficially, the film maintains this patchwork-like editing, presenting Bateman's life as a series of snippet views of life in 1980s New York. However, the film also uses this fragmentary style to refer to well-known cinematic genres, such as the slasher film. *American Psycho* has been compared to Alfred Hitchcock's *Psycho* (Paramount Pictures, 1960),[33] often considered one of the first slasher films, and also shares many characteristics with slasher films of the 1980s, which have been interpreted as the cultural representation of misogynist backlashes against feminism.[34]

American Psycho's early murder scenes borrow the darkness, fog, and creepy music which are token announcements of approaching evil in many slasher films, and stand out from the bright, airy atmosphere which characterizes the main storyline. Scenes such as the one in which Bateman kills a homeless man are almost-too-perfect examples of horror aesthetics. Bateman approaches the man in a dark, dirty alley, accompanied by John Cale's sinister sound effects, and stabs him to death as the music reaches its climax. Early in the film the murder scenes contrast sharply with colorful depictions of Bateman's restaurant visits and encounters with women; they are uncanny disruptions of his shiny corporate identity and highlight its violent undercurrent.

However, *American Psycho* ultimately departs from the slasher aesthetic that depicts violence as something which occurs in a dark "terrible place" and is committed by a mysterious invisible killer.[35] Instead, the film presents violent masculinity as occupying a central space within society as a crucial, yet deeply problematic, cultural metaphor. As the film progresses, it gradually brings the violence from darkness into the light, culminating in a scene where Bateman kills a prostitute in his own apartment and chases another one through the building with a chainsaw. In this scene there is no boundary between darkness and light, murder and corporate success, and marginality and mainstream. Bateman embodies the serial killer not as an "alien outsider"[36] but as "the blank surface that reflects back the commonplace anxieties and crises of his culture."[37] His choice of weapon nods to films such as *The Texas Chainsaw Massacre*, the final scene of which shows the murderous Leatherface (Gunnar Hansen) wave a chainsaw at the escaping heroine (Marilyn Burns). In *American Psycho*, however, there is no escape: Christie is caught and killed by the chainsaw in a brightly lit New York apartment building, which could not be more different from *The Texas Chainsaw Massacre*'s rural setting.

In *American Psycho*, violence is not only shown to exist in the heart of society, the film also suggests that violence is permitted *by* that society. No one responds to Christie's calls for help, and even though the scene may still be interpreted as a figment of Bateman's imagination, seeing the distressed woman being chased by a bloodied man with a chainsaw invites a very different response than the novelistic rendering of Christie's murder. By showing Christie interacting with Bateman, rather than portraying her as a victim solely seen through his eyes, the film attributes substance to her character and invites empathy, creating a much more complex power balance than the novel's perspective allows. Even though it could be argued that the film, by showing how Christie is murdered by Bateman, still perpetuates the violent masculinity it aims to criticize, it does settle for a much more complex and compelling depiction which questions the ethics of selling murder as entertainment.

This ethical criticism is enhanced by Harron's editing of the storyline and the creation of a mystery plot. Harron reorders the collection of vignettes about the antics of a yuppie in 1980s New York to create a much more plot-driven film in which the hunting of a serial killer by a detective becomes a metaphor for the critical dissection of violent masculinity. Many of the mystery scenes, such as the encounters between Bateman and detective Donald Kimball (Willem Dafoe), do appear in the novel, but they are isolated pastiches rather than plot-driving moments. In the film, in contrast, Kimball's visits to Bateman's office become increasingly disturbing disruptions of Bateman's life, and carry the suggestion that Bateman is about to be found out and put on trial for his crimes. The film increases this sense of threat by developing Bateman's violent chase through Manhattan, which occurs towards the end of the novel, into a pivotal moment which signals the unravelling of his carefully constructed persona. Both in the novel and in the film, Bateman's killing spree ends with him making a confession to his lawyer over the phone, but whereas the novel only briefly mentions this moment, the film features a much more extensive confession scene which consists solely of close up shots of Bateman's contorted face.

The surface of Bateman's yuppie persona is disrupted to offer a brief glimpse of humanity underneath, while simultaneously highlighting the inescapability of the cultural system of which he is a representation. The film also adds a significant line to the confession which does not occur in the novel: "I'm not sure I'm gonna get away with it this time." The novel never suggests that an arrest or conviction is a serious possibility, and Bateman's lawyer (Stephen

Bogaert) interprets his confession as a prank call. The same happens in the film version, but even though Bateman is never arrested or convicted, the introduction of a much more developed mystery plot opens up the possibility that Bateman's identity as a violent man could be subject to discipline and punishment.

The ending of the film does not depict this, but it does break down the final barrier between fiction and fact. Harron's reorganization of the novel ends with a metafictional statement that invites the viewers to reconsider their interpretation of the story and question the problematic nature of violent masculinity as a social metaphor. Just like the novel, the film ends in a bar, and shows how Bateman discusses dinner reservations with his friends. However, Harron ends the scene with a close-up of Bateman's face while he stares straight into the camera, breaking the artificial "fourth wall" which separates him from his audience. This is eerily similar to the shots that occur toward the ending of *Silence of the Lambs*, where the face of the serial killer, Buffalo Bill, gazes directly into the camera as he pursues Clarice. This creates a connection between fictional victims and the viewers. Buffalo Bill initially observes Clarice through his night-vision goggles before he attempts to kill her, but when he faces the camera the perspectives of the fictional Clarice and the non-fictional viewer temporarily merge. Even though Buffalo Bill is a fictional character confined by the boundaries of the story, the film creates the uncanny suggestion that his violent masculinity is an actual threat to the viewers. *American Psycho* combines this visual reference with sound by separating Bateman's voice from his body once more and turning it into a voice-over which states that "there are no more barriers to cross" and that "I want my pain to be inflicted on others." The ending of the film thus becomes a direct confrontation between the fictional violent masculinity idea and the viewer, inviting the viewer to consider the constructed nature of the concept, but also the danger it potentially implies. Harron suggests that, contrary to the claim films such as *Reservoir Dogs* seem to make, violent masculinity is ultimately a dangerous, morally void construct. Bateman's final statement that "this confession has meant nothing" becomes a terrifying dismissal of violent masculinity as a viable cultural metaphor.

CONCLUSION: READ, RECONSTRUCT, REVEAL

American Psycho is much more than a translation of a story from one medium into another. It is a feminist reinterpretation that uses the specific characteristics of film as an audio-visual medium to dissect the story's content and wider social significance. The film is an example of gendered metafiction and uses its experimental dissection of the boundary between fiction and non-fiction to interrogate cultural representations of violent masculinity. Harron uses a wide array of techniques, varying from audio-visual to editing, to explore the story's fictionality and its place within a wider social framework. Her interpretation highlights how *American Psycho*'s reception has been influenced by its masculine focalization and narration and opens up possibilities for feminine and feminist perspectives on the violent masculinity the film represents. This not only results in a more nuanced version of the story, which leaves more room for the representation of feminine characters as substantial actors, but also invokes questions about the place of *American Psycho* within a larger social framework of violent masculinity as a cultural metaphor. Instead of regarding violent masculinity as a metaphor for control, dominance and power, Harron highlights the moral void at the heart of this construct. Violent masculinity is not only an empty ideology with no significant potential for change or, as Bateman calls it, "catharsis," it facilitates the maintenance of gendered inequality and the promotion of gendered violence. Harron's film adaptation of Ellis' controversial novel thus moves beyond the use of violent masculinity as a satiric comment on 1980s American culture; it makes violent masculinity into its key concern. Even though Bateman insists that "no new knowledge can be extracted from my telling," the film invites the viewers to critically engage with his story and reconsider their own position within a violence-obsessed popular culture.

NOTES

1. Carla Freccero, "Historical Violence, Censorship, and the Serial Killer: The Case of *American Psycho*," *Diacritics* (Vol. 27, No. 2, 1997), 44–58.
2. Celia Quinnette, "3 Questions with *American Psycho* Director Mary Harron," *Sundance TV*, December 31, 2014, http://www.sundance.tv/blog/2014/12/3-questions-with-american-psycho-director-mary-harron. Accessed February 15, 2017.
3. Roger Ebert, "American Psycho," *Chicago Sun-Times*, April 14, 2000, http://www.rogerebert.com/reviews/american-psycho-2000. Accessed February 15, 2017.
4. Marc Maron, "Bret Easton Ellis," *WTF with Marc Maron*, episode 552, November 20, 2014, http://www.wtfpod.com/podcast/episodes/episode_552_-_bret_easton_ellis. Accessed February 15, 2017.
5. Unless otherwise specified, all discussions of *American Psycho* in this chapter refer to the film.
6. For more extensive critical discussions of the crisis of masculinity, see Faludi (1999) and Segal (2007).
7. Susan Faludi, *Stiff: The Betrayal of the Modern Man* (London: Chatto and Windus, 1999), 36.
8. Robert Bly, *Iron John: A Book About Men* (Shaftesbury: Element, 1990).
9. Faludi, *Stiff*, 10.
10. Though the full list of cast members mentions a few female characters, these are all very minor and include Linda Kaye as "Shocked Woman".
11. See, for example, Mulvey (2009) and Williams (2015).
12. See, for example, Clover (1992) and Halberstam (1995).
13. Trey Taylor, "How *American Psycho* Became a Feminist Statement," *Dazed*, 2014, http://www.dazeddigital.com/artsandculture/article/20751/1/how-american-psycho-became-a-feminist-statement. Accessed February 15, 2017.

14. Patricia Waugh, *Metafiction: The Theory and Practice of Self-Conscious Fiction* (London: Routledge, 1984), 2.
15. Mark Currie, "Introduction," *Metafiction*, edited by Mark Currie (London: Longman, 1995), 5.
16. Brian McFarlane, *Novel to Film: An Introduction to the Theory of Adaptation* (Oxford: Clarendon Press, 1996), 8.
17. George Bluestone, *Novels into Film* (1957; reprinted Berkeley: University of Los Angeles Press, 1969), viii.
18. See, for example, Deborah Cartmell and Imelda Whelehan (eds), *The Cambridge Companion to Literature on Screen* (Cambridge: Cambridge University Press, 2007).
19. Judith Butler, *Gender Trouble: Feminism and the Subversion of Identity* (1990; reprinted New York: Routledge, 2006).
20. R.W. Connell, *Masculinities*, Second Edition (Cambridge: Polity, 2005), 68.
21. Bly, *Iron John*, 2–8.
22. Jonathan Demme's *Silence of the Lambs* (1991), an adaptation of Thomas Harris's 1988 novel, won five Academy Awards, including awards for Best Picture and Best Director.
23. Linda Hutcheon and Siobhan O'Flynn, *A Theory of Adaptation*, Second Edition (Abingdon: Routledge, 2013), 38.
24. For more recent explorations of this idea, see Deborah Cartmell and Imelda Whelehan (eds), *Adaptations: From Text to Screen, Screen to Text* (London: Routledge, 2003), and Thomas Leitch, *Film Adaptation and Its Discontents: From* Gone With the Wind *to* The Passion of the Christ (Baltimore: Johns Hopkins University Press, 2009).
25. Mark Storey, "'And As Things Fell Apart': The Crisis of Postmodern Masculinity in Bret Easton Ellis's *American Psycho* and Dennis Cooper's *Frisk*," *Critique* (Vol. 47, No. 1, 2005), 57–72.
26. Laura Mulvey, "Visual Pleasure and Narrative Cinema," *Visual and Other Pleasures*, Second Edition (London: Palgrave Macmillan, 2009), 14–30, 16.
27. Clover, *Men, Women and Chainsaws: Gender in the Modern Horror Film* (Princeton: Princeton University Press, 1992), 12.
28. Ibid., 10.
29. Angelica Jade Bastién, "The Female Gaze of *American Psycho*: How Mary Harron Made Fantasy Into Timeless Satire," *Village Voice*, June 7, 2016, http://www.villagevoice.com/film/the-female-gaze-of-american-psycho-how-mary-harron-made-fantasy-into-timeless-satire-8707185. Accessed February 15, 2017.
30. Mary Ann Doane, *Femmes Fatales: Feminism, Film Theory, Psychoanalysis* (London: Routledge, 1991), 24.
31. Mulvey, "Visual Pleasure and Narrative Cinema," 20.
32. Elizabeth Young and Graham Caveney, *Shopping in Space: Essays on American "Blank Generation" Fiction* (London: Serpent's Tail, 1992), 112.
33. David Robinson, "The Unattainable Narrative: Identity, Consumerism and the Slasher Film in Mary Harron's *American Psycho*," *CineAction*, (No. 68, 2006).
34. Harry M. Benshoff and Sean Griffin, *America on Film: Representing Race, Class, Gender, and Sexuality at the Movies*, Second Edition (Malden: Wiley-Blackwell, 2009).
35. Clover, *Men, Women and Chainsaws*, 30.
36. Philip L. Simpson, *Psycho Paths: Tracking the Serial Killer Through Contemporary American Film and Television* (Carbondale: Southern Illinois University Press, 2000), 1.
37. Mark Seltzer, *Serial Killers: Death and Life in America's Wound Culture* (New York: Routledge, 1998), 126.

CHAPTER 5

"And Then I Met Lucy": Perfection, Same-sex Desire, and Social Control in Mary Harron's *The Moth Diaries*

Brittany Caroline Speller

INTRODUCTION

When describing the character of Lucy in a behind-the-scenes featurette for Mary Harron's *The Moth Diaries*, actress Sarah Gadon revealed "I like to think of her as the ideal girl. All the girls in the film look up to her, and she's popular and athletic. She just is that kind of epitome of teenage girl greatness, and they all want to be a part of that."[1] Lucy, though not the protagonist of the film, strives for perfection. However, Harron treats the character's struggle to be flawless as a horrific act. Much like the murdering psychopathic perfectionist of Harron's *American Psycho* or the all-too-perfectly planned neighborhood in the filmmaker's episode "Community" in the television series *Fear Itself* (NBC, 2008), *The Moth Diaries* expresses a distinct interest in the issue of real world perfection despite its exterior supernatural plotline. Harron's work on the film adaptation of Rachel Klein's modern Gothic tale illustrates a preoccupation with using horror to express social commentary. In this case, the message Harron wishes to send surrounds the nature of adolescent girls' relationships and how these connections can sometimes be toxic to all involved. As Harron notes, "there are loads of TV shows about teenage girls and it's almost like the most looked-down upon and despised category . . . I wanted to do something a little more dark and disturbing because adolescence is dark and disturbing."[2]

A fundamental characteristic of Harron's oeuvre is its frequent concentration on issues of female sexuality and the often negatively prescriptive expectations society places on women. Harron's *I Shot Andy Warhol*, *The Notorious Bettie Page*, and *Anna Nicole* all depict the narratives of unconventional women who are publicly misunderstood, by either society as a whole or those immediately around them, and who often resist being understood as a rejection of cultural norms. *I Shot Andy Warhol* captures the story of radical feminist Valerie Solanas, who, as the title suggests, shot Andy Warhol, and was the author of the *SCUM* (Society for Cutting Up Men) *Manifesto*. In *The Notorious Bettie Page*, Harron and frequent screenwriting collaborator Guinevere Turner offer an intimate look into the life of controversial 1950s pin-up model Bettie Page and her struggles against a sexually conservative society. *Anna Nicole* operates in a similar vein to *The Notorious Bettie Page* in that here, the biography of another international sex symbol explores public perception and the judgment of women's sexuality. Furthermore, Harron's television project, *Alias Grace*, released on Netflix, certainly fits into this category with the titular character Grace actively defying society's attempts to solidify a narrative of her personality. The series, adapted from Margaret Atwood's novel of the same name, represents Harron's fascination with social control and surveillance through embracing a closer look at how individuals participate in and are interpolated into hegemonic norms by means of identity. As the audience is faced with conflicting and unreliable portraits of Grace from others, as well as from the character herself, it becomes clear that identity is one of the key battlegrounds in the struggle between individuals and cultural structures.

SITUATING THE SUPERNATURAL

The Moth Diaries is seemingly a departure from Harron's prior works due to its inclusion of a supernatural storyline. However, the film explores the same essential themes as the rest of Harron's highlighted filmography above, and also expands her ability to discuss these topics through its break from the biographic genre. By centering this film on fictional teenage girls rather than the life story of real women, Harron demonstrates her talents as a director and adaptor through relocating the interrogation of female sexuality and prescriptive norms onto a new audience, while taking up these issues at a different stage of female development and socialization.

Like its source material, the film depicts the relationship between protagonist Rebecca (Sarah Bolger) and her best friend, Lucy. While all is idyllically calm at the start, the arrival of new student Ernessa (Lily Cole) to their all-girls boarding school throws the dynamic of the two girls off balance. Soon after befriending Ernessa, Lucy slowly begins to waste away due to a mysterious illness, which prompts the beginning of Rebecca's suspicions that Ernessa is a vampire bent on possessing and killing her friend. As the screenwriter, Harron chose to emphasize the relationship between the girls in the forefront of the story, with the Gothic narrative surrounding the question of Ernessa's potential vampirism serving as a backdrop for the internal struggles of each main character.

Figure 5.1 Lucy (Sarah Gadon) is drawn to Ernessa (Lily Cole)

While the film is a decidedly faithful adaptation of Klein's work, Harron changes the perspective of the story significantly by focusing on the power dynamics between the three main girls as it relates to their sexualities, rather than emphasizing questions of sanity or grief as Klein does. Harron highlights these endeavors by portraying Lucy's burgeoning sexuality as an intrusion into Rebecca's constructed world of perfection. Female sexuality, especially same-sex interest, underlines each of the main relationships between the characters in Harron's version of the story. It is Lucy's attraction to Ernessa that is the focal point of the film, with Rebecca and the antagonism between her and Ernessa, presented as a consequence of this relationship.

Harron's reframing of the story offers the portrait of a society in which lesbian desire is punished by the protagonist. Rebecca may or may not be repressing homosexual longings of her own. The narrative reflects same-sex preferences are antithetical to the character that Lucy represents as an ideal, golden girl. Lucy's rejection of heterosexuality, along with her striving to achieve a personality free of idealistic projections, allow Harron the opportunity to examine how the societal desire for perfection impacts women on a personal level. Using a Foucauldian and queer theory lens, I argue that *The Moth Diaries* portrays a panoptic environment in which protagonist Rebecca acts as a societal enforcer who punishes Lucy for exploring same-sex desire, and who later works to destroy any notion of queer futurity along with her own homosexual urges. Rebecca undertakes these actions with the goal of attaining perfection, which as she deems it, is strictly heteronormative.

THE WATCHFUL EYE: PANOPTICISM IN SOCIETY

In *Discipline and Punish*, Michel Foucault suggests that society utilizes constant surveillance to reinforce social norms while also operating to punish those who attempt to deviate from the prescribed notions of the cultural system. With Panopticism, Foucault theorizes that members of Western societies police themselves due to their internalization of the systemic measures used to maintain social control. Foucault bases this notion largely on an analysis of Jeremy Bentham's prison Panopticon structure, in which a central tower is used to watch over prisoners where "inspection functions ceaselessly" and "the gaze is alert everywhere," but whose insistent line of vision creates in the watched an instinct to internalize the gaze of the watcher.[3] This issue of watching and surveillance, which could alternately be deemed the gaze, is paramount to the social structure of Western society. For Jean-Paul Sartre, the gaze functions as a medium through which the self defines and redefines itself. Individuals only become self-aware as subjects when they encounter the gaze of the "Other" and its ability to make the self an object.

Due to its basic design, the Other and their gaze is not subject to one's control, and therefore, operates to objectify and deprives the self of its autonomy as a subject. Sartre acknowledges this power dynamic explaining, "insofar as I am the object of values which come to qualify me without my being able to act on this qualification or even to know it, I am enslaved," exemplifying the interlocked nature of the gaze and societal control that Foucault defines with Panopticism.[4] Alongside these theories, Lacanian notions of the mirror

Figure 5.2 Ernessa's "Other" gaze

stage have been helpful in analyzing the role of spectatorship and social identity in film theory. While children develop self-identification when confronted by their appearance in the mirror, spectators at the cinema form an identity when encountering images on screen.[5] Laura Mulvey uses Lacan to argue that film can function as a form of social control by allowing male subjects to employ the gaze as a method of dominating female bodies from both male and female spectatorship positions. This power transference takes place through forcing women into identification with the male gaze of the camera. Mulvey formulates that "in their traditional exhibitionist role women are simultaneously looked at and displayed, with their appearance coded for strong visual and erotic impact so that they can be said to connote to-be-looked-at-ness."[6] The final part of Mulvey's argument in the above quote attests to the surveilling quality inherent within the gaze, with this very feature being the crux of Panopticism. These developments on the theory of the gaze are useful in their ability to be applied to a visual text like *The Moth Diaries* given the high prioritization of gazing in the film and its role in the movie's world of social control. By recognizing Harron's tendency to reveal the surveilling power of the gaze as both a personal and public tool for social control, scholars can begin to understand how the filmmaker addresses censorship, sexuality, and heteronormativity in *The Moth Diaries* and her other films.

The Moth Diaries, along with *I Shot Andy Warhol* and *The Notorious Bettie Page*, each confront notions of surveillance, censorship, and social control. *The Notorious Bettie Page* is the most explicit example of these notions, particularly of censorship and social control, from Harron's previous filmography given its subject material. The court sequences of the film are the key evidence of this, with audiences seeing the hearings and witness testimonies that epitomized the importance censorship played in hindering freedom of sexual expression during the period. Constant references to postal service laws that prevented the mailing of certain types of materials are employed in the film as reminders of governmental surveillance and social regulation. *I Shot Andy Warhol* also discusses these themes, but in a larger sense, with an emphasis on gender and deviancy in relation to societal control. Valerie Solanas' position as an outsider is stressed through everything from her clothing to the scenes of her wandering around Andy's parties or studio, yet not taking part in the action within.

Following the outline of Foucault's Panopticism, it is important to note that the social environment of Brangwyn boarding school functions as a type of Panopticon structure in which discipline, surveillance, and punishment are ever present. The girls are regularly lined up, inspected, and reprimanded for everything from messy hair to dirty shoes. This chastisement is witnessed and announced in front of their classmates. Authority figure Miss. Bobbie (Kathleen Fee) supervises this disciplinary exercise in addition to her usual patrolling of the girls where she actively seeks out wrongdoers and stands as a symbolic threat of punishment. When one of the girls is penalized, Miss Bobbie is the executor of this sentence. For instance, she is the one in charge of detention and forces Ernessa to swim laps as penance for skipping gym every week even though Ernessa is afraid of the water. Rebukes are further dealt out to the girls during school assemblies, which are held in the chapel and sometimes before the beginning of a sermon, where detentions are given out publicly along with an announcement of what garnered the punishment. By openly humiliating each student who commits an infraction, the superstructure of Brangwyn encourages surveillance, self-policing, and social control.

SCHOOL AS A VAMPIRE

Several scenes in the film also point to Brangwyn's edifice of regulation. On their first day back, Rebecca and Lucy step out of their room to see Charley (Valerie Tian) riding a skateboard down the hallway. Lucy warns "you better hide it before Mrs. Rood sees," as Rebecca echoes "Charley, you can't get expelled on the first day."[7] By cautioning Charley, the girls serve as an example of the self-policing Brangwyn encourages on both internal and external levels. Their fear of the school's external punitive agenda works in tandem with their capacity and willingness to internalize and replicate the gaze of administrative watchers. The girls reproduce disciplinary techniques to an extreme through their incessant gossiping. Public reputations and the rumors that affect them oblige an internal scheme of social control within the group. After their admonition to Charley in the previous scene, the girls sit gossiping on Lucy's bed when Dora (Melissa Farman) exclaims, "you guys hear about Annabelle? She's been hooking up with two different boys from Langley College. Such a whore." This is also a scene where the girls discuss their sexual histories only to judge and mock each other based on this information. A few days later the girls sit in the lounge area when Lucy asks Rebecca about Mr. Davies' (Scott Speedman) class, when Kiki (Gia Sandhu) jumps in to embarrass Rebecca replying, "she has a huge crush on him and he's just lapping it up." Whether through their gossiping or admonitions of "not cool" when someone says something out of line, the girls often police each other without prompting and almost reflexively.

The claustrophobic atmosphere of the small, isolated girls' school also makes it a ripe environment for conscious policing through surveillance. Rebecca particularly seems fascinated with spying on others as a method of social control. On several instances she encourages the girls to spy on Ernessa. After Dora mentions a rumor about Ernessa sneaking out in the middle of the night, Rebecca takes this opportunity to persuade her friends to follow the new girl in order to "see where she goes, what she gets up to." Later that night Rebecca, Dora, and Charley hide behind a crop of trees, smoking pot while they watch for Ernessa, only to be disappointed at not seeing her or anyone else. A few scenes after this first night trip, Rebecca again enlists Dora to help spy on Ernessa. In the middle of the night she sneaks into Dora's room pleading, "I need your help. I'm going to go out on the gutters to see what's in Ernessa's room. Can you watch out?" The fact that Dora's first response is "what if Ernessa sees you?" rather than questioning the ethical implications of this request reinforces surveillance as an accepted social practice among the group. Although Rebecca's status as a societal enforcer is evident with her enthusiastic participation in gossiping and surveillance, this behavior becomes excessively aggressive as the film goes on, especially towards Ernessa and Lucy. The main reason for this intensification is her jealousy and anger at Lucy for exploring same-sex attraction.

The interactions between Lucy and Ernessa are encoded with same-sex desire in a multitude of ways, one of which is simply due to Ernessa's vampiric state. In her book *Phallic Panic*, Barbara Creed describes the vampire in film and literature as "the consummate sexual initiator."[8] To Creed, the vampire encompasses all erotic desire, and functions as a sapphic figure due to "its oral-sadistic character."[9] Harry Benshoff, like Creed, draws on classic horror films such as *Dracula* (Universal Pictures, Browning, 1931) for his analysis of homosexuality in the genre. In his seminal book *Monsters in the Closet*, Benshoff equates monstrosity in early horror cinema with homosexuality, stating "many monster movies (and the source material they draw upon) might be understood as being 'about' the eruption of some form of queer sexuality into the midst of a resolutely heterosexual milieu."[10] Vampirism, according to Lillian Faderman, has been a particularly common mythology in literature for repressing same-sex interest by working to make deviant and monstrous the potentially homosexual relationships embodied by nineteenth-century romantic friendships.[11] Benshoff even points out that "the girls' school is a staple cinematic setting for lesbian intrigue."[12] In this instance, Harron uses the vampire story as a metaphor to examine and destabilize the relationships between the three main girls, and how those friendships become entangled with sexuality and the striving of certain characters for perfection.

Furthermore, Harron employs this vampire allegory within the confines of the modern Gothic subgenre of horror and was intent on keeping those elements of the film intact while also capitalizing on them. In an interview with *Now Magazine*, she explains, "I loved the boarding school setting and in particular the intense, romantic crazy girlfriend shit. I felt like the supernatural element was just a fantastic metaphor to illustrate that and make the story a traditional Gothic, which I hadn't seen in a while."[13] Harron's decision makes sense considering the flexibility offered by the genre in exploring topics of social control and perfection. The modern Gothic is typically obsessed with "the social unconscious," and therefore serves as a perfect venue for investigating dominant mythologies within American culture.[14] Moreover, Charles L. Crow finds that within American strains of the Gothic, characters are often on a "common search for perfection," which certainly could describe Rebecca's journey throughout the film.[15]

PERFECTION *IS* HORROR

As with Lucy, a key element of Rebecca's character is her desire for a sense of perfection, and her view that perfection is an attainable reality. This longing stems from the family trauma of her father's (Julian Casey) recent suicide. Her father's death has made her home life unpleasant and painful for her, with Brangwyn becoming her haven away from the sadness at home. In the only scene where audiences see Rebecca at home, she is perturbed and anxious to return to school, and even tunes out her mother by thinking about school instead. This in part is due to a desire to avoid her mother's (Anne Day-Jones) grief, as it is incompatible with a world in which nothing is wrong and where everything is perfect. She tells Lucy when they first arrive back at school that her mother "just sat in her studio and painted, listening to the same music that my dad was listening to when he. . ." Rebecca's emphasis on perfection can be seen in a dream turned nightmare sequence in which she walks with her father in an Edenic garden where her father comforts and assures her that he would never leave her, surely an idealistic claim. For Rebecca, Lucy is now deemed with filling the void left by her father and plays a crucial role in Rebecca's search for perfection and happiness.

One way of explaining Rebecca's increasing fixation on Lucy, independent of any same-sex desire, is to consider how Lucy symbolizes the possibility of a perfect life. Rebecca's desire for perfection stems from her father's suicide, and she immediately makes clear Lucy's role in attaining perfection. As she sets up her room after arriving back at school, Rebecca reads from her journal, explaining to the audience that "every night I sat alone in my room aching for my father. And then I met Lucy. She was so confident, carefree, and normal. She taught me how to be happy again. That's why I love her so much." To emphasize this connection between the death of Rebecca's father, Lucy, and perfection, Harron focuses on the portraits Rebecca hangs as she narrates. The first of these pictures is a small framed headshot of her father. Next, is a smaller framed portrait of Lucy alone. The last is a photo booth strip of the two girls. Each of these pictures is placed with loving care, while their location also explains the relation of each character within them to Rebecca's happiness. Rebecca places the portrait of her father towards the back of her desk, slightly out of the lamp light. He is also seen in a dark turtleneck sweater, on a dim background, as he looks morosely at the camera. This dark image and its placement are juxtaposed with Lucy's picture and the photo booth roll. In her solo portrait, Lucy stands outside on a sunny day, blond hair down, slightly smiling at the camera. Although her picture is smaller than that of Rebecca's father, the frame is intricately designed and placed directly under the lamp facing anyone sitting at the desk, which maximizes the visibility of this photo and emphasizes its importance.

Meanwhile, the photo booth strip is stuck directly in the center of the mirror, positioning it as a focal point, while Harron places a smiling Rebecca in the frame as she hangs it. This technique of frames-within-frames is typical of Harron's aesthetics and can be seen throughout this film as well as her prior work. For instance, there are several scenes in *The Notorious Bettie Page* where Bettie is filmed looking in a vanity or compact mirror, with the perspective in the mirror being the one within the frame. *Anna Nicole* also features mirrors heavily. An early scene shows young Anna speaking to her future self who appears in the dresser mirror. In *I Shot Andy Warhol* there are moments where Valerie is framed from a diegetic camera perspective, which often cuts back and forth between these shots and the non-diegetic camera.

Another way that Harron accomplishes this frame-within-a-frame style is through the constant placement of characters within doorways and corridors to highlight either a sense of claustrophobia or their importance in that moment of the narrative. An example of this in *The Moth Diaries* is Ernessa's first glimpse of Lucy through the bathroom doorway as she appears over Rebecca's shoulder with Lucy brought into focus by the camera. Harron also employs reflections from mirrors, windows, or picture frames to isolate or emphasize elements within a shot, which works in tandem with Rebecca's literal peering into these fixtures and can be read as a subtle critique of this prying behavior.

To reiterate the normalcy that Lucy represents, Rebecca later echoes her previous fixation on Lucy's carefree life during a scene in the chapel. While they wait for assembly to start, the two girls gossip about their peers, focusing on the family problems of each classmate. Rebecca quips, "no one comes to Brangwyn unless something bad has happened to them," to which Lucy retorts, "except for me. I'm the only boring one." This prompts Rebecca to confide, "believe me, I wish I was like you." Despite the distraction of gossiping about their classmates, Rebecca still centers the conversation on Lucy in this scene. Harron mirrors this dynamic in an early group scene that demonstrates the innate hierarchy of the girls. When discussion turns awkwardly to the subject of Rebecca's dead father, which should put the emphasis on Rebecca's character in the scene, instead Lucy becomes the focal point with her cheerfully ordering "let's go play some hockey. . . that's exactly what we need. . . let's go, right now." Although the others protest or complain at the idea, their resistance is half-hearted, and they all move to follow her. It is also telling that Lucy is seated directly at the center of the table, making her the axis point for the camera, with most of the over-the-shoulder shots of the rest of the girls in conversation wrapping around her.

These early scenes that present Lucy as the golden girl character type soon give way to a darker, more conflicted version of her character as the story continues and as Rebecca's fixation grows increasingly toxic. Lucy's resistance to this behavior finally becomes vocalized when Rebecca confronts her one night about her recent personality changes. Under the guise of checking on her, Rebecca sees Lucy confined to bed and uses the opportunity to berate her for the close relationship she shares with Ernessa. Rebecca tells her that Ernessa is to blame for all the wrongdoings occurring at the school. When Lucy goes to defend Ernessa by pointing out that Rebecca scapegoats the other girl, Rebecca explodes with jealousy and asserts that she does this because "[Ernessa] is to blame for everything. If she hadn't come here this year, we would've had a great year. Don't you see, she's ruined everything for me. God, I hate her so much! I'd kill her if I had the chance." The emphasis in this diatribe against Ernessa is not explained by what Rebecca thinks the supposed vampire has done to her friend, but rather on the injustices she feels were performed against herself. Her dialogue in this scene reinforces the idea that Rebecca's real concern is not with the health of her friend, and instead is on maintaining what she deems a perfect existence, one in which Lucy was meant to play a pivotal role.

In the continuation of this scene Rebecca drags a physically enfeebled Lucy out of bed to stand in front of a mirror with the rebuke "look at yourself!", which she hopes will be a damning guilt trip. Lucy, however, rails against these attacks and destroys the other girl's attempts to define her personality for her by charging, "that's because you want to believe I'm still the old Lucy. It's sad. You don't care about the new me, the *real* Lucy. You don't even want to know her." With this exchange, Lucy identifies not only that she is determined to have her own personality, but that she demands the power to have a "real" selfhood independent of Rebecca's projections of perfection. Her attention to the dichotomy between the old and the new Lucy also marks her resistance to remaining the static figure Rebecca insists of her. Furthermore, her dialogue stresses that an essential part of her concept of selfhood is bound with the ability to change according to her own will. Taking her remonstrations a step further, Lucy announces her desire for physical, as well as mental, independence, stating, "Leave me alone. Please. I can't stand having you around me all the time, wanting me only for yourself. You're a fucking drag. You pull me down with all your pain." This exclamation comes as no surprise given that Rebecca counts on Lucy for a sense of happiness and fulfillment, which Lucy begins to find confining after her experiences in a fulfilling and healthy relationship with Ernessa. Following this scene, Rebecca shifts from the perspective that Ernessa is solely to blame for this new distance between herself and Lucy, but rather that the romantic relationship her friend shares with Ernessa is itself the threat to her intentions. Once she realizes this fact, Rebecca moves forward with a plot against both her own repressed same-sex desire for Lucy, as well as the romance of her friend and Ernessa through her efforts to destroy the new girl and all the spaces of Brangwyn associated with her.

HARRON'S VISUALIZATION OF THE BODY

For many film theorists, the dark and confined settings frequently found in horror movies represent areas of the female body. This trend roughly stems from Julia Kristeva's work with abjection, which other scholars including Barbara Creed and Isabel Cristina Pinedo have used a springboard for investigations of the female body in horror cinema. Using Sigmund Freud's discussion of the uncanny and anthropologist Mary Douglas' book *Purity and Danger* as a basis, Kristeva argues that the female body is one of abjection, meaning that it uncomfortably blurs homogenous boundaries, with the horrific maternal body being a key aspect to her study.[16] Famously, Barbara Creed draws on Kristevan notions of the maternal abject for her discussion of *Alien* (Twentieth Century Fox, Scott, 1979) in *The Monstrous-Feminine*, where she states that "when woman is represented in horror it is almost always in relation to her mothering and reproductive functions."[17] Creed additionally finds the dark, tunneling, uterine-like settings of the spaceship to be a further example of the abject feminine, contending that "these intra-uterine settings consist of dark, narrow, winding passages leading to a central room, cellar or other symbolic place of birth."[18] Laura Mulvey also makes an explicit link between place in film and female bodies. In her description of the home in Alfred Hitchcock's *Psycho*, Mulvey aligns the cellar with the abject female body, using the metaphor of Pandora's Box as a spatial representative of the inner female body.[19] These discussions of the abject feminine have led to what Rodney Farnsworth characterizes as "the basement-as-crotch/womb" in his examination of the primordial.[20] The principles presented by these readings are certainly viable tools for examining how the association between the settings and female characters in Harron's film operate.

In *The Moth Diaries*, "intra-uterine settings" dominate the landscape associated with Rebecca and Ernessa. One of the first things Rebecca finds odd about Ernessa is her predilection for the darker areas of Brangwyn, which symbolically tie the new girl to a desire for female genitalia. On one occasion, Rebecca finds Ernessa in a dark passageway and notes, "it's so dark I always just run straight through," while Ernessa explains "it's one of my favorite places here." Much like Rebecca flees from her own same-sex desire, she also seems to unconsciously fear the feminine encoded areas of Brangwyn. As perceptibly queer, Ernessa cherishes these spaces, which symbolically reinforces her status as queer and begins to explain why Rebecca finds this trait so unnatural. Later on, Rebecca wanders down a darkened hallway only to find Ernessa playing somber songs on the piano. The hallway itself features exposed pipes in the ceiling, is narrow, poorly lit, and leads to a doorway with light shining through. The pipes are uterine, the doorway like a vaginal opening, and her journey through these spaces, and fear of them, mark her unconscious desire for the female body.

The dark, cramped spaces of Brangwyn act not only as symbolic representatives of female genitalia, but also as an emblematic womb. When Rebecca decides to finally kill Ernessa, she begins an odyssey into the womb-like structures of Brangwyn. As a structure housing an all-girls school, Brangwyn is automatically coded female, and could be considered an embodiment of the feminine itself. Audiences see her travel through a series of dimly lit settings, that each go deeper and deeper downward, beginning with a room that holds keys to the basement, then down a hallway, and finally through the vaginal style opening of the basement. Once Rebecca descends the stairs, she wanders through various chambers separated by short arches in the ceiling, which resemble the ribbed inner structure of the vagina. At the end of this corridor, Rebecca finds a trunk belonging to Ernessa containing soil and a diary. In flashback, as Rebecca reads the diary, viewers witness Ernessa committing suicide by first stripping naked, then lowering herself into a tub where what is presumably blood begins to cloud the water stemming from her crossed arms over her chest. Her submergence into the womb-like structure of the tub, as well as her nakedness, further connect Ernessa to the womb. While this journey ultimately proves more as reconnaissance, Rebecca later returns the next day to fulfill her mission. When she finds Ernessa in the trunk, she douses her with gasoline then burns her alive, prompting the fire to spread to the entire basement.

If the coffin and basement spaces of the film stand for a symbolic womb, then the destruction of such places are equivalent to an annihilation of potential reproduction. In *No Future: Queer Theory and the Death Drive*, Lee Edelman draws on Lacanian principles to explain how the queer can function as what he terms a "sinthomosexual." He finds that like "sinthomes," these "sinthomosexuals" reveal not only what a culture hides, but also symbolizes death through their rejection of reproductive futurity. Through opposing the sense of heteronormative futurity represented by children, Edelman's "sinthomosexual" further acts as an example of the death drive given their status as a denial of "every form of social viability."[21] With this theory in mind, the symbolic significance Ernessa carries as a representation of the queer makes her ultimate destruction at the end subject to a larger discussion of how futurity appears in the film.

In fact, the threat of reproduction virulently haunts the film's narrative and *mise en scène*. Rebecca frequently wakes up to extreme cramps, or to find a large menstrual bloodstain on the bed, which serves as a reminder of the link between menses and pregnancy. This imagery was purposefully chosen by Harron, who

Figure 5.3 Rebecca (Sarah Bogler) becomes more traumatized by the decay of her relationship with Lucy and her repression

explained that "I always think that for teenage girls adolescence is your own personal horror movie because your body is transforming so rapidly and your moods swing are so intense. . . The supernatural is a way of expressing those inner fears about sex, about the body."[22] Harron's film could certainly be classified as what Erin Harrington calls "gynaehorror," which "deals with all aspects of female reproductive horror, from the reproductive and sexual organs, to virginity and first sex, through to pregnancy, birth and motherhood, and finally to menopause and post-menopause."[23] Furthermore, concerns around sexual experience and virginity are seen in Rebecca's voyeuristic dream of her friend Sofia's first time having sex turned nightmare of rape. The emphasis of the film on blood, menstruation, sexuality, virginity, and sex account for most of what is portrayed as horrific on-screen.

Because Rebecca cannot ultimately repress her same-sex desire, she instead chooses to destroy it. Creed's use of the Freudian uncanny can also be employed to examine Harron's film. In *Phallic Panic*, Creed notes that repression is central to horror films in that they innately contain references to the uncanny, which she defines as "that which should have remained repressed. . . but which has come to light."[24] Creed's synthesis of the uncanny relates directly to Rebecca's burgeoning same-sex desire. While the relationship between Rebecca and Ernessa can be read any number of ways, the reading I choose to emphasize here is one where Ernessa is an incarnation of Rebecca's same-sex desire, and as such is an example of the uncanny in the form of a double. The film accentuates a sense of doubling for the two girls both through dialogue and their mutual desire for Lucy. In a later scene Harron places the two girls in front of a framed photograph where the reflection of each is visible. While examining the photograph and their reflections Ernessa remarks, "have you ever considered how much we look alike?" As their reflections slightly face one another in the glass, Harron then has the two girls consider their appearance and push their hair behind an ear in mirrored unison. Rebecca further exemplifies this doubling with her assertions that Ernessa is always with her, and even seems to be a part of her own existence. Writing in her journal, Rebecca confides, "it's like she's invading my mind. Even when I'm alone I can't escape her." These two instances are complemented by the fact that Ernessa tends to appear regularly when Rebecca is alone, and that audiences rarely see Ernessa in a scene without Rebecca there as well. For example, the scene where Ernessa torments Rebecca by slitting her own wrists in the blood-soaked library illustrates this. This then leads Rebecca to finally destroy her.

After reciting a macabre nursery rhyme, Ernessa pulls up her sleeve to reveal several healed over scars across her wrists. Dramatically, she pulls out a razor blade, cutting her wrist again, and offers her arm to Rebecca. Blood begins to dramatically gush forth all over Rebecca in a stream, and moments later, rains from the ceiling with Ernessa raising her arms in oblivious pleasure as blood soaks her completely. The following shot shows Rebecca realizing none of the blood was real, and Ernessa nowhere to be found, with the only trace of the incident being the razor blade left on the table. The next scene finds Rebecca sitting in bed contemplating the razor and once again running it lightly over her own wrist. She then puts the razor blade away and the next shot is presumably the next day when Rebecca sneaks down to the basement with her bag of supplies to destroy Ernessa.

The destruction of her same-sex desire, as embodied by Ernessa, also destroys any notion of queer reproduction and futurity. With Lucy already deceased, Ernessa stands as the only clear representative of queer futurity left in the film. Because Ernessa is associated with the intra-uterine caverns of Brangwyn, Rebecca's decision to burn the coffin, basement, and Ernessa represents a three-fold destruction plan in which she destroys the figure of her repressed sexuality, a space that is symbolically vaginal, and the womb-like cocoon of Ernessa's coffin with all its symbolic reproductive power. After the elimination of such places, Rebecca is picked up by the police for questioning. While in the car, Rebecca discreetly slips her razor blade out of the window. By discarding her razor, which appeared in tandem with Ernessa and serves as a sign of queerness through this association, Rebecca signals to the audience her securely heteronormative futurity.

At the close of the film, both representatives of queer futurity are destroyed, and Rebecca's future is left uncertain. This restructuring of the finale is one of the few major alterations to the story Harron allows. In Klein's version of events, Rebecca includes an afterword in which she assures readers that she met a man, had two daughters, and remains happily married.[25] Harron's ending, however, features a soot-covered Rebecca in the back of a squad car, with a voice-over that sounds almost paranoid and delusional, rather than the lucidly triumphant tone of heteronormativity represented in Klein's prose. As the scene fades to black, Rebecca with her journal, *sans* symbolically queer razor blade of course, calmly looks out of the car window, and audiences are left to wonder if all is really as well as it now seems.

This ending is uncharacteristic of Harron's work, which often includes concrete finales through an afterword informing audiences of the fate of certain characters. The epilogues of *I Shot Andy Warhol*, *The Notorious Bettie Page*, and *Anna Nicole*, the three films most related thematically in terms of gender to *The Moth Diaries*, serve to bring closure to the stories in a structured manner. Alternatively, the ambiguous conclusion Harron chose for *The Moth Diaries*, as opposed to the neat close of the novel, prompts the viewer to question the future of the characters and disrupts audience security in Rebecca's decisions. The uncertainty of this ending exposes the destructively heteronormative mission Rebecca undertakes throughout the narrative, and firmly places the film within the thematic space occupied by Harron's other features, but this time in a modern setting and addressed to a younger audience.

CONCLUSION

Typically, Harron seeks to complicate notions of female sexuality in tandem with explorations of how women's roles in society are prescriptively derived by power structures. With this in mind, one can easily see the plot of *The Moth Diaries* as one sustained by social control. Whether this authority takes the form of larger institutional traits, such as public humiliation for messy hair or shoes, or the power exerted by individual characters over one another, regulatory mechanisms dominate the story. Rebecca is the character through which audiences witness Panoptic enforcement of societal norms taking place. Her maneuvers towards Lucy and Ernessa demonstrate a wide range of penalties toward what she deems deviant behaviors. While Rebecca mostly uses these enactments toward the other two girls, she also attempts to regain her sense of self control, which has been threatened by her same-sex desire towards Lucy. As Ernessa and Lucy grow closer, and later consummate their relationship, Rebecca moves from a system of attempts to control Lucy, to an exertion of punishment on both girls under the guise of the narrative that Ernessa is a vampire. While Harron's approach to same-sex attraction in the film may be foggy, one thing the film does make clear is how this desire is antithetical to the heteronormative world of perfection that Rebecca subscribes to. This becomes especially evident in the final removal of both sources and stressors of Rebecca's same-sex desire. When Rebecca seems freed at the end, one cannot help but wonder if it is really her repressed desire that was quelled by the flames.

NOTES

1. Sarah Gadon, "Behind the Scenes," *The Moth Diaries*, DVD, directed by Mary Harron (2011; Montreal, QC., Canada: Alliance Film, 2012).
2. Mary Harron, "The Moth Diaries: Mary Harron and Lily Cole on Vampires as a Metaphor," Interview by Melissa Leong, *National Post*, April 4, 2012, http://nationalpost.com/entertainment/the-moth-diaries-mary-harron-and-lily-cole-on-vampires-as-a-metaphor.
3. Michel Foucault, *Discipline and Punish: The Birth of the Prison*, Second Edition (New York: Vintage Books, 1995), 195.
4. Jean-Paul Sartre, *Being and Nothingness*, Reprinted Edition (New York: Washington Square Press, 1993), 358.
5. Todd McGowan, *The Real Gaze: Film Theory After Lacan (SUNY Series in Psychoanalysis and Culture)* (Albany: State University of New York Press, 2008), 2.
6. Laura Mulvey, "Visual Pleasures and Narrative Cinema," in *Issues in Feminist Film Criticism*, edited by Patricia Erens (Bloomington: Indiana University Press, 1991), 33.
7. *The Moth Diaries*, DVD, directed by Mary Harron (2011; Montreal, QC., Canada: Alliance Film, 2012).
8. Barbara Creed, *Phallic Panic: Film, Horror and the Primal Uncanny* (Vic: Melbourne University Press, 2005), 72.
9. Creed, *Phallic Panic*, 81.
10. Harry M. Benshoff, *Monsters in the Closet: Homosexuality and the Horror Film* (Manchester: Manchester University Press, 1997), 4.
11. Lillian Faderman, *Surpassing the Love of Men: Romantic Friendship and Love between Women from the Renaissance to the Present* (New York: Harper Paperbacks, 1998), 330.
12. Benshoff, *Monsters in the Closet*, 194.
13. Mary Harron, "Director Interview: Mary Harron," Interview by Phil Brown, *Now Magazine*, April 5, 2012, https://nowtoronto.com/movies/features/director-interview-mary-harron/
14. Jerrold Hogle, "Introduction: Modernity and the Proliferation of the Gothic," in *The Cambridge Companion to the Modern Gothic*, edited by Jerrold Hogle (Cambridge: Cambridge University Press, 2014), 7.
15. Charles L. Crow, *American Gothic (History of the Gothic)* (Cardiff: University of Wales Press, 2009), 53.
16. Julia Kristeva, *Powers of Horror: An Essay On Abjection (European Perspectives Series)*, Reprinted Edition (New York: Columbia University Press, 1982), 54.
17. Barbara Creed, *The Monstrous-Feminine: Film, Feminism, Psychoanalysis* (New York: Routledge, 1993), 7.
18. Creed, *The Monstrous-Feminine*, 53.
19. Laura Mulvey, *Fetishism and Curiosity* (London: Indiana University Press, 1996), 64.
20. Rodney Farnsworth, *The Infernal Return: The Recurrence of the Primordial in Films of the Reaction Years, 1977–1983* (Westport, CT, Praeger, 2002), 77.
21. Lee Edelman, *No Future: Queer Theory and the Death Drive* (Durham, NC: Duke University Press Books, 2004), 9.
22. Mary Harron, "Interview with Mary Harron—Director of *The Moth Diaries*," Interview by Melissa Silverstein, *IndieWire*, April 18, 2012, http://www.indiewire.com/2012/04/interview-with-mary-harron-director-of-the-moth-diaries-211491/
23. Erin Harrington, *Women, Monstrosity and Horror Film: Gynaehorror (Film Philosophy at the Margins)* (New York: Routledge, 2017), 3.
24. Creed, *Phallic Panic*, 5.
25. Rachel Klein, *The Moth Diaries* (New York: Bantam Books, 2002), 243.

CHAPTER 6

Charismatic Breadwinner Killer: Gender Power Relations in *Charlie Says*

Gemma Piercy-Cameron

INTRODUCTION

In these days of populism, there is a certain logic to the revival of interest in charismatic serial killers of the twentieth century. Furthermore, the women and wider public who seemingly fall under these killers' spell, either oblivious to or in denial of their crimes, have also become a curiosity. Recent examples in cinema include Ted Bundy biopic *Extremely Wicked, Shockingly Evil and Vile* (Netflix, Berlinger, 2019), and three recent interpretations of Charles Manson and the "Family" in *Charlie Says, Once Upon a Time In . . . Hollywood* (Columbia Pictures, Tarantino, 2019), and *The Haunting of Sharon Tate* (Skyline, Farrands, 2019). The fifty-year anniversary of the Tate murders has undeniably influenced the number of movies on the Manson murders, which already has an extended cinematic history.[1] Undeniably, artists in the creative industries and the general public are still fascinated with "why" the Manson murders happened and "how" did Manson influence so many people. A curiosity that is only intensified by Manson and the family's proximity to and links with Hollywood and the music industry.

    The purpose of this chapter is to address the conceptualization of masculinities in *Charlie Says*. First, there will be an examination of the way in which Harron depicts masculinity. Second, the chapter considers the temporal nature of gender power relations represented by the twentieth-century "breadwinner" gender contract and contradictions posed by the destabilization of that social contract that began in earnest in the time periods that the movie traverses. Third, the chapter discusses three main archetypes/tropes present, the motif of the rescuer as savior/controller, and the portrayal of alpha and beta masculinities.

Connell and Messerschimdt assert that masculinity is better conceptualized as operating at different levels (local, regional, and global) and that in these levels multiple and conflicting masculinities are at play.[2] This chapter will draw on this pluralist interpretation of masculinity to draw out tensions presented by multiple and conflicting masculinities. The terms "alpha" and "beta" as forms of masculinity will also be used to explore the portrayal of and movement between dominant and submissive masculinities in *Charlie Says*.[3] The concept of the alpha male, and more specifically patriarchal control, is a recurring theme within Harron's filmography. While the films mentioned in the first paragraph feature Manson as either a central or peripheral character, Harron's concern here is the impact of patriarchy on women,[4] as seen in her previous films *I Shot Andy Warhol*, *The Notorious Bettie Page*, and *Anna Nicole*. As such, Harron's exploration of the human condition, particularly the power and control exerted by her male characters, is further exemplified in *Charlie Says*. Significantly, the power and control of her male characters is enabled by the gender power relations that form part of the structural and everyday life aspects of the film's narrative. Therefore, it is important to contextualize gender power relations in this chapter.

SITUATING GENDER POWER RELATIONS

The first usage relates to Connell's explanation of hegemonic masculinity, which is "constructed in relation to various subordinated masculinities." An example is the practices associated with the beta male, "as well as in relation to women."[5] Messner and Messerschmidt argue that two key aspects of Connell's classification of hegemonic masculinity are: 1) the legitimization and protection of patriarchy, and 2) forms of masculinity that operate unequally in relation to femininity that are "practiced in complementary, compliant, and accommodating" ways.[6] This is termed "emphasized femininity." It is important to note that emphasized femininity operates in relation to hegemonic and certain forms of nonhegemonic masculinities.[7] Therefore, hegemonic masculinity requires a process of internalization for both sides of the relationship that justifies and enables the maintenance of unequal gender relations.[8] Thus, gender power relations refer to inequality between the genders that is maintained through discourse (gender orders and gender regimes) and material relations.[9] The power relations as conceptualized by Connell are dynamic. Consequently, the analysis of gender relations and the resistive practices on the part of the oppressed need to be acknowledged. Additionally, responses to social change/crisis that allow for progress and regression in gender relations is intrinsic to these discussions.[10] One such crisis to the maintenance of gender power relations/patriarchy was the second wave of feminism and the movement of women in greater numbers into the labor market from the 1970s. Gender power relations operate in this chapter as the social and gender contract termed the "breadwinner model"[11] and the concept of patriarchy as gender domination.[12]

The Industrial Revolution changed the nature of employment by moving work from the home or the domestic space to factories and the public sphere. As part of this transition, a new gender division of labor emerged that was legitimized by an emphasized femininity associated with domesticity. Domesticity as a form of emphasized femininity positions women's role not in the public space of work but in the private sphere of the home. This split between spheres reinforced already established practices of paying women less for their labor. As such women's entry into the labor market once industrialization began represented a threat to the employment of men. Thus, the labor movement in the nineteenth century turned its back on feminists, advocating that women's place was in the home.[13] These arguments were reinforced by policy in the early twentieth century that enshrined the social wage to place women in the position of economic dependence on men.[14] A representation of the breadwinner gender contract and its disadvantages for women is poignantly rendered in *Revolutionary Road* (DreamWorks Pictures, Mendes, 2008) set a decade prior to the events in *Charlie Says*. Despite the difference in time periods, the oppositional split between paid work (public sphere) being an aspect of masculinity and unpaid domestic work (private sphere) associated with femininity plays an important role in both films.

The conceptualization or framing of masculinity and femininity are designed to reinforce (or disrupt) social contracts such as the gender breadwinner contract. As part of these relational practices it is important to include the idea of gender performance. For the purposes of this chapter, gender performance is the way in which individuals embody practices associated with femininities and masculinities. This interpretation of gender performance is based on how the presentation of the self includes the management of impressions that are conceptualized by Goffman as performance in status games.[15] The process of performance between the player and the audience in the status game can engender a sense of belonging or exclusion, depending on the capacity for the "correct" impression to be made. The negotiation processes involved in social interactions of status games also influence the process of organization by the private inner "I" and could be perceived as interpellation. Performance in this sense, therefore, refers to: 1) the ways in which identities are conveyed to and recognized by an audience through specific situated and embodied practices, and 2) how identities reflect and reproduce structural and other ordering strategies in society.[16]

WAYS OF SEEING: FEMININE LENSES

The depiction of Charles Manson in *Charlie Says* is presented to us through a series of connected lenses. The first interpretation comes to us through the lens of Leslie (Lulu) Van Houten (Hannah Murray), a member of the Manson Family, the protagonist of the film. The second lens is through the interpretation of Leslie's stories by a women's studies lecturer Karlene Faith (Merritt Wever). Faith's PhD thesis on Leslie was used by the screenwriter Guinevere Turner, who provides the third lens. The fourth and final lens is through the eyes of Harron and her direction of actor Matt Smith, who portrays Manson.

In *Ways of seeing* (1974), Berger points out in historical art that women are always defined in relation to men.[17] However, Fanon suggests the black man is always defined in relation to white men.[18] Berger argues that women are traditionally represented in art as an object of the male gaze, thus representations of femininity are defined by men. Women internalize these representations, resulting in an interpretation of femininity and masculinity, both of which are constructed from a patriarchal standpoint. By implication, then, to define oneself from a different standpoint is to other oneself, effectively alienating your identity from the dominant order, an aspect featured in *I Shot Andy Warhol* and *The Notorious Bettie Page*.

For the purposes of understanding the portrayal of masculinity in *Charlie Says*, Berger's and Fanon's arguments are important in two central ways. First, they allow us to see the ways in which identities are othered. Second, that the consideration of gender roles or racial identities are underpinned by the argument that women define gender roles, including that of femininity, using an internalized patriarchal or masculine frame, as blackness is defined in relation to whiteness. Therefore, my rationale on the importance of pointing to the lenses of Harron, Turner, Faith, and Van Houten is that they are all women seeking to understand and portray gendered experiences in relation to men or, in this case, a man, Charles Manson. What is also significant is that these feminine lenses mean that the portrayals of masculinities are derived through a gendered lens, one informed and deliberately sharpened to bring out the power relations between genders.[19]

The recent portrayals of Ted Bundy (Zac Efron) and Manson (Smith) could be argued to be a decision to cast against type, given the tempered masculinity represented in previous roles, of note *High School Musical* (Disney, Ortega, 2006) and *Doctor Who* (BBC, 2005–present) respectively. The diminutive Efron and lean Smith force us as viewers to reconsider the traditional portrayals of dominant masculinity through the display of larger size and physical strength. Additionally, these roles provide us with opportunities to reflect on the way charismatic individuals can exert control and influence that seems unbelievable and contradictory. The casting of these characters illustrate how dominance can be asserted in gender power relations in ways that are not linked to physical size and strength. The characters present masculinities in a fluid sense indicating how gender performance is not stable, or fixed, and alters in accordance with the context and the social interactions. Status games emphasize how gender performances can be carefully gauged to exploit the appearance of a soft or caring masculinity.

In comparison, *Once Upon a Time In ... Hollywood* features Manson (Damon Herriman) as a peripheral but important character. However, the female characters are given little development, focus, or screen time, and instead the film concentrates on the two male protagonists Rick Dalton (Leonardo DiCaprio) and Cliff Booth (Brad Pitt). Again, though Manson features in both Tarantino's and Harron's films, each filmmaker has differing approaches that reflect their lens, or their interpretation of what masculinity means in the context of such an infamous character. The decision to cast against type illustrates that as a director Harron is more subversive, while Tarantino reflects a stance uncritical of patriarchy, reflecting the tendency in the re-telling of history to marginalize or render invisible the stories of women.[20]

Another important aspect of Harron's gendered lens was not just to tell the story of the women but to do so by narrowing in on the "tiny moments" that led to the women becoming trapped or stuck in the Manson Family.[21] As I indicated at the beginning of this chapter, there is a fascination with the how and why people fall under the thrall of men who seem unlikely charismatic leaders. By focusing on tiny moments, Harron skillfully depicts how these women become part of the Manson Family and later become murderers themselves. Without relying on the bluntness of a dual narrative, as utilized in *Sliding Doors* (Miramax Films, Howitt, 1998), Harron uses these small moments to show how different paths could have been taken, particularly that of Van Houten. These moments of reflection engage the audience further with the character's internal conflict, illustrated distressingly at the end of the movie with a reprise of a biker driving away from the ranch, a person who wanted to take Leslie away from the family.

Figure 6.1 Harron utilizes this image of at the end of the movie to portray a different path (tiny choice) where Leslie (Hannah Murray) left the ranch with her biker rescuer

Hannah Murray's casting as Leslie may or may not have been against type but it was inspired. Murray's performance of Leslie is compelling: through her eyes, forehead, and mouth she conveys a multitude of emotions to the audience. It is through her that we see how someone who is not just ordinary but a high achiever (Homecoming Queen) and from a loving family becomes enthralled by the psychotically unhinged Manson. More than just moments of decision-making, Leslie's reactions to the Family's behavior highlight the tension between what was promised and what in the end is realized. In key scenes, crinkling her eyes and nose, she allows the audience to share her own puzzlement in trying to understand the contradictions posed by Manson's rhetoric of freedom that contrast with the strict limitations he imposes that often manifest as abusive control.

In the re-telling of Leslie's story, Harron utilizes a non-linear approach, unfolding the narrative in flashbacks from Leslie's perspective on death row.[22] Faith visits Susan/Sadie (Marianne Rendón), Patricia/Katie (Sosie Bacon) and Leslie at the request of the prison warden (Annabeth Gish), initially to provide adult education classes for the women to cope with their boredom. One of Faith's roles is to help them come to terms with their actions. Later, Faith wants them to admit guilt but to also see the role of the abuse at the hands of others, particularly Manson, which played a substantial part in their decisions. However, as Faith converses with the women about their situation, and the choices they made to commit murder based on Manson's "Helter Skelter" vision, the refrain "but Charlie says" is a constant from each of the inmates. It becomes an instant representation of how Manson had complete control over the women, even years later as they languish on death row. Leslie is the first to accept that Faith's alternative version of events could be valid. At this point, we are taken back to Leslie's first encounter with the Family and to her moments of doubt and conflict with the philosophy of Manson. Together we are invited by Harron to reflect on moments with the Family that reveal Faith's position of Manson as an abuser/brainwasher.

The different standpoints—the controlled (Leslie), the challenger (Faith), and the portrayer (Harron)—define what it meant to be "the man" Manson presented himself as. However, it is from their gendered standpoint. Does this matter? It is intrinsic to Harron's film as masculinity is defined through the eyes of these different women, highlighting the difference of how men might define themselves and their gender role performance. It is also important because in the binary context of this film, the gender roles of men and women, are defined in relation to each other. I refer to gender in binary terms because of the way the movie focuses on heteronormative gender power relations. Heteronormativity operates on the basis that heterosexuality is assumed to be the "norm," and that social systems and interactions work to promote and idealize it. Heteronormativity has gender binaries (i.e. male + female) as a cornerstone and dominates these "gendered sexualities."[23]

Queer identities are only referred to once explicitly when Faith is asked if she is a lesbian.[24] The question posed to Faith by Leslie, Patricia, and Susan was stated in such a way that being a lesbian is "other," reinforcing the dominant social norm of heterosexuality. Their justification of the positioning of Faith as a lesbian was due to the supposed "unfeminine" way she dressed and the lack of reference she made to a husband despite talking about her children. Their stance sends a strong signal that even though sharing sexual favors with men and women and wearing swinging sixties clothes was the norm on the ranch, the three women now isolated on death row had returned to the emphasized femininity of the breadwinner gender contract.

The othering of the lesbian identity suggests that Harron made a deliberate decision to emphasize gender roles in a heteronormative fashion in the movie. Perhaps this was to recall the oppositional binaries that the radicals in the second wave of feminism sought to disrupt through the dialectic.[25] One such binary in the film is the inclusion of men in the position of public and decision-making roles, while women were part of the private domain and submitted to orders given to them by the men in the Manson Family.[26] Given the time period in which the film is set, the enduring nature of the 1950s traditional gender hierarchy associated with the breadwinner gender contract that is part of the public dominant and private submissive divide illustrates the enduring nature of some cultural traditions during times of societal change.

CONTRADICTIONS: EMERGENT, RESIDUAL, AND DOMINANT GENDER ROLES

The different representations of masculinity and gendered power relations in *Charlie Says* provide an opportunity to reflect on how masculinities, hegemonic or otherwise, are a temporal and dynamic construct. The portrayals of the men and women in *Charlie Says* shift between time periods, in relation to specific settings and within social interactions. Harron draws our attention to these shifts cinematically as well as through performances. In collaboration with cinematographer, Crille Forsberg, Harron visualizes scenes at the ranch with yellow tones designed to reinforce warmth, love, open spaces, freedom, and possibility that attracted women such as Leslie to join the Family. In contrast, the prison scenes are dominated by blue light and closed spaces, cold, clinical, and oppositional to the ranch.[27] Another aspect of representation that illustrates change and shifting gender norms (discussed in detail below) is adornment and the body itself in the expression but also reification of control between men and women throughout the time periods within the film. Therefore, the performances or representations of masculinity and femininity highlight pre-emergent, emergent, traditional (residual) practices that are part of dominant gender relations.

The terms pre-emergent, emergent, and traditional (residual)[28] stem from Raymond Williams' challenge to epochal analysis in the study of cultural practices.[29] Williams does not reject epochal analysis but instead argues that the fixed way change is conceptualized needs to be altered. Cultural shifts inevitably include ideas and practices that are part of past traditions, which are still considered salient or current (residual) to the dominant way of being. He also argues that new practices take time to be incorporated into the dominant and exist in a pre-emergent state that remain as an outlier to cultural practice. Essentially, not all new practices that are pre-emergent will become part of the dominant order. For example, the women embraced free love, but given their conversation on death row with Faith they had not incorporated an acceptance of homosexuality as part of their gender identity. Thus, it is only once practices become more generalized or more widely accepted that the cultural practices become emergent and with aspects perhaps later incorporated as dominant. Cultural shifts are, therefore, always made up of ideas old and new that shift as norms are challenged, re-established, altered or removed.[30] The gender performances in *Charlie Says* present us with contradictions that stem from the movement between emerging understandings of womanhood and the retreat into the traditional gender roles.

The pre-emergent and emergent forms of femininity present in the film are linked with the societal changes in the US that had been signaled by the beatniks in the 1950s and ultimately expressed by social movements associated with counter-culture[31] and hippies of the late 1960s.[32] These emergent ideas associated with gender represented a strong challenge to traditional institutions of marriage and maternity on the part of women,[33] while for men, their counter-culture performance challenged the traditional conservative clean-cut, straight-edge, and dominant form of masculinity by rejecting shaving, haircuts and paid work.[34] These new ideas where part of rejecting an adherence to breadwinner gender contract.

These fashion and clothing choices also represented new ways of performing masculinity (pre-emergent) that were about crossing over into femininity, challenging an oppositional representation of gender. In place of the minimalist, space-oriented, modernist aesthetic of the 1950s, fabrics like velvet, corduroy, and colorful prints dominated, softening the image of the black-and-white IBM man or the blue jeans/flannel shirt wearing working-class man. Women embraced waistcoats, jeans, miniskirts, and bikinis, asserting control over their bodies via the freedom bestowed by the contraceptive pill and penicillin.[35] As part of counter-culture, these choices signaled a deliberate mixing up of the gender appearance and performance designed to destabilize what was understood to represent twentieth-century gender roles of men and women. The film incorporates these feminized depictions of masculinity, utilizing the fashion of counter-culture to visually indicate what it meant to be a hippie. The lead characters, both male and female, wear jeans, with gender only being signaled through facial hair and/or the removal of clothing as different members of the Family were often only partially clothed.

The lack of clear gender roles exemplified by clothing was reinforced by various "new age" or "hippie" language in conversations as well as shifting dynamics between the gendered performances. For example, the opening scene depicts Leslie, Patricia, and Tex (Chace Crawford) dumping their bloody clothes before hitching a ride with Pete (Christopher Gerse). Leslie sits in the front and excitedly engages Pete in conversation. She offers to buy him breakfast and by the time they are in the diner they animatedly discuss the musician Tiny Tim. Pete criticizes Tiny Tim's voice as effeminate and uses expletives to describe him, and by doing so presents a traditional view of gender norms whereby men who are not dominant or masculine enough are ridiculed using feminine traits.[36] Unlike her companions, the guarded Patricia and Tex, Leslie is confident and chatty. She holds control of the narrative having asked for the ride, paying for breakfast and betraying no fear: Leslie occupies the public domain and makes decisions. Here is a product of these changing social mores and the counter-culture narratives. Within moments and despite the gender bending or blending suggested by the clothes, Leslie's dominant and public role is shown to have thin veneer. Her companion Patricia observes and wipes away some clotted blood off Leslie's face. The power dynamics within the group visibly shifts, suddenly Leslie folds in on herself, cowed by the threat she has imposed on the group by not washing off all the blood. Her dominating public persona is shed, she falters in her conversation but then reasserts herself and gets them all to leave and continue on with their journey back to the ranch.

The contradiction presented to us by Leslie's initial powerful demeanor and its sudden removal is integral to the depiction of gender roles in *Charlie*

Figure 6.2 Leslie in charge of the conversation

Says. Leslie's hesitation and urge to leave illustrate the resumption of traditional heteronormative gender roles, despite the clothes and the language worn by the characters. Leslie retreats from the public domain and takes a submissive stance of emphasized femininity, a role that she assumes for the rest of the film. This early moment in the narrative illustrates to the audience that gender roles associated with counter-culture as well as the breadwinner gender contract are present. The masculinity portrayed by the language and clothes used in the film are in line with the social movements of the 1960s, and indicate an emergent understanding of a softer, submissive form of masculinity.

However, the continuous shift between traditional forms of masculinity and their swinging sixties softer forms, particularly by Manson, creates a jarring effect in the film, designed by Harron to generate discomfort. The shift to traditional Western understandings of men as dominant and powerful, and women as submissive and weak, is often accompanied by the threat of or actual violence. These shifts by Manson from emergent softer forms of masculinity to its traditional and hegemonic structures are part of the patterns of abuse and control experienced by the Family members.

MASCULINE MOTIFS: THE PROTECTOR/RESCUER, THE DOMINANT ALPHA, AND THE SUBMISSIVE BETA

The archetypes of the alpha and beta males and the rescuer/protector role are recurring motifs in Harron's work, especially in both *American Psycho* and *Anna Nicole*. However, they are analyzed further, and, arguably, in more depth in *Charlie Says*. While alpha and beta terms are common terms in animal research, their usage in gender studies literature is scarce. In studies of masculinity there is a clear preference for terms such as hypermasculinity and dominant masculinity to represent characteristics associated with the term "alpha male." This could be due to the association of these terms with pop psychology but also because alpha and beta are Greek terms that mean first and second respectively. In a pack setting it makes sense to identify one male or female as the lead and another as the second but in most human interactions, either group based or between two individuals, power relations are more dynamic. However, the Family could be considered a pack and Manson, most definitely, their alpha. Furthermore, certain gender studies film literature utilizes the terms alpha[37] and beta[38] or both[39] in their analyses. Mclean's usage of alpha male as an interpretation of the hypermasculine performance requirements of men (and some women) working in the finance industry draws on wider literature, reflecting a much wider acceptance of the term alpha. While Greven labels the new softer forms of masculinity associated with Judd Apatow films, such as *This Is 40* (Universal Pictures, 2012), as a type of beta masculinity. These terms also have a new salience in the vernacular through discussions of masculinity online with men identifying themselves as beta or incels railing against women and the alpha males they purported prefer.[40]

For the purposes of the remainder of this chapter, I will utilize the terms alpha and beta not to discuss hypermasculinity or softer caring versions of masculinity per se but to capture the way the male characters' stances shift between a dominant and submissive role. These shifts are part of status games and reflect the classifications of alpha and beta in a relational and hierarchical way where the performance rather than the person is identified based on the presence of other males and the type of interaction being depicted.[41] Such classification is not identity based. As such when I use the term alpha, I am referring to performances of masculinity that reflects dominant and domineering behavior, and beta is associated with submissiveness.

Tex's interactions with Manson reflect a submissive presentation of the self, where he often takes the stance of a beta male in their exchanges, only reluctantly taking on a public and dominant role when it is asked of him. For example, in the murders of the couple Rosemary (Jackie Joyner) and Leno LaBianca (Dan Olivo), the women call on Tex to help them subdue the wife, when he was already dealing with killing Leno. Significantly, Smith's depiction of Manson includes performances in all of these roles as he sought to resolve threats to his sense of self as well as his assert his control over the Family. The following section charts Manson's shifts between these different interpretations of masculinity and outlines Tex's stance as a beta male. Manson's role as rescuer/protector is also contrasted with Faith's position with the three women, and the biker who provides a significant tiny moment of Leslie's life.

When we are first introduced to Manson, it is through Leslie's perspective, which depicts him as rescuer/protector. The first flashback depicts the moment Leslie is introduced as a "new girl" to Manson, who proceeds to interrogate her. He is reassured no one will come looking for her and she is permitted to stay. It is worth pausing though to consider the significance of these questions. On a surface level the questions are clearly about managing risk of unwelcome company and attention from parents and boyfriends seeking to rescue their "girl," but these questions are also a way to gauge the levels of abandonment experienced by the "new girl." But at the time they are posed as a way to show Leslie that Manson and the Family will rescue her off the street and meet her needs.

When the Family take Leslie on her first garbage run in the bus, we are told how one day Manson got annoyed with the Family and drove the bus away. He came back for them telling them it was a joke. In this snippet of early Family history given to Leslie we are again shown that while Manson can rescue you, he can take everything away if you do not comply with his commands. A tension and contradiction that keeps the Family addicted to retaining his good will as a means to be safe but also keep being rescued.

Faith's role as rescuer/protector could be perceived as a different way in which control by others is imposed on the lives of the Manson girls. Her irritation with the refrain "but Charlie says" is made clear and she engages in deprograming techniques, even introducing the women to an African-American academic in order to disrupt "Helter Skelter." However, even when irritated by their dedication to Manson and his promise of metamorphosis, Faith is patient, calm, supportive, and predictable. Sitting on the ground together in a separate empty cell Faith meets the women at their level and shares literature designed to be part of consciousness-raising. Initially drawn to the women by the sense of voyeurism shared by so many, including her colleagues, Faith realizes that the abandonment experiences of the women mean that her role is to be a steadfast, constant presence in their lives.[42] The kind of loyalty she provides to the three women on death row is something that Turner argues kept the women at the ranch even when escape was offered.[43]

When Charlie begins preparing the Family to put his vision of "Helter Skelter" into place, the motif of the rescuer/protector returns to the narrative. At this point in the film, the tension between tenderness and dominance is removed with only anger and frustration in its place. The parties and the pleasure fade into the background. Instead, Family members train for the coming war and put their lives on the line at Manson's orders. In order to get access to weapons, Manson commoditized the Family and the women become prostitutes in all but name. Leslie and a biker wake in the early morning light and Charlie bursts in yelling. Leslie fearfully gazes up at Manson as he kicks the man out of the barn and the ranch. Manson tells Leslie no more hippies as they are just getting in the way of the scene. Later in the storyline, the biker comes back to the ranch and he asks, pleads even, with Leslie to go with him. Leslie looks into his eyes and then at Manson, who shrugs his shoulders dismissively at her and then makes a shooing motion. She looks at the biker and then back at Manson, and then confidently tells him no and assures him that she is fine and the biker leaves. This moment is significant for Leslie and, as noted above, Harron reprises this scene in the film's finale, but this time she drops the broom and jumps on the back of the bike. We are left with the reflection: if only she had left with the biker, she would have never participated in the murders. For me, this choice also raised further questions. Why did she still need a man to rescue her? Despite his kind words of unconditionality, would a hippie biker be any safer than Charles Manson?

The dominance of men is signaled in so many scenes where women's bodies (not their being) are presented as foils. For example, the access to the ranch is explained as the owner, a very old man, blind and voiceless, is shown sitting on a couch with the TV blaring and being masturbated by a young woman. Through Leslie, we are told that he is a friend and the young woman is not compromising herself or doing something distasteful: she is being "nice." The message sent here is that to belong to the Family is about performing an essentialized femininity focused on satisfying male desire. The women's identities were being remade as needing to meet the physical desires of Manson and other men.

Another example in the film that powerfully reflects the dominance of men that contrasts the "free love" hippie rhetoric is illustrated in the idea that being part of the Family means letting go of your ego. The group gathers around a fire and a young woman, Sandy (Julia Schlaepfer), is singled out by Manson. He calls to her and makes Sandy stand up, stating "Take your clothes off." She looks tearful, reluctant, until he commands: "DO IT!" Still, Sandy hesitates. Manson looks to the group and explains "She's spoilt, so she can't let go of her ego." Letting go of your ego, we are told, is essential so you can live in the now. In this scene we learn that personal ego is to be surrendered but not to the universe, to God, but to Manson. By making the women vulnerable in public spaces through their bodies, Manson exerts the kind of control associated with alpha males. He demonstrates to all that he is able take away everything—their clothes, their dignity, their ego, and their past and name.

By emphasizing these kinds of moments, Harron makes the traditional patriarchal gender power relations visible through the mechanisms used to control the Family members. During mealtime, as Leslie, now renamed Lulu, starts to serve herself, "No, men first," she is told. The rhetoric of freedom, equality, and of being in the "now" is overlain with the additional requirement to do so within the parameters that Manson sets, parameters that reflect gender roles associated with the breadwinner gender contract. There is serious contradiction here between what the Family members left behind (the breadwinner model) and what they have been promised by the social movements of the 1960s and the rhetoric of Manson that reflect freedom and love. This is made clear by Tex's uncertainty because as Leslie accepts the command, she gives the plate to Tex first. As viewers we are given permission to see the tension imposed by Manson's command not just on Leslie but on Tex as well as a beta male in the group. In an interview with Nicolas Rabold, Harron revealed that it was very important to her vision that the viewers be aware that Mason controlled men as well as women.[44]

The depiction of Tex as a beta male is reinforced by a subsequent scene where the Family are exhorted to enjoy themselves sexually, by themselves or with each other, their responsibility to experience fulfilment and to not hold back. Two perspectives are used to frame our understanding of the room's dynamics—Manson's and Leslie's. Harron continues to highlight Leslie's naivety and Murray utilizes her wide eyes to present this: she takes it all in, as she has in all the preceding scenes, desperate to learn the rules and ensure she maintains stability. Sandy is crying again, Manson observes Leslie watching and tells her not to worry, that it is just her inability to let go of her ego, reinforcing the need once more for Leslie to let go of hers. In this moment, as with others, Harron has set up the audience with an opportunity to identify with Leslie—through Murray's performance and manifest fascination we become the voyeurs mirroring the fascination with Manson, the Family and the murders that has endured now for over fifty years.

Manson breaks the moment, seeking to distract Leslie and anyone else from Sandy's crying and the tension it raises (as how can those who have come to a place of freedom and love be sad?), and shifts attention to Tex who is having oral sex with a female member of the Family. As Manson draws everyone's attention to Tex's behavior, Tex demonstrates that this is not the first time this has happened. As he knows what is coming, Tex seeks to prevent what follows, asking Manson "Don't do this." However, in order to reinforce Tex's position as a beta male Manson cannot spare him. Tex is told publicly to start again and do it better this time in full view under Manson's instruction. Tex is disciplined publicly for doing it wrong, he is humiliated and shamed.

Smith's performance of Manson's overt and public displays of asserting dominance as an alpha male is not one-dimensional. Manson's vulnerability comes to the fore when he takes and is also placed into a beta male role. For example, when the Beach Boys cover one of Manson's songs, he pressures Dennis Wilson (James Trevena) to get music producers to come to the ranch so he can get a record deal. Dennis convinces Terry Melcher (Bryan Adrian) to come and listen to Manson perform. It is big moment for Manson and Smith conveys his excited desperation compellingly. He struts around stating that it is his moment and piles demands on the Family. Some of the women work on making Manson a brown suede fringed leather suit, while others become his back-up singers and dancers. Over time, however, Manson's behavior becomes more frenetic and aggressive; correspondingly the women become more fearful. Manson is demanding, unreasonable, and unforgiving of any errors. His cruel and abusive demands are made most clear when the dancing and singing required by the women morph into a striptease. His control over the women and their bodies through verbal abuse and criticism is powerful, clearly unsafe to resist.

Once the record producers arrive, the formerly ferociously angry Manson greets them in a subservient manner. Indicating that he is at the ranch under sufferance Terry insists on listening to the music. In this moment Terry is the alpha male and Manson the beta. Manson, cowed and nervous, begins the performance outside with the girls on elevated land behind him, they harmonize with his singing and slowly remove their clothes until they are mostly topless. Terry cuts the song short and pulls Manson to one side thanking him but quietly refuses to sign him. Money is exchanged, "for the girls" Terry says, thanking Charlie for the striptease.

Talking with Rabold, Harron draws parallels between Smith's performance as a rampantly insecure Manson and Christian Bale's portrayal of Patrick

Figure 6.3 Charles Manson (Matt Smith) as beta male

Bateman in *American Psycho*. Harron reveals that she wanted to show in both films that dominating, violent, alpha males are really ridiculous figures, made pitiful through their insecurities.[45] Manson's insecurity is demonstrated again when a young woman Bobby Beausoleil (Cameron Gellman) comes to the ranch. Charlie is taking a bath, with Leslie by his side, evoking the earlier scene when it was Patricia presenting Leslie to Charlie for acceptability. For the first time in the film, Manson is naked and vulnerable, a state normally reserved for the women. Manson, relaxed and joking around, leaps up in the bath, giving the pretty blond newcomer full frontal exposure. She is repelled—when asked by Manson if his body offends her, she says no, stating that he is being rude. Assertive, she is the alpha in this exchange and her rejection of Charlie in this moment places him as a beta, a figure of disdain. He pushes back immediately, refusing to stay in a subservient role, turning on Bobby, he yells at her saying "she doesn't belong here." Bobby, confused, apologizes, and Leslie promptly takes her away. The young woman had a strong sense of self and saw Manson for what he was: a fool, idiot, and disrespectful to women. Unlike Leslie, this newcomer refused to take on the essentialized femininity Manson's hegemonic masculinity practices are paired with.

CONCLUSION

Harron's gendered lens gives us a much more nuanced interpretation of masculinity. It is not essentialized or deterministic, or a fixed quality of identity. The portrayals by Smith and Crawford present masculinity as a variable and at times contradictory set of practices. Harron and Turner's storytelling reinforces the conceptualization of masculinity as a dynamic construct, as presented at the start of this chapter.

In the idyllic moments of the ranch, bathed in the yellow tones of the sun and fire, the promise of social change promised to alter stable social norms, such as those associated with the breadwinner social contract. The sexual revolution offered a liberal equality, and the ranch represented freedom and love. However, Manson's embrace of hippie counter-culture that drew his followers to him meant that his status as an alpha male was impermanent. He constantly renegotiated his dominant stance through social interactions. In tangled dialogue designed to preserve the message of freedom from everything except Manson, he asserted control over the Family members, both men and women, taking their names, ego, and bodies for his own. The more tenuous his hold on his status as an alpha, the more abusive and controlling he became. The more abusive he was, the more the women shifted into the submissive stance of essentialized femininity and Tex becomes a beta male. The metamorphosis that Manson promised did happen, but rather than becoming the fairies Patricia dreamed of, Susan, Leslie, and Patricia were pushed into the domesticity associated with breadwinner gender contract that they had come to the ranch to escape.

Taking these values into the prison environment, the three women's work with Faith revealed not just their sins of needless murder but their loss: loss of life within society, loss of their potential futures, and the loss of the dreams they had weaved around Manson. Entwined within these dreams are the pre-emergent social shifts in terms of gender freedom but also the loss of the domesticity promised to them as part of the breadwinner gender contract. Patricia, Susan, and Leslie would never be mothers, never have a home to call their own. As Murray shared in an interview, we do not necessarily sympathize with or condone their horrific acts but through these gendered lenses we can understand.[46] In particular we can understand the role of masculinity and gender power relations that led to their enthrallment and imprisonment long before they were sentenced to death row.

NOTES

1. Elizabeth Yuko, "Rolling Stone: Manson Family Movies: 11 Streaming Film Go Inside Terrifying 1969 Cult," *Rolling Stone* (2019). Accessed 4 April, 2020. Available: https://www.rollingstone.com/movie-lists/manson-family-movies-streaming-864045/
2. Michael A. Messner and James W. Messerschimdt, "Hegemonic, nonhegemonic and 'new' masculinities," in *Gender Reckonings: New Social Theory and Research*, edited by James. W. Messerschmidt, Patricia Yancy Martin, Michael A. Messner, and Raewyn Connell (New York: New York University Press, 2017), 40, 35–56.
3. Rudy Dunlap and Corey W. Johnson, "Consuming contradiction: media, masculinity and (hetero) sexual identity," in *Leisure/Loisir* (Vol. 37, No. 1, 2013), 69–84, 75.
   Debbie Ging, "Alphas, Betas, and Incels: Theorizing the Masculinities of the Manosphere," in *Men and Masculinities* (Vol. 22, No. 4, 2017), 638–57, 640.

David Greven, "'I Love You, Brom Bones': Beta Male Comedies and American Culture," in *Quarterly Review of Film and Video* (Vol. 30, No. 5, 2013), 405–20, 405 Kate Maclean, "Gender, Risk and the Wall Street Alpha Male," in *Journal of Gender Studies* (Vol. 25, No. 4, 2015), 427–44, 431.
4. Steven Saito, "The Moveable Fest: Interview: Mary Harron and Guinevere Turner on Restoring the Female Voice to History in *Charlie Says*," *Moveable Fest* (2019). Accessed April 5, 2020. Available: http://moveablefest.com/mary-harron-guinevere-turner-charlie-says/
5. Raewyn Connell, *Gender and Power: Society, the Person, and Sexual Politics* (Palo Alto: Stanford University Press, 1987), 183.
6. Messner and Messerschimdt, "Gender Reckonings," 37.
7. Ibid.
8. Ibid., 38.
9. Ibid., 36.
10. Ibid., 40.
11. Colette Fagan, Jacqueline O'Reilly, and Jill Rubery, "Part time work: Challenging the 'breadwinner' gender contract," in *The Gendering of Inequalities: Women, Men and Work*, edited by Jane Jenson, Jacqueline Laufer, and Margaret Maruani (Farnham: Ashgate, 2000), 174–86, 175.
12. Sonya O Rose, "Gender at Work: Sex, Class and Industrial Capitalism," in *History Workshop Journal* 21 (1986), 113–31, 114.
13. Ibid., 124.
14. Colette Fagan, Jacqueline O'Reilly, and Jill Rubery, "Part time work: Challenging the 'breadwinner' gender contract," in *The Gendering of Inequalities: Women, Men and Work*, edited by Jane Jenson, Jacqueline Laufer, and Margaret Maruani (Farnham: Ashgate, 2000), 174–86, 175 and 184.
15. Erving Goffman, *The Presentation of the Self in Everyday Life*, (Harmondsworth: Penguin Books, 1959), cited in Gemma. L Piercy, *Baristas: The Artisan Precariat* (PhD Thesis, University of Waikato, Hamilton, New Zealand, 2018), 153–4. Accessed March 8, 2020. https://researchcommons.waikato.ac.nz/handle/10289/12038
16. Ibid.
17. John Berger, *Ways of Seeing* (New York: Penguin Books, 1972), 46.
18. Franz Fanon, *Black Skin, White Mask* (New York: Grove Press, [1952] 2008), 92, cited in Elizabeth Wissinger, "Managing the semiotics of skin tone: Race and aesthetic labor in the fashion modelling industry," in *Economic and Industrial Democracy* (Vol. 33, No. 1, 2012), 125–43, 131.
19. Ricky Camilleri, Interview with Mary Harron, Guinevere Turner, Marianne Rendón, and Hannah Murray, *Build series NYC*, YouTube, Filmed at 692 Broadway, New York, May 1, 2019. Video: 27.22, https://www.youtube.com/watch?v=NILkGykqZl8
20. For example, David Bodanis, *Passionate Minds: The Great Enlightenment Love Affair* (London: Little, Brown, 2006), xviii.
21. Abbey White, "'Charlie Says' Director Mary Harron Talks Depicting the 'Tiny Choices' of the Manson Women," *The Hollywood Reporter* (2019). Accessed April 28, 2020. Available: https://www.hollywoodreporter.com/news/charlie-says-director-mary-harron-interview-1209251
22. Nicolas Rapold, Interview with Mary Harron, *Film at Lincoln Center*, May 17, 2019. Video: 49.26. https://www.youtube.com/watch?v=IKXJV9ByyCY
23. Virginia E. Rutter and Braxton Jones, "The Sexuality of Gender," in *Handbook of the Sociology of Gender*, edited by Barbara Risman, Carissa Froyum, and William Scarborough (Cham: Springer, 2018), 285–9, 286.

24. Barbara J. Risman, "Gender as a Social Structure," in *Handbook of the Sociology of Gender*, edited by Barbara Risman, Carissa Froyum, and William Scarborough (Cham: Springer, 2018), 19–43, 28.
25. Theresa Man Ling Lee, "Feminism: Government and Politics," *Encyclopedia of Life Support Systems* (EOLSS) (2002). Accessed January 17, 2020. http://www.eolss.net. Victor J. Seidler, "Differences: Feminisms/enemies/equalities," in *Embodying Identities: Culture, Differences and Social Theory* (Bristol: The Policy Press, 2010), 53–69, 53.
26. Lee. "Feminism", 6.
27. Rapold. Interview with Mary Harron.
28. Raymond Williams, *Marxism and Literature* (Oxford: Oxford University Press, 1977), 123.
29. Ibid., 120.
30. Ibid., 124.
31. J. Hoberman, "The Other Charles Manson Movie Has a Lot to Say," *The New York Times* (2019). Accessed April 28, 2020. https://www.nytimes.com/2019/11/19/movies/charlie-says-mary-harron.html
32. Mark Kurlansky, *1968: The Year the Rocked the World* (London: Vintage Random House Publishing, 2005), 180.
33. Lee, "Feminism", 7.
34. Kurlansky. *1968: The Year the Rocked the World*, 184.
35. Ibid., 189.
36. Maclean. "Gender, Risk and the Wall Street Alpha Male," 436.
37. Ibid., 431.
38. Greven, "'I love you Brom Bones'," 405.
39. Dunlap and Johnson, "Consuming contradictions," 75.
40. Ging. "Alpha, betas and incels," 640.
41. Dunlap and Johnson. "Consuming contradictions," 75.
42. Camilleri, Interview with Harron et al.
43. Ibid.
44. Rapold, Interview with Mary Harron.
45. Ibid.
46. Camilleri, Interview with Harron et al.

PART III

Television and Short Film Production

CHAPTER 7

Death to Disposal: Echoes of *American Psycho* in "The Rainbow of Her Reasons" (*Six Feet Under*)

Gareth Schott

INTRODUCTION

This chapter draws attention to the thematic association between Mary Harron's second feature film *American Psycho*, and "The Rainbow of Her Reasons" (2005), the sixth episode of the fifth and final season of HBO television series *Six Feet Under*, which she guest directed. Harron's interpretive art as a director is more typically examined in relation to her feature film work. Her adaptation of Bret Easton Ellis' controversial and negatively received novel *American Psycho* (1991) has gathered significant attention for the manner in which she successfully emphasized the satirical nature of the source material that had previously been defined by its graphic physical and sexual violence. By contrast, the extent to which Harron was able to exert her influence in the industrialized process of an established television series with a highly coded aesthetic is much more difficult to discern. As a result, her directorial contribution to *Six Feet Under* has received little scholarly attention to date. Indeed, reflecting on her role as director for *Six Feet Under*, Harron commented: "You don't set the tone. The really important people in TV are not the directors; they're the writers." Further clarifying that for the final season of *Six Feet Under*, "you're obviously not going to shape the style at that point."[1] Nevertheless, her contribution to *Six Feet Under* is worthy of consideration for the manner in which it clearly echoes and amplifies key themes accentuated by Harron and her co-writer Guinevere Turner, known for her acting role in Rose Troche's *Go Fish*, in their cinematic interpretation of one of the great sociopathic misogynists of contemporary fiction—Patrick Bateman.

Both *American Psycho* and *Six Feet Under* share a curiosity with characters grappling with their sense of purpose, whilst experiencing feelings of emptiness and disconnection. Harron's Patrick Bateman (Christian Bale) is portrayed as stifled and constantly outwitted by the shifting burdens and pressures of a materialist, status-driven corporate climate. A culture that possesses an ever-evolving set of refined codes for projecting status and success that has to be bettered in a game of one-upmanship (e.g. material and design of business cards, capacity to make table reservations in exclusive restaurants, apartment living, personal grooming and appearance etc). The epicurean routines attached to Bateman's corporate existence and excessive yuppie lifestyle, are offset by his "apparent" loss of control and expulsive acts of viciousness. The unconscionable acts "performed" by Bateman equipoise his otherwise lack of distinctiveness within a system that exhibits a different kind of pathology—corporate abuse and financial manipulation.[2] The television series *Six Feet Under* also offsets its psychodrama against a socially constructed expectation of a veneer of control associated with the social role of a funeral director. It achieves this by highlighting the personal vulnerabilities and fragility of the family members behind Fisher Family & Sons funeral services. When assessed as part of Harron's body of work, her association with the television series, created and written by Alan Ball, who penned the screenplay for the award-winning *American Beauty*, exposes common themes between her work and *Six Feet Under* that may otherwise go unnoticed. Additionally, it also serves to further reinforce the social satirical intent of Harron's adaptation of *American Psycho*.

FIONA LENORE KLEINSCHMIDT, 1948–2005

Following the convention established from the first season of *Six Feet Under* onwards, its final season continued the practice of opening each episode with a prelude that depicts the death of the person that Fisher Family & Sons are subsequently entrusted to prepare for viewing and burial. While the series chronicles the changing relationships and family ties that connect individuals to Fisher Family & Sons, each episode tells its own story—the story of the deceased. In this way, the episode directed by Harron is the story of Fiona Lenore Kleinschmidt (Lee Garlington). Unlike the majority of cases handled professionally by the Fisher sons, in this episode the deceased is known to the family as the friend of Aunt Sarah (Patricia Clarkson), sister of Ruth (Frances Conroy), mother of Nate (Peter Krause), David (Michael C. Hall), and Claire Fisher (Lauren Ambrose). The episode also reveals Fiona to be the woman to whom the eldest Fisher son, Nate (Nathaniel), lost his virginity when he was only fifteen years of age.

This chapter aims to illustrate the degree of equivalence between the way *American Psycho* emphasizes how Bateman's emptiness is compensated by his "excessive and erotic [narcissistic] interest in his own body," which serves to critically emphasize how he inhabits a culture that values appearance above all else, and its relationship with the role of appearance in our engagement with the dead.[3] Furthermore, "The Rainbow of Her Reasons" also serves to connect the culture of work with modern consumer culture, and the emergence of a new conception of the self, "namely, the self as performer—which places great emphasis upon appearance, display, and the management of impressions."[4] The episode of *Six Feet Under* directed by Harron serves as a provocation, chiefly prompting questions concerning the nature and role of appearance for the dead within mourning and burial rites. By virtue of its setting the drama normalises preparatory death rites. Indeed, it often presents casual everyday exchanges between established characters as they go about the routine of embalming or performing cosmetic restorative practices on the unknown dead. The routine nature of this process is, however, confronted and unsettled in "The Rainbow of Her Reasons" by the personal connection that exists between key characters and the deceased. The veneer of objectivity associated with performing the professional identity of a funeral director is ruptured by Nate's prior subjective experience of the body he is being asked to treat dispassionately. Taken together, both of Harron's projects bestride the boundaries of life/death, subjectivity/objectivity, and reality/pretence.

CADAVER COSMETICS

The responsibility associated with the extraordinary position that funeral directors assume in dealing with the body of the deceased should be read as a counterpoint to the disrespect with which Patrick Bateman desires the mutilation and destruction of the bodies of others. However, there is a level of equivalence suggested by the deference with which Bateman objectively treats his own body and the clinical practices performed on the dead by funeral directors, as represented and portrayed in *Six Feet Under*. A connection is established that initiates a closer inspection and evaluation of the practices performed on individuals as part of death rites. At the beginning of *American Psycho* film audiences are introduced to Bateman via his complicated daily cleansing routines. His voice-over account of his daily routine runs through the various products he applies:

> I use a deep pore-cleanser lotion. In the shower, I use a water-activated gel cleanser, then a honey-almond body scrub, and on the face an exfoliating gel scrub. Then I apply an herb mint facial masque which I leave on for ten minutes while I prepare the rest of my routine. I always use an after-shave lotion with little or no alcohol because alcohol dries your face out and makes you look older. Then moisturizer, then an anti-aging eye balm, followed by a final moisturizing "protective" lotion.[5]

Bateman's applications of anti-aging and beauty enhancing products constitute an excessive projection of pathological narcissism that masks his nihilism. Through his routine Bateman desperately tries to communicate and associate substance with appearance. Yet, like a human cadaver, Bateman reveals he is lifeless within, a cypher rather than a character.[6] He reveals:

> There is an idea of a Patrick Bateman, some kind of abstraction, but there is no real me, only an entity, something illusory, and though I can hide my cold gaze and you can shake my hand and feel flesh gripping you and maybe you can even sense our lifestyles are probably comparable: I simply am not there.[7]

Echoing Bateman's confession, Harron's adaptation of the source material constitutes a graveyard for ephemera from the 1980s.[8] Viewed upon its release in 2000, the *American Psycho* morning routine scene cites products that had lost their exclusive status (e.g. Vidal Sassoon), dropped out of fashion or simply no longer existed (e.g. Gruene natural revitalizing shampoo; Baume des Yeux). Bateman's insatiable emptiness leads him to subscribe to the notion that particular expensive in vogue idealised beauty products constitute pure representation of social power firmly linking organizational identity to culture and image.[9]

Like the superfluous products consumed by Bateman, the treatment of a cadaver, when applied by funeral directors, shares a similar level of redundancy and convention. In many Western cultures, embalming (the injection of chemical solutions into the arterial network of the body in order to "disinfect" and "slow" the decomposition process) is presented as a normal and necessary procedure. However, in countries like the US, where embalming is an expected

Figure 7.1 Patrick Bateman's morning routine

part of most funeral arrangements, it is not actually a requirement of law nor, as some argue, is there much legitimate need for it.[10] The highly toxic chemicals used in the physically invasive process of embalming pose a real health risk to those who perform the procedure. The premise that embalming sanitizes the body, which has become a source of contagion, to make it "safe" for viewing is inaccurate. The procedure is primarily used to temporarily slow decomposition in order to preserve a more "life-like" appearance. Embalming has been so convincingly marketed to the funeral-buying public that it became routine and ordinary within American society.[11] To this effect, embalming constitutes part of a broader range of temporary cosmetic restorative processes that seek to reduce the appearance of death (hypostasis) in order to preserve the last elements of an individual's social identity.[12]

In Mark Harris' *Grave Matters* (2007) he provides a case study of the method for escalating funeral costs. In his account of the experiences of the Johnson family, responding to the loss of their only child, eighteen-year-old Jenny, Harris chronicles how a basic funeral package ranging between $3,295–$3,595 increased to a total of $12,376.[13] Returning to the gratuitous daily cleansing routine performed by Patrick Bateman, as articulated as an itemized list of products, the funeral director is revealed as leading the Johnson family through an itemized set of costs that are added gradually, using one decision to require further consequential obligatory purchases. As Harris highlights, because the initial funeral package offered to the family included a viewing, they then also had to agree to embalming at an extra cost of $825, which in turn adds hair-styling services (a beautician at a cost of $90) and dressing and "casketing" of the remains ($50) to the consideration. Harris is able to financially trace and chronicle the way dignity and presentational concerns permit funeral directors to be able to upsell supplementary services, such as "professional funeral wear," where garments have the back cut out for minimum disruption of the body and easy dressing ($135). What is an emotional process for the family is used to drive a financial process for the funeral director.

Accounts provided by individuals of first encounters with a dead body, in otherwise death-denying cultures of the West,[14] describe how separate and disconnected the dead appear to the living, often causing individuals to respond by being with the body.[15] Pre-funerary rituals violate that vulnerability in order to prepare the deceased for one last mode of social connectivity. For the grieving it is a final opportunity to be with the person that will be physically gone forever. It will also constitute a notable last memory of the deceased. The funeral directors charge is therefore to avoid having mourners recoil at the grotesqueness of the natural order of events connected with the decomposition of the body, for autolysis (or self-digestion) begins immediately after death as the body has no way of getting oxygen or removing waste. Muscle stiffness (or rigor mortis) also gives the body sheen, due to ruptured blisters, causing the skin's top layer to begin to loosen. In the last moments with the deceased artificiality prevails as a means of disguise and diversion. Much like Bateman, "where nothing is internalized" because he is defined by his body, the practices portrayed in *Six Feet Under* represent the wider practices of an industry that reinforces Bateman's visual orientation as a predominant communicational device.[16]

DEATH EVERY DAY

Six Feet Under captures how death, when it occurs, is perceived as a "matter out of place," a phenomenon that is separate from the composition of everyday life thus leading to the surrender of control to others deemed more equipped and professional.[17] Protocols, conduct and convention provide substance and guide the grieving through an aberrant experience, filling the void at a time when individual worlds have been emptied and drained. A key area where mourner conformity is expected and reinforced is in the area of restoration services, which has sparked its own industry in specialized cosmetic products. For example, a cadaver requires non-thermogenic make-up as conventional make-up for the living is designed to be absorbed by the skin and applies more uniformly—on the flesh of the dead conventional make-up simply blotches. The artificiality of the surface veneer pervades most post-death rituals. An aptly named Australian florist company, "Absolutely Unreal," recommends to its prospective customers that they "may wish to consider hiring artificial floral tributes" for funeral and service flowers. It appears that nothing should trigger thoughts of decay. Conventions surrounding how the dead are laid out are "deeply ingrained in the specific death culture in which the corpse and its mourners are situated."[18] In modern Western societies laying out the dead often presents the corpse legs extended, arms folded with hands placed on top of the chest—a demeanor that suggests the dead are resting. Yet, there are examples of grieving families opting to preserve the memory of the deceased in "living" postures, in denial of decay and departure. In New Orleans, USA, Charbonnet-Labat Funeral Home has gained distinction for the manner in which it stages bodies in an "out of the box" fashion in what might be described as death dioramas. The body of fifty-three-year-old Miriam Burbank was posed sat at a table, cigarette in hand, surrounded by her preferred alcoholic beverages, as if sitting in the corner of a party. While in San Juan (Puerto Rico) Christopher Rivera, a boxer who was shot to death, was propped up standing in a fake boxing ring for his wake.

CLINICAL PRACTICE(S)

In *American Psycho* Harron deploys Gideon Ponte's set design to great effect, using Bateman's apartment to reflect his inhuman perfectionist ideals. It screams superficiality and materialism and refuses any suggestion of homely warmth or comfort. Bateman's kitchen resembles a sterile environment rather than a slaughterhouse, while his all-white bedroom shines like a surgical space. His tendency to itemize products, possessions and bodies, in lieu of profundity, further adds to the dehumanization of his victims.

By comparing *American Psycho* and *Six Feet Under* there are clear parallels in terms of Bateman's lifestyle and the funeral industry. The "hard sell" and "add-on" tactics employed by the funeral industry, as exposed by Jessica Mitford in her landmark work of investigative journalism, *The American Way of Death* (1963), reveal a comparable element between the Fishers' business and Bateman's investment banking.[19] Furthermore, Bateman is driven by an intent that equals the funeral industry's aim to achieve the same, as Harris describes, "pleasant demeanor" for their cadavers. During "The Rainbow of Her Reasons," Nate consults with Aunt Sarah over the arrangements for Fiona's funeral. While the series avoids repeating discussions of the cost attached to Fisher Family & Sons services to its audience, Sarah does make a request of Nate to "make her [Fiona] beautiful."

Harron's work on *Six Feet Under* shares a similar treatment of violent events employed with *American Psycho*, in that "she finds the aftermath of violence more interesting than the actual act."[20] In the case of "The Rainbow of Her Reasons" she lingers on bodily trauma. Nate re-encounters Fiona in the most unusual of circumstances. Having had his first sexual encounter with Fiona at the age of fifteen years, Nate beholds her naked, older, and inert body—this time not by mutual consent but by circumstance. As Nate enters the mortuary, his ordinary everyday place of work, he reacts with "whoa" to which his brother David acknowledges: "Yep, first person you ever slept with." This statement takes restorative artist Federico (Freddy Rodriguez), who is working on the body, by surprise ("Really?"). Looking down at the body, subjectively discerning the naked person before him, Nate states: "For real." David then vocalizes what Nate might be thinking when he asks: "I bet you'd never thought you'd see her naked again?" Federico then pushes the thought too far by asking, "Hey, how'd she hold up? What's the difference on her twenty years later?" To which Nate responds: "In case you haven't noticed she's all bruised and busted up you fucking idiot" before covering the body with a sheet in a gesture of protection.

Harris' account of embalming eighteen-year-old Jenny Johnson's dead body describes a set of highly intrusive and aggressive practices, which seem to incriminate practitioners in the desecration of the dead in the name of conjuring a likeness to the physical exterior of the living. Harris' description reads like a passage from Ellis' *American Psycho* as he describes the process, instrumentation, and techniques used on the body. For example, we are introduced to the sharp two-foot-long "trocar" used to pierce the abdominal wall in order to siphon out its contaminants. This instrument is required to be firmly driven into the body (termed "belly punching"). Learning about some of the measures performed on the body provokes a response of physical empathy for what such actions would mean for a living, feeling, and pain-sensing individual. For instance, the use of packing forceps to push "wads of cotton soaked in phenol into Jenny's anus and vagina,"[21] gluing eyelids to an "eyecap" placed on the eyeball, shooting barb-tipped wire into the mouth filled with "mortuary putty" in order to draw it and keep it shut, "running a half-curved needle threaded with suture into each breast at a point just off the nipples and pulling the suture taut," all evoke a sense of horror and body trauma.[22] At the very least it requires the body to suffer indignity in order to achieve a "peaceful" appearance to console the living. Appearance is everything, in accordance with Bateman's rationale: "All it comes down to is: I feel like shit but look great." To this effect, Nate's aggressive retort can also be read as acknowledgment of the funeral director's culpability in the state of Fiona's appearance.

Further liability for Fiona's current state also extends to Sarah (the aunt), as she was the individual responsible for dragging Fiona out on the early morning hike, during which she slipped and fell to her death down a ravine. In the episode's self-contained impact of Fiona's death, a drunk and grieving Sarah wallows in her complicity. Having initially explained away Fiona's death as being her "time" during her consultation with Nate and Federico at the funeral parlour, she later repeals this initial platitude. In her subsequent drunken outburst, later on in the episode, she declares: "Shit just goes wrong, because there is evil in the world, like me. I'm evil," then asking: "Am I the anti-Christ?" Her outburst clearly mirrors Bateman's proclamation that: "Reflection is useless, the world is senseless. Evil is its only permanence." Next morning, a hungover Sarah mocks herself, labels herself a narcissist and an "asshole at the center of the universe."

TORTURE AND SOCIAL DEATH

Parallel to Fiona's storyline, "The Rainbow of Her Reasons" constitutes a significant change in the nature of Ruth's marriage to George. Unable to cope with his psychotic depression any longer, unbeknown to George, Ruth is moving him out. Prior to learning about Fiona's death, which provides Ruth with an excuse to extract herself from George in order to be with her sister Sarah, the married couple are shown settling into a new apartment. George is blissfully unaware that his and Ruth's new start in a new apartment that also includes new furniture, appliances, cutlery, and linen is in fact just his new start. In this scene, the windows of the apartment fail to reveal an exterior or a vista, but instead form panels of bright light that flood the living space illuminating the space. A heavenly kind of atmosphere thus pervades the space, mirroring the fade to white after Fiona's death, suggestive of George's "social death."[23]

Much like Patrick Bateman's inability to contain his "disordered self," the dismemberment and scattering of his persona throughout *Six Feet Under* is again revealed. Here George's unnoticed and disregarded plight (save by his daughter Maggie) is symptomatic of how Bateman too is indistinguishable—he frequently goes unnoticed and is often confused as someone else. Despite being driven by "radical individualism" Bateman is urged by a compulsive need to fit in, in order to be able to compete.[24] Yet, his efforts are rarely recognized or attributed to his name. At the conclusion of *American Psycho* a sweat drenched Bateman agitatedly approaches his lawyer, having left a phone message for him in which he confessed to killing Paul Allen. Yet, in this encounter his lawyer understands him to be, and refers to him as Davis, informing him that the prank message "was amusing, but c'mon man, it had one fatal flaw. Bateman is such a dork, such a boring spineless lightweight. Now if you said Bryce, or McDermot."

The concept of social death has been used to understand a number of different social contexts, for example slavery.[25] However, in death studies it has served to distinguish a loss of identity, role, social activity or connectivity in advance of physical or clinical death. In George's case social death describes his banishment, removal and isolation from the Fisher family—an action that receives little interrogation or opposition from the Fisher children David, Claire or Nate when they learn of Ruth's plan. While, for Bateman, who is subject to the "illusion of difference," his failure to recognize his lack of distinction and the homogeneity of his slavish acts of conformity to corporate culture ultimately fulfils his self-erasure.[26] To reiterate Bateman's final deliberations in the book's conclusion, Harron divides them in two, opting to use the first half to introduce Bateman at the beginning of the film, in which he firstly states "you can shake my hand and feel flesh gripping yours and maybe you can even sense our lifestyles are probably comparable: I simply am not there." Here Bateman is akin to the impermanent existence of a corpse. He is someone or something that has no feelings under the flesh. Then, in bringing the film to its end, Bateman declares: "There are no more barriers to cross." He is not expiring physically and no one cares for his confessions, but he has reached the end of his degradation, resulting in cessation of his ability to function as a social being: he is speaking of his social death.[27]

Connected to Bateman's fate, Harron's "The Rainbow of Her Reasons" also revisits the eradication of self that comes with adopting corporate codes of behavior. During the episode youngest sibling Claire signs up with an office temp agency while she awaits the results on her application for an art grant. On her very first job assignment, she quickly discovers the sterile nature of the white-collar corporate environment with its "fluorescent lighting, nondescript cubicles, and buzzing fax machines."[28] Although used as an establishing shot for Claire's workplace scenes, the exterior shot of two indistinct corporate buildings possesses no depth of field. The buildings are so tightly framed in a medium shot that it creates the impression of a single flat surface. Unlike *American Psycho*'s use of the expressive power of lower Manhattan's architecture to convey corporate philosophy, "The Rainbow of Her Reasons" holds more in common with the Slough-based paper merchants featured in the UK satire and mock-documentary television sit-com *The Office* (BBC, 2001–2003) that anatomises white-collar woes. Harron avoids applying architecture as a "mode of domination," as a space that celebrates the performance of the corporate identity, preferring instead to suggest how the workplace inhibits individual desires of the white-collar worker.[29]

In Richard Donkin's *The History of Work* (2010), he states that the meaningless nature of white-collar work has created a new leisure ethic focused on the weekend.[30] He cites C. Wright Mills' (1956) assertion that work has been "split from the rest of life, so the idols of work have been replaced by the idols of leisure."[31] Yet, upon first arriving to her workstation, Claire discovers her most immediate colleagues to be unnervingly positive about the company and prevail strongly upon her how fortunate she would be if she could attain the position on a permanent basis (much to Claire's horror). The first question from Claire's most direct booth mate, is: "Are you having fun yet?" The overselling of the otherwise monotony of their desk-bound existence troubles the otherwise cynical and superior Claire, who has little intention of extending her association with the firm beyond the current "temp" nature of the role. In this episode Claire assumes a similar role to *The Office*'s Tim Canterbury (Martin Freeman)—a university dropout and reluctant Wernham Hogg employee who torments his bumptious desk-mate Gareth Keenan (Mackenzie Crook) for his career aspirations with the company. Above all else, Harron has described Patrick Bateman in *American Psycho* as a pathetic character: "Trying to be cool and failing so badly."[32] There appears to be one in every workplace. *The Office* has David Brent (Ricky Gervais) and for Claire it is the male worker across the way that communicates primarily through popular culture aphorisms—"Wassup!" from the 2001 award-winning Budweiser campaign and Mike Myers' Austin Powers catchphrase "yeah baby!" In the case of "Wassup," campaign creative director Vinny Warren attributes the success of their appropriation of Charles Stone III's (1999) short film *True*, to the way "it was physically cathartic to say the phrase . . . It was just magically irresistible on some level. And 'wassup' is American for 'hello,' so everyone had lots of excuses to say it in a day" (AdAge, 2000). Fine and de Saucey (2005) support this account when they state that every "interacting social group develops, over time, a joking culture: a set of humorous references that are known to members of the group to which members can refer."[33] They argue that the social function of such a "joking culture" is to "*smooth*" group interaction, "*share*" affiliation, and "*separate*" the group from outsiders.

DEDICATING YOUR LIFE TO THE COMPANY

The eagerness with which Claire's workmates instantaneously seek to draw her into the culture of their workplace (and persuade both her and themselves how satisfying their worklife is) is evident when she is asked to sign a birthday card for Beverly within moments of arriving at her workstation. Upon retorting with the obvious observation that she has yet to meet Beverly, a colleague from across the way interjects with: "She won't even read it. Last time I signed it Hitler and she never said a word." Bateman's imperceptibility is again evoked, cuing the nightclub scene where, during casual conversation, he utters that he is into "murders and executions." The disinterested recipient of the comment mishears this as "mergers and acquisitions." Similarly, Bateman's confession to a bartender: "I like to dissect girls. Did you know I'm utterly insane?" goes undetected. As Bateman breaks up with his fiancé Evelyn over dinner, Bateman states: "My need to engage in homicidal behavior on a massive scale cannot be corrected." As he utters these words, Evelyn is ignoring every word, instead looking across the restaurant and acknowledging the entrance of a friend or acquaintance and silently mouthing her appreciation ("It's lovely") for some sort of adornment on her arm. Few take notice of Bateman's declarations or his confessions, reinforcing the empty and worthless nature of his existence. While Bateman's behaviors have been frequently interpreted as exhibiting narcissistic traits of grandiosity, lacking in empathy for others, and preoccupation with fantasies of success, power, and beauty he does not necessarily demonstrate the same need for admiration, kindness or devotion. While Claire tolerates a workplace acquaintance giving her an unwanted embrace with a perceptible level of unease, Bateman instead snaps cruelly at Louis when he merely touches his suit in admiration, stating that: "The compliment was sufficient Louis." Bateman does not tolerate Evelyn touching his neck in the restaurant and reprimands a prostitute ("Don't touch the watch") when her arm accidently touches his Rolex Datejust 16013 whilst lying next to him in bed.

When Claire was assigned to her first temp assignment, the agency warned her that she was going into a very conservative company, and asks: "you have corporate attire right?" Unlike the expensive comfort of Bateman's Valentino couture suits, Claire suffers in her (unnatural) work attire, complaining:

> It is these pantyhose. I just feel like I can't breathe, none of this work would seem that hard if I didn't have to sit in some kind of torture chamber all day. I don't understand how having your legs sheathed in this, like, smooth plastic Barbie leg, like being encased in this sausage casing, will help you do your job better.

Harron, in an interview with *The Guardian*, reflected on how her film career was sparked by the chance discovery of Valerie Solanas' *SCUM Manifesto*

Figure 7.2 Claire Fisher (Lauren Ambrose) describes the confinement of pantyhose through a musical number

(1967), written by the radical feminist who attacked Andy Warhol and the subject of Harron's debut feature film *I Shot Andy Warhol*. With the acronym referring to the Society for Cutting Up Men, the work is widely regarded as satirical in its critique of patriarchy. Harron identified the dark humor in Solanas' work but also discovered a different way to examine the world. As she states: "take the world of Warhol, tell it through the least important person... it really opened up the world." Furthermore, she describes Solanas' text as highlighting "how women were propping up the male ego, colluding in their own oppression."[34] Claire's endurance finds defiance in a reverie performance of the song "You Light Up My Life," with lyrics amended so that she sings: "I've never been this fucking uncomfortable, never again to wear pantyhose, You ride up my crotch, you ride up my thighs, you're tight on my ass, you climb up my crotch, you ruin my day." Claire's loss of identity and transformation however is complete when Aunt Sarah comments: "You look nice, like a business lady," followed by "Maybe you're not an artist? Did I hurt your feelings when I said that?" Claire: "Yeah." Sarah: "Maybe I'm right, if you were an artist you would have laughed."

CONCLUSION

For Leiss et al, both "lifestyle groups" featured in *American Psycho* and the episode of *Six Feet Under* directed by Mary Harron are structured by "self-administered codes of authority for dress, appearance... customary places of assembly, and behavior rituals" that interpellate and take possession of individual identity from the office worker, the funeral director, to the investment banker.[35] Each of these groups develop surface traits that make them indistinguishable from others within the same professional group. Both Harron-directed texts are therefore dark and pessimistic accounts of the angst and fears attached to these realities on those who are not resigned, or feel ensnared by their lifestyles. These lives are however ruptured by dreams, fantasies and visions that contest corporeality. Harron's adaptation of *American Psycho* leans audience interpretation heavily toward the explanation that the homicidal machinations and actions of Patrick Bateman are ultimately figments of his imagination. Whereas *Six Feet Under* points to clandestine realities that are performed to perpetuate pretence and deception to create a surface that quells the fear of bodily death amongst the living. As American economist Akerlof (1983) argued: "There is a return to appearing honest, but not to being honest."[36] Both Harron's works visually present the psychodrama of "fluid compensation," psychological phrasing that conveys how challenges to meaning in one aspect of life can be compensated in another.[37] Bateman's nihilism for his superficial existence is maintained by finding meaning in cruel, vicious slaughter. Bateman uses murder to live an alternative life that is a finite commodity. Indeed, a similar veneer of professionalism has now come to represent death and death rites. Bodies of loved ones are avoided and outsourced to a profession that attempts to soften unwelcome truths. The ultimate blow to the "American way of death" is delivered toward the end of the final season of *Six Feet Under* when Nate passes away. This enabled the series to bring green burial to mainstream television audiences for the first time, as Nate finally rejects the professional practices that represented him in life.

NOTES

1. Anisse Gross, "Mary Harron: 'Mostly I'm just not American'," *Believer* (2014), accessed March 30, 2018. Available from: https://www.believermag.com/issues/201403/?read=interview_harron
2. William K. Tabb, "The Criminality of Wall Street", *Monthly Review* (Vol. 66, No. 4, 2014), accessed March 1, 2018. Available from: https://monthlyreview.org/2014/09/01/the-criminality-of-wall-street/
3. Sorin Floti, "Narcissism and Criminality on Wall Street: the Sociology of *American Psycho*", *Culturised* (2017), accessed March 1, 2018. Available from: https://culturised.co.uk/2017/09/narcissism-and-criminality-on-wall-street-the-sociology-of-american-psycho/
4. Llewellyn Negrin, *Appearance and Identity: Fashioning the Body in Postmodernity* (New York: Palgrave Macmillan, 2008), 9.
5. Mary Harron and Guinevere Turner, *American Psycho Screenplay* (1998). Available from: https://www.dailyscript.com/scripts/American_Psycho_Harron_Turner.html

6. Elizabeth Young, *Shopping in Space: Essays on America's Blank Generation Fiction*, edited by Elizabeth Young and Graham Caveney (New York: Atlantic Monthly Press/Serpent's Tail, 1993).
7. Harron and Turner, *American Psycho Screenplay*.
8. Dave Schilling, "*American Psycho*'s Morning Ritual: Would Patrick Bateman's routine work today?", *The Guardian* (2016), accessed March 14, 2018. Available from: https://www.theguardian.com/stage/2016/apr/22/american-psycho-musical-film-morning-routine-patrick-bateman
9. Theodor Adorno and Max Horkheimer, *The Culture Industry: Enlightenment as Mass Deception, Dialectic of Enlightenment* (New York: Seabury Press, 1972).
10. Suzanne Kelley, *Greening Death* (Lanham, MD: Rowman & Littlefield Publishers, 2017).
11. Joshua Slocum and Lisa Carlson, *Final Rights: Reclaiming the American Way of Death* (Hinesburg, VT: Upper Access Books, 2011).
12. Alison Chapple and Sue Ziebland, "Viewing the Body After Bereavement Due to a Traumatic Death: Qualitative study in the UK", *BMJ* (340, 2010).
13. Mark Harris, *Grave Matters: A journey through the modern funeral industry to a natural way of burial* (New York: Scribner, 2007).
14. Ruth McManus, *Death in a Global Age* (Basingstoke, Palgrave Macmillan, 2013).
15. In "The Rainbow of Her Reasons" Ruth breaks the rules and leads Fiona's friends down to the Fisher Family and Sons mortuary to be with the body.
16. Anne-Marie Bowery, "The Practical Self: A test case for Foucault," in *Analectra Husserliana: The yearbook of phenomenological research (Vol LIV)*, edited by A-T. Tymieniecka (New York: Springer Science & Business, 1995).
17. Mary Douglas, *Purity and Danger: An analysis of concepts of pollution and taboo* (London: Routledge 2003).
18. Sian Mui, "Dead Body Language: Positioning, posture, and representation of the corpse," Theoretical Archaeology Group Conference, Southampton, 19–21 December, 2016. Accessed 24 March 24, 2018. Available from: https://www.southampton.ac.uk/tag2016/sessionsabstracts/session3.page
19. Jessica Mitford, *The American Way of Death* (New York: Simon & Schuster, 1963).
20. Angelica Jade Bastién, "The Female Gaze of 'American Psycho': How Mary Harron Made Fantasy Into Timeless Satire," *Village Voice* (2016). Accessed March 14, 2018. Available from: https://www.villagevoice.com/2016/06/07/the-female-gaze-of-american-psycho-how-mary-harron-made-fantasy-into-timeless-satire/
21. Harris, *Grave Matters*, 17.
22. Ibid., 19.
23. Jana Králová, "What is Social Death?" *Contemporary Social Science* (Vol. 10, No. 3, 2015), 235–48.
24. Robert N. Bellah, Richard Madsen, William M. Sullivan, Anne Swidler, and Steven M. Tipton, *Habits of the Heart: Individualism and Commitment in American Life* (Berkeley: University of California Press, 2007).
25. Orlando Patterson, *Slavery and Social Death: A comparative study* (Cambridge, MA: Harvard University Press, 1985).
26. Jonah Berger, *Invisible Influence: The hidden forces that shape behaviour* (New York: Simon & Schuster, 2016).
27. Jana Králová, "Why We Need to Find a Cure for 'Social Death'," *The Conversation* (2016). Accessed March 28, 2018. Available from: https://theconversation.com/why-we-need-to-find-a-cure-for-social-death-59997
28. Jessica Birthisel and Jason A. Martin, "'That's What She Said': Gender, satire, and the American workplace on the sitcom *The Office*," *Journal of Communication Inquiry* (Vol. 37, No. 1, 2013), 64–80.

29. Pierre Bourdieu, "*Les modes de domination, actes de la recherché*," *Sciences Sociales* (Vol. 2, No. 2–3, 1976), 122–32.
30. Richard Donkin, *The History of Work* (Berlin: Springer, 2010).
31. Charles Wright Mills, *White Collar: The American Middle Class* (New York: Oxford University Press, 1956), 236.
32. Gross, "Mary Harron: 'Mostly I'm just not American'".
33. Gary Alan Fine and Michaela de Soucey, "Joking Cultures: Humor themes as social regulation in group life," *Humor: International Journal of Humor Research* (Vol. 18, No.1, 2005), 1–22, 1.
34. Kate Bussman, "Interview: Cutting edge," *The Guardian* (2009). Accessed March 30, 2018. Available from: https://www.theguardian.com/lifeandstyle/2009/mar/06/mary-harron-film
35. William Leiss, Stephen Kline and Sut Jhally, *Social Communication in Advertising: Persons, products and images of well-being* (New York: Routledge, 1997), 344.
36. George A. Akerlof, "Loyalty Filters", *American Economic Review* (Vol. 73, No. 1, 1983), 54–63, 57.
37. Steven J. Heine, Travis Proulx and Kathleen D. Vohs, "The Meaning Maintenance Model: On the Coherence of Social Motivations," *Personality and Social Psychology Review* (Vol. 10, No. 2, 2006), 88–110.

CHAPTER 8

Sartorial Interventions: When Fashion and Film Collide

Elena Caoduro

INTRODUCTION

Clothes are never simple embellishments of the body: garments might be basic facts of social life, worn to protect from weather or for modesty, but they also reveal and reflect the ways in which individuals inhabit their bodies and negotiate group relationships and cultural conventions. As Roland Barthes suggested, clothing carries out a signifying function, they were invented to be noticed: "Clothing concerns all of the human person, all of the body, all of the relationship of Man to body as well as the relationships of the body to society."[1] According to Joanne Entwistle the role of fashion in human culture seems also to indicate that clothing is "one of the means by which bodies are made social and given meaning and identity. The individual and very personal act of getting dressed is an act of preparing the body for the social world."[2] This signifying activity is even clearer in cinema, where costumes, along with make-up and hair styling and performance, play a crucial role in building a character's story in terms of class, gender, and status. In *Undressing Cinema* Stella Bruzzi re-evaluates film costumes from mere accessories to pivotal elements in the creation of cinematic identities, arguing that clothes serve as mediators to narrative and character, or as an independent art spectacle.[3] In particular, couturier designs and garments lent or specifically created by fashion designers function within films as "spectacular interventions that interfere with the scenes in which they appear and impose themselves onto the character they adorn," and work as independent authorial statement suspending or disrupting the film narrative.[4]

Beside a character's exterior presentation, costumes provide insight about the emotional status, implying that the outward appearance often reveals aspects of the inner self. This is particularly evident in the works of Mary Harron, where costumes act not as mere anchor to a specific historical time (the mid-nineteenth century for *Alias Grace*, the 1950s in *The Notorious Bettie Page*, the 1960s in *I Shot Andy Warhol*) but their aim is ultimately to mediate between the actor's body, the character's identity, and narrative, thus establishing and facilitating the development of the story. This chapter reconsiders Mary Harron's works in light of the ways in which fashion items and period costumes operate. After a brief consideration of the role of costumes in *Alias Grace* and a film such as *American Psycho*, where couture designs and made-for-the-screen clothing strike a fine balance between issues of verisimilitude and spectacle, a separate set of questions are raised with regards to Harron's collaboration with the fashion house Giorgio Armani S.p.A. in their fashion film *Armani*.[5] Differently from film and TV drama, where costume designers create garments around pre-existing characters or gather fashion items to accommodate a director's or producer's requests and adapt them to the actor's body, in fashion films pieces of clothing pre-exist the story, and cinematic narratives are created around them, or better, inspired by them. This chapter seeks to ultimately problematize the notion of an "authored fashion film," exploring the symbiotic relationship between filmmaker and fashion designer in order to reach a more organic understanding of collaborative authorship.[6]

THE TENSION BETWEEN FASHION AND COSTUME

To begin with, it is important to note the existing body of work on fashion and costume in film. Traditionally studies on fashion theory mark a clear distinction between these two terms: fashion and costume. This is epitomized by the explanation of Deborah Nadoolman Landis, the head of the American Costume Designers' Guild, who emphatically argued that "fashion and costumes are not synonymous; they are antithetical."[7] On the surface the tension might be real; fashion and costume design are perceived as two distinct disciplines: with fashion more as a creative industry, and costume design, instead, as a creative art. Yet, they frequently intersect. Booth Moore mends the divide underling the different agencies behind their works, but also their crossovers: "Fashion designers are beholden to sales, and costume designers are beholden to stories, but they both deal with fantasy and reality. Costume designers create clothing to help an actor find a character."[8] But, how can we approach costume in a film such as *American Psycho*, which we know from interviews and press articles features designer suits and other branded apparel in vogue during the 1980s and favored by the rampant yuppie culture? Although it remains relevant classifying and providing precise definitions, positioning film and costume at the antithesis, in the same way as Landis claims, is unproductive and reductive since in the contemporary media landscape these can often coexist. It is under these auspices that this chapter explores the blurred distinction between fashion and costumes, a malleable variation, which is perhaps even more evident when discussing *Armani*, the fashion film Harron directed to showcase the 2012 fall/winter collection designed by Giorgio Armani. In this case, the branded garments become at the same time symbolic products of the fashion house Armani—we find indeed his favorite color, a sea of grays, and the ubiquitous pantsuit, but, by leaving the setting of the catwalk and entering the fictional realm created by Harron, these items of clothing, like costumes, become narrative, their job is in fact to tell a cinematic story, to shape a character and tell his/her journey.

There has been a long-standing debate concerning fashion's role in film on the grounds of narrative and characterization, based on the assumption that fashion primarily acts as a distraction to the narrative flow. In her influential article "Costume and Narrative," Jane Gaines maintains that during classical Hollywood cinema costumes work to serve the narrative: the story and realism. The economics of film dictates costumes, not the other way around, and a failure to remain "subservient" to the higher purpose of storytelling would "distract the viewer from the narrative."[9] In other words, clothing sustains the characters' roles because of their empathetic power, fulfiling the requirements of plot and story. As previously mentioned, Bruzzi's *Undressing Cinema* is one of the few academic studies that challenges the hierarchy narrative/*mise en scène*, proposing a "discourse not wholly dependent on the structure of narrative, and character for signification."[10] Bruzzi not only acknowledges the role of certain iconic costumes as pure visual pleasure and "spectacular interventions" but also draws attention to the role of fashion designers when called in by a film production and the symbolic roles costumes play in relation to class and gender.

As well as being informed by the above debates on costume, fashion and cinema, I approach the functions of on-screen fashion and costumes in the works of Mary Harron from different angles, including a consideration of extra-textual discourses related to the new industrial synergies between the fashion and media industries. It is not surprising, therefore, that the British newspaper *The Guardian* has elevated Canadian writer Margaret Atwood and the television series based on her novels, *Alias Grace* and *The Handmaid's Tale* (Hulu, 2017–present), as "the unlikely style soothsayer of 2017."[11] According to journalist Hannah Marriott, last year's catwalks presented references to the TV shows and their main characters, whose clothes reflected their subjugation to the rules of patriarchy and servitude, in particular through the use of the bonnet as a symbol of imposed modesty, repression, and limitation to the female gaze. In the case of *Alias Grace*, period costumes convey not only the historical condition of servants, immigrants, and, more broadly, women in nineteenth-century Canada, but also the eerie foresight of the power of "style" in media-covered trials. Harron and Sarah Polley adapt Atwood's book about the real-life trial of Grace Marks (Sarah Gadon) and James McDermott (Kerr Logan) accused of murdering their employer, Thomas Kinnear (Paul Gross) and his housekeeper and mistress, Nancy Montgomery (Anna Paquin). As well as channeling the zeitgeist and mood of the series, costumes and more broadly textiles become crucial narrative devices. It is sufficient to think of the theme of quilting represented in Grace's attachment to her knitted bedspread and the fact that she sews quilt blocks during her sessions and conversations with Simon (Edward Holcroft). Quilting becomes a metaphor for the whole series as it relates to issues of female labor and friendship, Grace's patchwork memory and personality, and the complex narrative of *Alias Grace* itself, given that the mystery of the murders is slowly revealed in small pieces and not through an omniscient and unbiased narrator.[12]

The trial, in particular, seems to put great emphasis on clothing, timidly inferring that Grace killed Nancy in part to rob her of a voluptuous pink dress. In fact, during the arbitration we see Grace wearing a grandiose bonnet full of frills, which overwhelms her minute face, as well as the same dress worn by Nancy at the moment of her death. Simonetta Mariano, the costume designer of the series, underlines the importance of the "pink dress" in her vision of Grace during the trial, and her tribulations to convince Harron of her sartorial choices.[13]

While Harron wanted to preserve the simplicity of Grace's character through a more demure attire, Mariano insisted, to convey the class warfare occurring

Figure 8.1 Grace (Sarah Gadon) in Nancy Montgomery's (Anna Paquin) pink dress after her murder

in the courtroom and evidenced in the trial reports still accessible today: the pink dress and more significantly the bonnet make Grace a fish out of water, offering the overall effect of an unsophisticated teenaged pauper playing dress-up. However, Grace wears the pink dress with a simple undergarment rather than the more precious chemisette owned by Nancy, thus indicating a possible mediation between the creative visions of director and costume designer. In any case, the color of the dress conveys the difficult positions of both characters: on the one hand the softly washed peony pink symbolizes Grace's youthfulness and naivety; on the other, the hue equally marks out Nancy, a woman who bends social norms, fancying colorful attires and having an affair with her wealthy employer.[14] In *Alias Grace* on-screen clothes and textiles play multiple functions: narrative, iconic and symbolic. First and foremost, they are storytelling devices: Grace is, in fact, easily identified by the authorities because of her dress, but at the same time costumes are stand-out performances in their own right as well as a symbolic token. The richness of the attires in the church and courtroom scenes transform costumes into moments of pure visual pleasure, such as in the case of the much-observed pink dress.

Given that Harron's distinct body of work is characterized by the recurrent themes of consumption and masquerade, it is surprising how scholarly and critical studies have paid little attention to fashion, privileging instead the sole notion of the body—and gender—with little consideration for the fashioned or clothed body. I seek to rebalance this and analyze the complex relationship between costumes, narrative, and character, a connection which is neither expressive nor excessive as previous studies might indicate. As suggested in the case of *Alias Grace*, on-screen clothes, whether borrowed from archival collections or specifically made by costume designers, can be read through a rubric that combines "the symbolic," "the supportive," and "the iconic" functions of garments. These are not to be intended as mutually exclusive categories; rather they are tendencies that can cohabit within the same piece of fashion and in the same scene. This new model is particularly useful when the fashion film *Armani* will be discussed in conjunction with the idea of authorship championed in a new media genre, namely the fashion film. However, it is first important to contextualize the unique case of the fashion film *Armani* in relation to *American Psycho*, where period costumes give way to brand garments, operating a peculiar system of codes between made-for-the-screen clothes and fashion items.

FASHIONING *AMERICAN PSYCHO*: THE SYMBOLIC, THE SUPPORTIVE, AND THE ICONIC

Providing a complete overview of how costumes operate in Harron's four feature films and television work would go beyond the scope of this chapter. However, by highlighting some moments from *American Psycho* I want to focus on the corporate environment and a businesswear attire that link the promotional short and the full feature, despite the different temporal setting.

Set in the late 1980s, *American Psycho* highlights the importance placed on personal appearance and the disparity between the external and internal selves engulfing a rampant Wall Street broker, Patrick Bateman (Christian Bale). The film not only showcases his impeccable beauty routine, namely face scrubs and masks, special shampoo and lotions, strict diet and exercise regime, but also his flawless wardrobe. Bateman wears tailor-made suits that reflect his power and status: his starched shirts with contrasting white collars are often striped and decorated with colorful ties: red, green, and blue. Everything is well studied, including the legendary braces symbolizing his class. Mid gray or dark blue, four-on-one-breasted suit with peaked lapels are his careful corporate uniform. This style, reminiscent of an era before World War Two, creates an imposing allure, which is very much looked for in the business world he inhabits. According to Pamela Church Gibson, "The suit indicated, historically, that its wearer was either a man of leisure and wealth, or a member of the rapidly expanding middle classes. Since its revival it has had 'aspirational' associations [. . .]."[15] And indeed Bateman's and his associates' position is all reflected in the same series of suits, shirts, and patterned ties they display to hide a vacuum within. In this sense, these costumes work as symbols of his attitude, his wealth, loudness, and obsession with superiority. Bateman's associates compare their business cards and value their worthiness with the brands they are wearing and what restaurant they can get reservations at. Fashion labels are a big part of the sartorial competitiveness between Bateman and his male friends in the office and names are thrown around to show their prowess. However, despite functioning as symbol of his status, these fashion items do not stand as true signifiers of his character and identity; they work as a façade, a uniform, and hiding masquerade.

In an interview featured in the DVD extras, costume designer Isis Mussenden reveals the difficulties in securing designer items for the film. Cerruti or Armani suits could have been realistically employed during the shooting, since they were fashionable at that time, but several brands decided not have their name associated with the film, and did not allow their branded items to feature due to the controversial nature of *American Psycho* and the damage it could potentially lead to.[16]

Consumerism is at the center of the film and interestingly, Bateman places an almost fetishistic love and protection towards his apparel. For example, every time someone at work touches his suit, he reacts angrily or during the sex scene with the two prostitutes he warns them not to touch his precious Rolex. This could suggest that not only does he have little tolerance toward challenges to his personal look, but it also feels like these attempts could shatter and break through the illusion that he has so carefully constructed and controlled through luxury garments. On another occasion clothing accessories are used to hide his identity as a shield. When Bateman attempts to strangle an associate because of his supposed superiority in terms of business cards, he dons a pair of black leather gloves in a fashion similar to the classic killers in 1970s Italian *giallos* (cheap crime and mystery paperbacks). This is not a mere example of postmodern intertextual reference to the notorious *filone* (genre) of horror cinema where misogyny was the norm, but also an instance of Harron's cinephilia. Moreover, this works also as her tongue-in-cheek approach to deconstruct and ironically play with genres.

Harron's film constantly emphasizes the importance of costume. In the scene where Bateman murders Paul Allen (Jared Leto) with an axe, he wears a transparent plastic raincoat covering his immaculate office uniform comprised of pale blue shirt and red tie. In this case the film provides a vivid representation of how clothing can disguise, confuse and horrify an audience. This morbidly spectacular piece of clothing has become iconic, as the naked body of Bateman waiving a chainsaw in the corridor. Wearing dark glasses and dancing in the raincoat, Bateman prolongs the suspense; by deferring the frenzy attack it allows a moment of ironic indulgence of his preposterous attire. After swinging the axe, the camera stops on his clothes and shoes, completely unaffected by blood in comparison with his splattered face. In short, the look is everything to Bateman: fashion brands are supportive of his constructed image of superiority, narcissism, and cover for his lack of humanity and emotions.

It is worth remembering, however, that the composition of the film wardrobe is not solely determined by Harron. Collaboration with the costume designer and writers is crucially important. As the interviews with Mussenden confirm, director and designer work together to create an overall conception of the film's look. And it is in this collaborative effort and exchange between technical figures that a process of demythologizing the granted authority of the director can take place in order to offer a more organic envisaging of a film's style.

COLLABORATIVE AUTHORSHIP AND THE FASHION FILM GENRE

In essence, auteur theory champions the director as the author of a film, an artist who is able to give expression of his/her own personality in his/her work. Film authorship debates can be traced back to Alexandre Astruc's article "The Camera-Stylo" published in 1948. For the first time the director's camera was equaled to an author's pen, painting a romantic vision of the director as the sole individual giving shape and vision to a film and in total control of the creative ownership of the final product.[17] The initial formalization of *la politique des auteurs*, however, developed in the 1950s around the writings of a series of

French critics, François Truffaut and Jacques Rivette among others, connected to the journal *Cahiers du Cinema*. The publication of "A Certain Tendency in French Cinema" by Truffaut in 1954 and the later reformulation of American critic Andrew Sarris' "Notes on Auteur Theory" in 1962 took the world by storm, but remain strong manifestos of classical auteur theory.[18] Given the changing cultural context in the late 1960s brought about by structuralism and later by post-structuralism, auteur theory was put under scrutiny, problematized and eventually evolved under the influences of reception theory. But outside academic writing, film journalism and the film industry itself continue to celebrate the triumph of the director, turning critically acclaimed directors into brands. It suffices to think how in promotional material "directed by Spike Lee" becomes "a film by Spike Lee," or "a Spike Lee joint."

As far as fashion films are concerned, the centrality of the role of the director is crucial, because fashion houses and brands commission promotional short videos in a manner akin to advertising due to the distinct style of certain filmmakers. According to Nikola Mijovic:

> In the context of the promotional fashion film and celebrity culture, the circle is complete and auteurism reaches its antithetical closure: maverick directors have themselves become brands, involved in a sort of brand fusion when commissioned by fashion companies to recycle their "signature style" in a short format for online consumption.[19]

For example, contemporary auteur, Wes Anderson, created promotional short films for H&M, their Christmas advertisement *Come Together* (2016), and the narrative fashion film *Castello Cavalcalti* for Prada (2013), among many other commercials featuring his elaborate sets, obsession for retro props and costumes, peculiar color palettes and well-balanced centered composition.[20] One could therefore assume that auteurism reached a point where the director has now become a form of commodity. As far as Harron is concerned, it is difficult to pinpoint her specific signature style, therefore challenging the contemporary interpretation of the notion. Mary Harron's name might not be the first one that comes up in the mind when thinking of contemporary auteurs, nonetheless, the predilection for strong-willed female characters, the ironic tone and the playfulness in working with generic conventions are crucial in defining her authorial voice. A voice that is able to adapt to different media: film, television, and online videos, but also a voice that does not impose a strong unilateral vision, and instead is perhaps reinforced and enhanced by the symbiotic relationship with other figures: writers, actors and, in this case, fashion designers.

Before exploring the authorial collaboration underscoring *Armani*, it is important to unpack the characteristic features of fashion films that make them distinct from more traditional moving image commercials. Scholars such as

Natalie Khan and Marketa Uhlirova seem to agree that at its heart the fashion film does not blatantly promote fashion, since it does not address viewers as simply consumers; its intention is not to persuade, but to extend the experience of a brand.[21] Specifically, Khan interprets fashion films as a new media genre that transforms viewer-consumers of ads into real cinematic spectators.[22] Unconventional communication strategies have in fact taken over more traditional marketing campaigns as print advertising got increasingly expensive and new markets, the digital natives, need to be reached through different channels. In addition, a notable appeal of fashion films is represented by the aura of prestige that is associated with having a filmmaker, or better, an auteur, associated with the project. The brand, in fact, exploits the cultural capital of a director and his/her style in an act similar to Renaissance patronage.[23] Harron's intervention in the project legitimizes the cultural status of the short *Armani* and positions it at the interstice between commerce and art, fashion rhetoric, and cinematic tropes. As a result, we ought to consider the fashion film closely related to advertisement: it is a commodity that is consumed on digital platforms, but because of its less direct promotional approach, it also sits in its own logic intertwining commerce and art in a manner similar to fashion photography.

Intention is not only a crucial issue for understanding the hybridity of this new genre in between advertisement and art, but also it is the core concept behind more recent interpretation of authorship, for instance Paul Sellors' formulation of collaborative authorship.[24] Drawing on communication studies, Sellors maintains that the author intentionally makes an utterance, an expression of an idea, a story. He argues that a single individual cannot be the sole creator of a film; the contribution of the cinematographer, editor, and other artists and technicians involved in a collective effort for a common goal ought to be recognized.[25] Intentionality and exercise of control are the two key issues at the basis of this position, as well as the mutual collaboration between creators. Audiences might be attracted to the coherence of the film as a single entity, and not capture the significance of costume choices, sound mixing or acting performance, but it is the concerted effort of multiple artists that creates the whole picture. Collaborative theories have therefore several advantages: on the one hand, they allow not to fall within the arbitrary and dogmatic conundrums of classical approaches to authorship. On the other hand, they give credit to other figures beyond the director. As such this approach seem perfectly suited to better comprehend the dynamics of a complex project such as the commissioned fashion film *Armani*, where the artistic spirit of Harron marries the style and meaning conveyed by Giorgio Armani's collection. It is not my intention to diminish or deny the role of auteur to Harron, rather to shed light on other members of the cooperative activity, as authorship is dependent on contribution. While Giorgio Armani's contribution might have been small, providing the location and fashion items for the shooting, nonetheless the clothing carries its significant meaning. While in the preceding section I discussed how made-for-the screen costumes support or challenge the narrative, hence highlighting the contributing effort of costume designers, in the following, I explore how a fashion author and a film author interact to create a choral vision and expression.

ARMANI: A FASHION FILM DIRECTED BY MARY HARRON

Shot in black-and-white at the five-star Armani Hotel in Milan, the short film narrates how a woman (Julie Ordon) checking out and leaving the premises meets by chance a former lover (Teddy Sears). Dialogue-free and lasting around two minutes, the fashion film captures this serendipitous moment, which elicits strong memories and feelings between the couple. It also showcases clothes and accessories from the 2012 fall/winter collection, in particular sequin eveningwear, gray tweed pantsuits, and leather wallets and bags.

Three flashbacks intercut by gazes between the protagonists recount the beginning, middle and ending of their romance: from passionate moments in the early stages of their story, to arguments and reconciliation, until a final separation. Released on the Internet in December 2012, the fashion film promotes not only the "Easy Chic"-themed women's collection, including a few items from the men's collection showcased on the Milanese catwalks the previous February, but also the latest business venture of Giorgio Armani S.p.A.: a branded hospitality venue that reflects the classic, elegant, and understated

Figure 8.2 The couple meet for the first time in *Armani* (2012)

brand style. As Mark Tungate explains, the complex at Via Manzoni 31 (in close proximity of the upscale shopping street, via Montenapoleone, part of the so-called *Quadrilatero della moda*, where many designers have their high-end boutiques in Milan) constitutes a perfect example of brand extension.[26] Differently from other fashion corporations, such as LVMH or OTB who follow a strategy of acquiring existing brands, the Armani group has preferred to create and reinforce a "branded environment": the giant space in Milan includes a ninety-five-room luxury hotel, the Armani spa, a flower shop, bar, restaurant, and a café. The Giorgio Armani boutiques of course take center stage in this enterprise, but also these ancillary ventures function to channel and promote an Armani lifestyle.

Following common practices in fashion films, Harron's work does not present itself as a blatant advertisement of the most recent coats, dresses, and accessories of the collection, nor a direct promotional video of the hotel. Rather it provides glimpses of the hall and the bar, giving little indication of the geographical location—there are no postcard images of Milanese tourist sights: only an attentive eye can catch an old tram passing in front of a window with a large "A" logo and a roofscape with an medieval belltower. In addition, logos, which in any case are not usually prominent in Armani collections, disappear even when a leather bag is shot in an extreme close-up.

Written by Harron and her husband John C. Walsh, the film resembles many other narrative fashion films as the plot is simplified in order to encourage the viewer to experience the emotions that the images suggest and absorb the spectacle of the designer items. We see the woman dropping a pair of dark shades on the floor and being caught by the sight of her former partner; here the sunglasses and the exchange of gazes function as a Proustian madeleine revealing a montage of scenes that chronicle their love story. These subjective flashbacks follow conventional cinematic cues, such as the initial close-up and the subsequent dissolve, and are therefore reminiscent of the quintessential example of chronicling the memories of past love: *Casablanca* (Warner Bros., Curtiz, 1942). In this case we first see the couple in love, undressing along the corridors of the hotel as they reach their room. Then the flashback turns to an argument, followed quickly by a reconciling embrace. And eventually, the final segment reveals the woman packing a small purse and leaving a bedroom. As the viewer comes back from this trip down memory lane, it is revealed that the woman has found happiness somewhere else and is now a mother to a little curly-haired girl. As the man leaves the hotel wondering "what if," mother and daughter stand by some armchairs before the credits appears showing the name Armani for the first time. Harron as a navigated director understands the basic premise of cinema: one should tell a story through visual means and not though exposition, and therefore, by trusting the medium, avoids any line of dialogue and prefers the instrumental tune of "Wild Heart Can't Be Broken" by Piano Dreamers to guide the viewer through this emotional journey.

Despite being set in a glamorous location and showcasing luxury garments and accessories, this is not a flagrant celebration of consumption, consistent with the understated elegance of Armani's brand identity and the more subtle communication strategies of fashion films. Even the choice of costumes, the selected items from the "Easy Chic" collection, mirror this tamed sense of glamor and luxury: the chosen garments range from loose pantsuits, elongated jackets, pleated trousers and fedora hats. These relaxed pieces of garments are typical of Armani's innovative style, which can be simply defined as "logical, rational, and wearable."[27] Giorgio Armani created his first menswear independent collection in 1974 and then founded his eponymous *maison* in 1975 in Milan, after a few years of apprenticeship as assistant to Nino Cerruti, an Italian textile businessman and designer. Armani's most notorious innovation in terms of fashion design is represented by the informal liberated jacket for both men and women, where internal supports such as padding and interlinings are eliminated, buttons moved, and traditional proportion adjusted for a more relaxed wear and look. The Armani unstructured jacket was the culmination of new trends that Farid Chenoune traces to the changing habits of the late 1960s, when sportswear became more popular on the streets as did looser jackets for business wear. In his *A History of Men's Fashion*, Chenoune argues that, "The goal of unstructured garments was to make suits and jackets lighter and more comfortable, putting an end to the sartorial schizophrenia of white-collar professionals."[28]

Having abandoned his studies in medicine, Armani's early designs wanted to emphasize the typical V shape, a male anatomy characterized by a muscular build with broad shoulders and a slim waist, making his suits synonymous with rampant independence and ambition. Therefore, Bruzzi is correct when she claims that "it is in the nebulous intersection between masculinity and narcissism that Armani's muted radicalism is represented."[29] When, in the 1970s, formal dressing became démodé, Armani imitated and adapted French ready-to-wear also to his women's collections in order to offer a more relaxed but refined figure. The female protagonist of Harron's short promotional video embodies this idea of womanhood according to Armani: strong, independent, and elegant. She puts on her sunglasses and stands strong in the hall of the hotel, holding her child as her former lover leaves. She does not wear heels (the fall/winter 2012 collection featured flat loafers), and her sleek gray pantsuit accentuates her tall and slim figure: she is still standing without regrets. According to Christopher Laverty these are the trademarks for professional women wearing Armani: "Right or wrong, women who achieve are dressed in Armani because of an inbuilt association with mannish tailoring. To succeed in a man's world, women must apparently adopt their silhouette."[30]

The fact that the film was shot in black-and-white, thus enhancing the famous hues of gray that made Giorgio Armani famous, renders the costumes more sober and self-contained than those displayed on the catwalk itself. In fact, as Tim Blanks report for *Vogue*, the 2012 fall/winter collection was characterized by flashes of color: magenta, cerise, and tangerine, a continuation of the experimental warm colors employed in the previous Armani summer collection. The suit that Julie Ordon is wearing features a prominent colorful brooch, which on the Milanese catwalks stood out for its sheer brilliance but is toned down by the antique patina provided by the black-and-white film. Furthermore, Blanks notices Armani's provocation also in the way models were directed to walk down the catwalk during the 2012 fashion week: staring directly at the audience, as opposed to the usual frosty stare.[31] This is mirrored in several moments of the short film, where the female protagonist is in charge of her action: she initiates the romance, she decides to terminate it, and she stares at the camera. What is interesting in this fashion film is that viewers are sutured to a specific way of experiencing fashion through conventional cinematic narratives. Fashion is not displayed here to be admired as a designed object or work of art, as it could be in exhibitions or on traditional catwalks, rather the aesthetic qualities of the items are shadowed by the symbolic value, the aspirational identity that they embody. They are not "spectacular" to use Bruzzi's term, allowing the flow of narration without disruption.

Trying to incorporate a two-minute video within the oeuvre of Harron could be a stretch, as there is a difference between what can be developed in a two-hour film and a short online video. However, it does share the themes, and the emotional and personal concerns of Harron's feature films. For instance, giving a voice to female figures who otherwise are sidelined or shadowed by

Figure 8.3 The couple meet again years on

other events. In this case the constant with her previous work is the attempt to deploy the stylistic conventions of the genre and then subvert them. In an interview for *The Believer*, Harron argued:

> I always say to my husband: I make unpopular versions of popular things. I make a horror film and it's not a horror film. None of my genre movies function as genre movies. When people see the conventions, they think they're going to get the straightforward genre—I don't give them that and they get mad. People see that and they think I don't understand the conventions because I'm not a good filmmaker.[32]

Also, in this case the fashion film *Armani* seems to follow the conventions of a typical romance story, boy meets girl, but the audience expectations are disrupted at the end, since the fortuitous encounter does not lead to a rapprochement between the couple. This is a fresh take that demonstrates the feminist ethos moving many of Harron's works: romantic love is not what a woman needs to be happy and successful. Nonetheless, it fails to critically engage with the fashion world: this fashion film celebrates women as subjects of desire, rather than objects, but any critical or ironic take is neutralized. There are no veiled critiques on contemporary beauty standards, the cast actor could have walked on a catwalk in a fashion show given her tallness and thinness. It is therefore surprising that a director so involved in demystifying consumerism in a film such as *American Psycho* or giving agency and a voice to pin-up model Bettie Page becomes complicit of a system which reinforces fashion's paradigms and the status provided by fetishized luxury commodities.[33]

One of the aims of this chapter has been to explore the multiple ways in which clothing interacts with the body to create meaning: as a symbol, as a spectacle or as a supportive and verisimilitude utterance. Even a cursory viewing of Harron's works reveals their richness as sources of fashion inspiration. While in drama these modalities interact with each other and coexist, in the short film *Armani* the clothes discourse seems to solely rely on imagination and the power of allusion rather than making a sartorial statement. I hope to have demonstrated that, as Sarah Street argues, "studying films 'through clothes' enhances an appreciation of cinema which is primarily visual."[34] The emergence of the fashion film genre is proof of the never-ending symbiosis between these two forms of art, both nourished by dreams, obsessions, and fantasy.

NOTES

1. Roland Barthes, *The Language of Fashion*, translated by Andy Stafford, edited by Andy Stafford and Michael Carter (London: Bloomsbury, 2013), 96.
2. Joanne Entwistle, *The Fashion Body*, Second Edition (Cambridge: Polity Press, 2015), 7.

3. Stella Bruzzi, *Undressing Cinema. Clothing and Identity in the Movies* (London and New York, 1997).
4. Ibid., xv.
5. In the course of this chapter I will be using the term fashion film to denote those promotional videos commissioned by fashion houses as part of their marketing campaigns. These can take different forms, from experimental to narrative short films. For a detailed mapping of this new format see: Nikola Mijovic, "Narrative forms and the rhetoric of fashion in the promotional fashion film," *Film, Fashion & Consumption* (Vol. 2, No. 2, 2013), 175–86, and Gary Needham, "The Digital Fashion Film", in *Fashion Cultures Revisited: Theories, Explorations and Analysis*, Second Edition, edited by Stella Bruzzi and Pamela Church Gibson (London and New York: Routledge, 2013), 103–11.
6. Here I am employing Needham's definition of a specific genre of fashion films, namely those shorts directed by renowned filmmakers with their distinct style. Examples include works such as David Lynch's *Lady Blue of Shangai* (2010), Roman Polanski's *A Therapy* (2013), and Spike Jonze's *Kenzo World* (2016).
7. Deborah Nadoolman Landis, *Screencraft: Costume Design* (Burlington: Focal Press, 2003), 8. Nadoolman Landis' position stems from the assumption that even when fashion designers collaborate in the costume department of a film, for instance in the case of Jean Paul Gautier with Pedro Almodovar's *Kika* (1993) or Giorgio Armani with *American Gigolo* (Schrader, 1980), their contribution always needs to be re-adjusted to the actor and the story.
8. Booth Moore, "Unfashioning Costume Design," in *Hollywood Costume*, edited by Deborah Nadoolman Landis (London: V&A Publishing, 2012), 151.
9. Jane Gaines, "Costume and Narrative: How Dress Tells the Woman's Story," in *Fabrications: Costume and the Female Body*, edited by Jane Gaines and Charlotte Herzog (London and New York: Routledge, 1990), 193.
10. Bruzzi, *Undressing Cinema*, xvi.
11. Hannah Marriott, "Margaret Atwood: the unlikely style soothsayer of 2017," *The Guardian*, December 27, 2017. Accessed July 1, 2018. https://www.theguardian.com/fashion/2017/dec/27/margaret-atwood-the-unlikely-style-soothsayer-of-2017
12. Each section of the novel has a symbolic quilt pattern name: rocky road, broken dishes, and jagged edge, mirroring difficult phases in Grace's condition. Significantly, at the end of the novel Grace makes a Tree of Paradise quilt using fabric from clothes that marked her existence: a scrap from Mary's petticoat, Nancy's pink dress, and her own prison nightgown.
13. Jennifer Vineyard, "How a Pink Dress Made It Into Margaret Atwood's Murder Mystery," *Racked.com*, November 30, 2017. Accessed July 1, 2018. https://www.racked.com/2017/11/30/16715278/alias-grace-costumes
14. Ibid.
15. Pamela Church Gibson, "Brad Pitt and George Clooney. The Rough and the Smooth: Male Costuming in Contemporary Hollywood," in *Fashioning Film Stars. Dress, Culture, Identity*, edited by Rachel Moseley (London: BFI Publishing, 2005), 69.
16. I am making reference to the on-set interviews present in the Region 2 Entertainment in Video DVD.
17. John Caughie, *Theories of Authorship: A Reader* (London: Routledge, 1981), 24.
18. For a history of authorship theories see also David A. Gerstner and Janet Staiger (eds), *Authorship and Film* (New York and London: Routledge, 2003), and Barry Keith Grant (ed.), *Auteurs and Authorships: A Film Reader* (Malden, MA, and Oxford: Blackwell, 2008).
19. Mijovic, "Narrative Forms and the Rhetoric of Fashion," 181.

20. Several renowned auteurs have channels their themes, style, and personal obsessions in commercials. The list includes Federico Fellini, Ingmar Bergman, Jean-Luc Godard, and David Lynch, among many others.
21. Natalie Khan, "Cutting the Fashion Body: Why the Fashion Image is No Longer Still," *Fashion Theory* (Vol. 16, No. 2, 2012), 235–50, and Marketa Uhlirova, "100 Years of the Fashion Film: Frameworks and Histories," *Fashion Theory* (Vol. 17, No. 2, 2013), 137–58.
22. Khan, "Cutting the Fashion Body," 237.
23. I further explore this issue in relation to Miu Miu's project *Women's Tales* in Elena Caoduro, "'Women's Tales': Postfeminist Adventures into Consumerville," *Comunicazioni Sociali: Journal of Media, Performing Arts and Cultural Studies* (1, 2017), 37–42.
24. Paul C. Sellors, "Collective Authorship in Film," *The Journal of Aesthetics and Art Criticism* (Vol. 65, No. 3, 2007), 263–71.
25. Ibid., 268.
26. Mark Tungate, *Fashion Brands: Branding Style from Armani to Zara* (London: Kogan Page, 2012), 129.
27. Giorgio Armani, "A certain style," *Vogue* (143, No. 3, March 1986), 398.
28. Farid Chenoune, *A History of Men's Fashion*, translated by Richard Martin (Paris: Flammarion, 1993), 292.
29. Bruzzi, *Undressing Cinema*, 25–6.
30. Christopher Laverty, *Fashion in Film* (London: Laurence King Publishing, 2017), 82.
31. Tim Blanks, "Fall 2012 Ready-to-Wear Giorgio Armani," *Vogue.com*, February 27, 2012. Accessed February 2, 2018, https://www.vogue.com/fashion-shows/fall-2012-ready-to-wear/giorgio-armani
32. Mary Harron, "Mostly I'm Just Not American," interview by Anisse Gross, *Believer Magazine*, March/April 2014, https://www.believermag.com/issues/201403/?read=interview_harron
33. This is the conundrum behind many fashion films: commissioned by fashion brands, directors have the limitation of only showcasing some garments from a recent collection. The celebratory mode is difficult to escape from and just a few examples try to expose a veiled criticism, sometimes with a tongue-in-cheek spirit. Lucrecia Martel's *Muta* (2012) for Miu Miu represents an enigmatic critique towards beauty standards for models as it depicts the female protagonists of this film as humanoid stick insects. Moreover, the recent emergence of fashion mockumentaries, for instance *The Life of Pitti Peacocks* (Aaron Christian, 2016), *Unravelled: The Greatest Story Never Told* (Isaac Lock, 2017), and *La Chaise Ironique* (Rankin, 2017) seem to demonstrate that a more ironic look at the fashion world is possible.
34. Sara Street, *Costume and Cinema: Dress Codes in Popular Film* (London: Wallflower Press, 2001), 11.

Filmography

DIRECTOR

2020 *The Expecting* (TV series, 11 episodes)
2018 *Charlie Says*
2017 *Alias Grace* (TV mini-series, 6 episodes)
2015 *Graceland* (TV series, 1 episode)
2015 *The Following* (TV series, 1 episode)
2015 *Constantine* (TV series, 1 episode)
2014 *We the Economy: 20 Short Films You Can't Afford to Miss* (documentary, segment)
2013 *Anna Nicole* (TV movie)
2008 *Fear Itself* (TV series, 1 episode)
2007 *The Nine* (TV series, 1 episode)
2006 *Six Degrees* (TV series, 1 episode)
2006 *Big Love* (TV series, 1 episode)
2005 *Six Feet Under* (TV series, 1 episode)
2004 *The L Word* (TV series, 1 episode)
2002 *Pasadena* (TV series, 1 episode)
1998 *Oz* (TV series, 1 episode)
1998 *Homicide: Life on the Street* (TV series, 1 episode)
1994 *Winds of Change* (TV documentary)
1991 *Without Walls* (TV series, Documentary, 1 Episode)
1988 *The Late Show* (TV Series, documentary, 1 episode)

WRITER AND DIRECTOR

2012 *Armani* (written by, with John Walsh)
2011 *The Moth Diaries* (written by, based on the novel by Rachel Klein)
2010 *Sonnet for a Towncar* (short, written by, with John Walsh)

2008 *Holding Fast* (short, written by, with John Walsh)
2005 *The Notorious Bettie Page* (written by, with Guinevere Turner)
2000 *American Psycho* (written by, based on the novel by Brett Easton Ellis)
1996 *I Shot Andy Warhol* (written by, with Daniel Minahan, based on research by Diane Tucker, and additional scenes and dialogue by Jeremiah Newton)

Bibliography

About Schmidt. Directed by Alexander Payne. New Line Cinema, 2002.
Adorno, Theodor, and Max Horkheimer. *The Culture Industry: Enlightenment as Mass Deception, Dialectic of Enlightenment*. New York: Seabury Press, 1972.
Akerlof, George A. "Loyalty Filters." *American Economic Review* 73, No. 1 (1983), 54, 63.
Alexander, Scott and Larry Karaszewski. *Man on the Moon: The Shooting Script*. New York: Newmarket Press, 1999.
Alias Grace. Created by Sarah Polley. CBC, 2017.
Alien. Directed by Ridley Scott. Twentieth Century Fox, 1979.
Allen, Kim. "Girls Imagining Careers in the Limelight: Social Class, Gender, and Fantasies of 'Success'," in *In the Limelight and Under the Microscope: Forms and Functions of Female Celebrity*. Edited by Sue Holmes and Diane Negra. New York: Continuum, 2011.
Amanda Knox: Murder on Trial in Italy. Directed by Robert Dornhelm. Lifetime, 2011.
American Beauty. Directed by Sam Mendes. DreamWorks Pictures, 1999.
American Horror Story. Created by Ryan Murphy. FX, 2011–present.
American Splendor. Directed by Shari Springer Berman and Robert Pulcini. Fine Line Features/HBO Films, 2003.
Anderson, Carolyn. "Biographical Film," in *Handbook of American Film Genres*. Edited by Wes D. Gehring. Westport: Greenwood, 1988.
Armani, Giorgio. "A certain style." *Vogue* 143, 3 (March 1986), 398.
Asanova, Svetlana. "Consumerism and Madness in Mary Harron's *American Psycho*." *Gender Forum* 40 (2012), 1–13.
Atwood, Margaret. *Alias Grace*. Toronto: McClelland & Stewart, 1996.
Badley, Linda, Claire Perkins, and Michele Schreiber. "Introduction," in *Indie Reframed Women's Filmmaking and Contemporary American Independent Cinema*. Edited by Linda Badley, Claire Perkins, and Michele Schreiber. Edinburgh: Edinburgh University Press, 2016.
Barthes, Roland. *The Language of Fashion*. Translated by Andy Stafford. Edited by Andy Stafford and Michael Carter. London: Bloomsbury, 2013.
Basquiat. Directed by Julian Schnabel. Miramax Films, 1996.
Bastién, Angelica Jade. "The Female Gaze of *American Psycho*: How Mary Harron Made Fantasy Into Timeless Satire." *Village Voice*, June 7, 2016. Accessed February 15, 2017.

Available: http://www.villagevoice.com/film/the-female-gaze-of-american-psycho-how-maryharron-made-fantasy-into-timeless-satire-8707185.

Bastién, Angelica Jade. "The Female Gaze of 'American Psycho': How Mary Harron Made Fantasy Into Timeless Satire." *The Village Voice* (2016). Accessed April 9, 2019. Available: https://www.villagevoice.com/2016/06/07/the-female-gaze-of-american-psycho-howmary-harron-made-fantasy-into-timeless-satire/

Bellah, Robert, Richard Madsen, William M. Sullivan, Anne Swidler, and Steven M. Tipton. *Habits of the Heart: Individualism and Commitment in American Life.* Berkeley: University of California Press, 2007.

Benshoff, Harry M. *Monsters in the Closet: Homosexuality and the Horror Film.* Manchester: Manchester University Press, 1997.

Benshoff, Harry M., and Sean Griffin. *America on Film: Representing Race, Class, Gender, and Sexuality at the Movies.* 2nd Edition. Malden: Wiley-Blackwell, 2009.

Benson-Allott, Caetlin. "'Made for Quality Television?' *Behind the Candelabra* (Steven Soderbergh, 2013), *Anna Nicole* (Mary Harron, 2013)." *Film Quarterly* 66, No. 4 (2013), 5–9.

Berger, John. *Ways of Seeing.* New York: Penguin Books, 1972.

Berger, Jonah. *Invisible Influence: The hidden forces that shape behaviour.* New York: Simon & Schuster, 2016.

Bingham, Dennis. *Whose Lives Are They Anyway?: The Biopic as Contemporary Film Genre.* New Brunswick, NJ: Rutgers University Press, 2010.

Birds of Prey. Directed by Cathy Yan. Warner Bros., 2020.

Birthisel, Jessica, and Jason Martin. "'That's What She Said': Gender, satire, and the American workplace on the sitcom *The Office.*" *Journal of Communication Inquiry* 37, No. 1 (2013), 64–80.

Black Widow. Directed by Cate Shortland. Walt Disney Studios Motion Pictures, 2019.

Blanks, Tim. "Fall 2012 Ready-to-Wear Giorgio Armani." *Vogue.com,* February 27, 2012. Accessed February 2, 2018. Available: https://www.vogue.com/fashion-shows/fall 2012-ready-to-wear/giorgio-armani

Blow. Directed by Ted Demme. New Line Cinema, 2001.

Bluestone, George. *Novels into Film.* Reprinted Edition. Berkeley: University of Los Angeles Press, [1957] 1969.

Bly, Robert. *Iron John: A Book About Men.* Shaftesbury: Element, 1990.

Bodanis, David. *Passionate Minds: The Great Enlightenment Love Affair.* London: Little, Brown, 2006.

Bonnie and Clyde. Directed by Arthur Penn. Warner Bros., 1967.

Bordwell, David. *The Way That Hollywood Tells It: Story and Style in Modern Movies.* Berkeley/Los Angeles/London: University of California Press, 2006.

Bourdieu, Pierre. "Les modes de domination," *Actes de la recherché en sciences sociales* 2, Nos. 2–3 (1976), 122–32.

Bowery, Anne-Marie. "The Practical Self: A Test Case for Foucault," in *Analectra Husserliana: The yearbook of phenomenological research* LIV. Edited by A-T. Tymieniecka. New York: Springer Science & Business, 1995.

Brand, Madeleine. "Mary Harron and 'The Notorious Bettie Page'." *NPR,* April 14, 2006. Available: http://www.npr.org/templates/story/story.php?storyId=5342546

Bronson. Directed by Nicolas Winding Refn. Magnet Releasing, 2008.

Brown, Jeffrey A. "Class and Feminine Excess: The Strange Case of Anna Nicole Smith." *Feminist Review: Bodily Interventions* 81 (2015), 74–94.

Brown, Phil. "Director Interview: Mary Harron." *Now Magazine,* April 5, 2012. Available: https://nowtoronto.com/movies/features/director-interview-mary-harron/

Brunsdon, Charlotte. "Problems with Quality." *Screen* 31, No. 1 (1990), 67–90.

Bruzzi, Stella. *Undressing Cinema. Clothing and Identity in the Movies.* London and New York, 1997.
Bussmann, Kate. "Interview: Cutting Edge." *The Guardian* (2009). Accessed May, 23 2018. Available: https://www.theguardian.com/lifeandstyle/2009/mar/06/mary-harronfilm
Buszek, Maria Elena. *Pin-Up Grrls: Feminism, Sexuality, and Popular Culture.* Durham, NC: Duke University Press, 2006.
Butler, Judith. *Gender Trouble: Feminism and the Subversion of Identity.* New York: Routledge, 2006.
Caoduro, Elena. "'Women's Tales': Postfeminist Adventures into Consumerville." *Comunicazioni Sociali: Journal of Media, Performing Arts and Cultural Studies* 1 (2017), 37–42.
Captain Marvel. Directed by Anna Boden and Ryan Fleck. Walt Disney Studios Motion Pictures, 2019.
Cartmell, Deborah and Imelda Whelehan (eds). *The Cambridge Companion to Literature on Screen.* Cambridge: Cambridge University Press, 2007.
Casablanca. Directed by Michael Curtiz. Warner Bros., 1942.
Castello Cavalcalti. Directed by Wes Anderson. Prada, 2013.
Catch Me If You Can. Directed by Steven Spielberg. DreamWorks Pictures, 2002.
Caughie, John. *Theories of Authorship: A Reader.* London: Routledge, 1981.
Chaplin. Directed by Richard Attenborough. TriStar Pictures, 1992.
Chapple Alison and Sue Ziebland. "Viewing the Body After Bereavement Due to a Traumatic Death: Qualitative study in the UK." *BMJ*, No. 340 (2010).
Chenoune, Farid. *A History of Men's Fashion.* Translated by Richard Martin. Paris: Flammarion, 1993.
Cherniavsky, Eva. *Incorporations: Race, Nation, and the Body Politics of Capital.* Minneapolis: University of Minnesota, 2006.
Church Gibson, Pamela. "Brad Pitt and George Clooney. The Rough and the Smooth: Male Costuming in Contemporary Hollywood," in *Fashioning Film Stars. Dress, Culture, Identity.* Edited by Rachel Moseley. London: BFI Publishing, 2005, 62–74.
Clover, Carol J. Men. *Women and Chainsaws: Gender in the Modern Horror Film.* Princeton: Princeton University Press, 1992.
Color Me Kubrick. Directed by Brian Cook. Magnolia Pictures, 2005.
Come Together. Directed by Wes Anderson. H&M, 2016.
Connell, Raewyn. *Gender and Power: Society, the Person, and Sexual Politics.* Palo Alto: Stanford University Press, 1987.
Connell, R.W. *Masculinities.* 2nd Edition. London: Polity, 1995.
Creed, Barbara. *Phallic Panic: Film, Horror and the Primal Uncanny.* Carlton, Vic: Melbourne University Press, 2005.
Creed, Barbara. *The Monstrous-Feminine: Film, Feminism, Psychoanalysis.* New York: Routledge, 1993.
Crow, Charles L. *American Gothic (History of the Gothic).* Cardiff: University of Wales Press, 2009.
Currie, Mark. "Introduction," in *Metafiction.* Edited by Mark Currie. London: Longman, 1995.
Custen, George F. *Bio/Pics: How Hollywood Constructed Public History.* New Brunswick, NJ: Rutgers University Press, 1992.
D'Acci, Julie. "Introduction," in Special Issue on Lifetime: A Cable Network 'For Women.' *Camera Obscura: Feminism, Culture, and Media Studies* Vols. 11–12 (1994), 7–11.
Dancyger, Ken. *The Director's Idea: The Path to Great Directing.* Burlington, MA: Focal Press, 2006.

Debord, Guy. *The Society of the Spectacle*. Translated by Donald Nicholson-Smith. New York: Zone Books, 1994.
Doane, Mary Ann. *Femmes Fatales: Feminism, Film Theory, Psychoanalysis*. London: Routledge, 1991.
Dr. Doolittle. Directed by Richard Fleisher. Twentieth Century Fox, 1967.
Doctor Who. Created by Russell T. Davies. BBC, 2005–present.
Donkin, Richard. *The History of Work*. Berlin: Springer, 2010.
Douglas, Mary. *Purity and Danger: An analysis of concepts of pollution and taboo*. London: Routledge, 2003.
Dunlap, Rudy, and Corey W. Johnson. "Consuming contradiction: media, masculinity and (hetero)sexual identity." *Leisure/Loisir* 37, No. 1 (January 2013), 69–84.
Dyer, Richard. *Heavenly Bodies: Film Stars and Society*. 2nd Edition. London: Routledge, [1986] 2004.
Dyer, Richard. *White*. London: Routledge, 1997.
Easy Rider. Directed by Dennis Hopper. Columbia Pictures, 1969.
"*Easy Rider* Box Office." World Wide Box Office. Accessed April 4, 2018. http://www.worldwideboxoffice.com/movie.cgi?title=Easy%20Rider&year=1969
Ebert, Roger. "American Psycho." *Chicago Sun-Times*, April 14, 2000. Accessed February 15, 2017. Available: http://www.rogerebert.com/reviews/american-psycho-2000
Ed Wood. Directed by Tim Burton. Touchstone Pictures, 1994.
Edelman, Lee. *No Future: Queer Theory and the Death Drive*. Durham, NC: Duke University Press, 2004.
Ellis, Bret Easton. *American Psycho*. London: Vintage, 1991.
Entwistle, Joanne. *The Fashion Body*. 2nd Edition. Cambridge: Polity Press, 2015.
Extremely Wicked, Shockingly Evil and Vile. Directed by Joe Berlinger. COTA Films/Ninjas Runnin' Wild Productions/Voltage Pictures, 2018.
Faderman, Lillian. *Surpassing the Love of Men: Romantic Friendship and Love between Women from the Renaissance to the Present*. New York: Harper Paperbacks, 1998.
Fagan, Colette, Jacqueline O'Reilly, and Jill Rubery. "Part time work: Challenging the 'breadwinner' Gender Contract," in *The Gendering of Inequalities: Women, Men and Work*. Edited by Jane Jenson, Jacqueline Laufer, and Margaret Maruani. Farnham: Ashgate, 2000.
Faludi, Susan. *Stiff: The Betrayal of the Modern Man*. London: Chatto and Windus, 1999.
Farnsworth, Rodney. *The Infernal Return: The Recurrence of the Primordial in Films of the Reaction Years, 1977–1983*. Westport, CT: Praeger, 2002.
Fear Itself. Created by Mick Garris. NBC, 2001.
Fight Club. Directed by David Fincher. Twentieth Century Fox, 1999.
Fine, Gary Alan, and Michaela de Soucey. "Joking Cultures: Humor themes as social regulation in group life." *Humor: International Journal of Humor Research*, 18, No. 1 (2005), 1–22.
Fleetwood, Nicole R. *On Racial Icons: Blackness and the Public Imagination*. New Brunswick, NJ: Rutgers University Press, 2015.
Floti, Sorin. "Narcissism and Criminality on Wall Street: the Sociology of *American Psycho*." *Culturised* (2017). Accessed March 1, 2018. Available from: https://culturised.co.uk/2017/09/narcissism-and-criminality-on-wall-street-the-sociology-of-american-psycho/
Foltyn, Jacque Lynn. "Bodies of Evidence: Criminalizing the Celebrity Corpse." *Mortality* 21, No. 3 (2016), 246–62.
Foucault, Michel. *Discipline and Punish: The Birth of the Prison*. 2nd Edition. New York: Vintage Books, 1995.

Freccero, Carla. "Historical Violence, Censorship, and the Serial Killer: The Case of *American Psycho*." *Diacritics* 27, No. 2 (1997), 44–58.
French, Marilyn. *The Women's Room*. London: Sphere Books Ltd, 1978.
Gadon, Sarah. "Behind the Scenes." *The Moth Diaries*, DVD, directed by Mary Harron (2011; Montreal, QC., Canada: Alliance Film, 2012).
Gaines, Jane. "Costume and Narrative: How Dress Tells the Woman's Story," in *Fabrications: Costume and the Female Body*. Edited by Jane Gaines, and Charlotte Herzog. London and New York: Routledge, 1990.
Gerstner, David A., and Janet Staiger (eds). *Authorship and Film*. New York and London: Routledge, 2003.
Gilchrist, Todd. "American Psycho Director Mary Harron Talks Anna Nicole." *Hitflix*, February 20, 2014. http://uproxx.com/hitfix/american-psycho-director-mary-harrontalks-anna-nicole/
Ging, Debbie. "Alphas, Betas, and Incels: Theorizing the Masculinities of the Manosphere." *Men and Masculinities* 22, No. 4 (May 2017), 638–57.
Goffman, Erving. *The Presentation of the Self in Everyday Life*. Harmondsworth: Penguin Books Limited, 1959.
Grant, Barry Keith (ed.). *Auteurs and Authorships: A Film Reader*. Malden, MA and Oxford: Blackwell, 2008.
Greven, David. "'I Love You, Brom Bones': Beta Male Comedies and American Culture." *Quarterly Review of Film and Video* 30, No. 5 (June 2013), 405–20.
Gladiator. Directed by Ridley Scott. Dreamworks/Universal, 2000.
Go Fish. Directed by Rose Troche. Samuel Goldwyn Company, 1994.
Goldman, Robert, Deborah Heath, and Sharon L. Smith. "Commodity Feminism." *Critical Studies in Communication* 8 (1991), 333–51.
Gopalan, Nisha. "*American Psycho*: the story behind the film." *The Guardian* (2000). Accessed May 2, 2018. Available: https://www.theguardian.com/film/2000/mar/24/fiction.breteastonellis
Griggers, Camilla. *Becoming-Woman*. Minneapolis: University of Minnesota Press, 1997.
Gross, Anisse. "Mary Harron: 'Mostly I'm just not American'," *Believer* (2014). Accessed November, 2017. Available: https://www.believermag.com/issues/201403/?read=interview_harron
Haight, Sarah. "WWD: Women's Wear Daily." *Los Angeles* 196, No. 125 (2008), 14.
Halberstam, Judith. *Skin Shows: Gothic Horror and the Technology of Monsters*. Durham, NC: Duke University Press, 1995.
Harrington, Erin. *Women, Monstrosity and Horror Film: Gynaehorror (Film Philosophy at the Margins)*. New York: Routledge, 2017.
Harris, Mark. *Grave Matters: A journey through the modern funeral industry to a natural way of burial*. New York: Scribner, 2007.
Harron, Mary. Interview by Nicolas Rapold on *Charlie Says/Film Comment Talk*. Film at Lincoln Center, May 17, 2019. Video: 49.26. https://www.youtube.com/watch?v=IKXJV9ByyCY
Harron, Mary. "Introduction," in *I Shot Andy Warhol* (Screenplay), Mary Harron, and Daniel Minahan. London: Bloomsbury Publishing, 1996.
Harron, Mary, Guinevere Turner, Marianne Rendon, and Hannah Murray. "The Film Charlie Says." Interview by Ricky Camilleri. *Build series NYC*. YouTube. Filmed at 692 Broadway, New York, May 1, 2019. Video: 27.22. https://www.youtube.com/watch?v=NILkGykqZl8
Heaven's Gate. Directed by Michael Cimino. United Artists, 1980.

Heine Steven. J., Travis Proulx, and Kathleen D. Vohs. "The Meaning Maintenance Model: On the Coherence of Social Motivations." *Personality and Social Psychology Review* 10, No. 2 (2006), 88–110.

Heise, Thomas. "*American Psycho*: Neoliberal Fantasies and the Death of Downtown." *Arizona Quarterly: A Journal of American Literature, Culture, and Theory* 67, No. 1 (2011), 135–60.

Heller, Dana. "Shooting Solanas: Radical Feminist History and the Technology of Failure," in *Feminist Time against Nation Time: Gender, Politics, and the Nation State in an Age of Permanent War*. Edited by Victoria Hesford, and Lisa Diedrich. Lanham, MD: Lexington Books, 2008.

Hewitt, Nancy A. "Solanas, Valerie," in *Notable American Women: A Biographical Dictionary Completing the Twentieth Century*, Vol. 5. Edited by Susan Ware. Cambridge, MA: Harvard University Press, 2004.

High School Musical. Directed by Kenny Ortega. Disney, 2006.

Hoberman, J. "The Other Charles Manson Movie Has a Lot to Say." *The New York Times*. Accessed April 28, 2020. Available: https://www.nytimes.com/2019/11/19/movies/charlie-says-mary-harron.html

Hogle, Jerrold. "Introduction: Modernity and the Proliferation of the Gothic," in *The Cambridge Companion to the Modern Gothic*. Edited by Jerrold Hogle. Cambridge: Cambridge University Press, 2014.

Holmes, Sue, and Diane Negra. "Introduction," in *The Limelight and Under the Microscope: Forms and Functions of Female Celebrity*. Edited by Sue Holmes, and Diane Negra. New York: Continuum, 2011.

Homicide: Life on the Street. Created by Paul Attanasio. NBC, 1993–99.

House of Cards. Created by Beau Willimon. Netflix, 2013–18.

Hurd, Mary G. *Women Directors and their Films*, Westport: Praeger Publishers, 2007.

Huyssen, Andreas. *After the Great Divide: Modernism, Mass Culture, Post-Modernism*. Bloomington: Indiana University Press, 1986.

I'll Cry Tomorrow. Directed by Daniel Mann. Metro-Goldwyn-Mayer, 1955.

Imre, Anikó. "Gender and Quality Television." *Feminist Media Studies* 9, No. 4 (2009), 391–407.

Iocco, Melissa. "Addicted to Affliction: Masculinity and Perversity in *Crash* and *Fight Club*." *Gothic Studies* 1, Vol. 9 (2007), 46–56.

Jaws. Directed by Steven Spielberg. Universal Pictures, 1975.

Joyrich, Lynne. "All That Television Allows: TV, Melodrama, Postmodernism, and Consumer Culture," in *Private Screenings: Television and the Female Consumer*. Edited by Lynn Spigel, and Denise Mann. Minneapolis: Minnesota University Press, 1992.

Juarez. Directed by William Dieterle. Warner Bros., 1939.

Kapica, Steven S. "Multivalent Feminism of *The Notorious Bettie Page*." *Jump Cut: A Review of Contemporary Media*, No. 55 (Fall 2013).

Kaplan, E. Ann. "Troubling Genre/Reconstructing Gender," in *Gender Meets Genre in Postwar Cinema*. Edited by Christine Gledhill. Urbana: University of Illinois Press, 2012.

Kavka, Misha. *Reality TV*. Edinburgh: Edinburgh University Press, 2012.

Kelley, Suzanna. *Greening Death*. Lanham, MD: Rowman & Littlefield Publishers, 2017.

Kennedy, Todd. "Off with Hollywood's Head: Sofia Coppola as Feminine Auteur." *Film Criticism* 35, Vol. 1 (2010), 37–59.

Khan, Natalie. "Cutting the Fashion Body: Why the Fashion Image is No Longer Still." *Fashion Theory* 16, No. 2 (2012), 235–50.

King, Geoff. *Indiewood USA: Where Hollywood Meets Independent Cinema*. London: I. B. Tauris, 2009.

King, Geoff. *New Hollywood Cinema: An Introduction*. London and York: I. B. Tauris, 2002.

King, Larry. "Interview with Anna Nicole Smith." *Larry King Live* (CNN), May 29, 2002. http://edition.cnn.com/TRANSCRIPTS/0205/29/lkl.00.html/
Klein, Rachel. *The Moth Diaries*. New York: Bantam Books, 2002.
Králová, Jana. "Why We Need to Find a Cure for 'Social Death'." *The Conversation* (2016). Accessed March 28, 2018. Available: https://theconversation.com/why-we-need-to-find-a-cure-for-social-death-59997.
Králová, Jana. "What is Social Death?" *Contemporary Social Science* 10, No. 3 (2015), 235, 248.
Kristeva, Julia. *Powers of Horror: An Essay On Abjection (European Perspectives Series)*. Reprinted Edition. New York: Columbia University Press, 1982.
Kolker, Robert. *A Cinema of Loneliness*. 4th Edition. New York: Oxford University Press, 2011.
Krämer, Peter. *The New Hollywood: From Bonnie and Clyde to Star Wars*. New York and Chichester: Columbia University Press, 2005.
Kuhn, Annette. *Women's Pictures: Feminism and Cinema*. London: Pandora, 1982.
Kurlansky, Mark. *1968: The Year that Rocked the World*. London: Vintage Random House Publishing, 2005.
Lady Sings the Blues. Directed by Sidney J. Furie. Paramount Pictures, 1972.
Laine, Tarja. *Shame and Desire: Emotion, Intersubjectivity, Cinema*. Brussels: P.I.E. Peter Lang, 2007.
Landis, Deborah Nadoolman. *Screencraft: Costume Design*. Burlington, MA: Focal Press, 2003.
Lang, Alison. "Mary Harron." *Cutthroat Women: A Database of Women who Make Horror* (2018). Accessed April 2, 2019. Available: https://www.cutthroatwomen.org/harron 2018
Laverty, Christopher. *Fashion in Film*. London: Laurence King Publishing, 2017.
Leave No Trace. Directed by Debra Granik. Bleecker Street, 2018.
Lee, Dan P. "Paw Paw & Lady Love." *New York Magazine*, June 5, 2011. Accessed February 10, 2018. Available: http://nymag.com/news/features/anna-nicole-smith-2011-6/
Lee, Theresa Man Ling "Feminism: Government and Politics." *Encyclopedia of Life Support Systems (EOLSS)*. Edited by Masashi Sekiguchi. Oxford. Published 2002. Accessed January 17, 2011. Available: http://www.eolss.net
Leiss, William, Stephen Kline, and Sut Jhally. *Social Communication in Advertising: Persons, products and images of well-being*. New York: Routledge, 1997.
Leitch, Thomas. *Film Adaptation and Its Discontents: From Gone With the Wind to The Passion of the Christ*. Baltimore: Johns Hopkins University Press, 2009.
Leong, Melissa. "*The Moth Diaries*: Mary Harron and Lily Cole on Vampires as a Metaphor." *National Post*, April 4, 2012. Available: http://nationalpost.com/entertainment/the-moth-diaries-mary-harron-and lily-cole-on-vampires-as-a-metaphor
Levy, Emanuel. *Cinema of Outsiders: The Rise of American Independent Cinema*. New York: New York University Press, 1999.
Liz & Dick. Directed by Lloyd Kramer. Lifetime, 2012.
McCabe, Janet and Kim Akass. "Introduction: Debating Quality," in *Quality Television: Contemporary American Television and Beyond*. Edited by Janet McCabe, and Kim Akass. London: I. B. Tauris, 2007.
McFarlane, Brian. *Novel to Film: An Introduction to the Theory of Adaptation*. Oxford: Clarendon Press, 1996.
McGowan, Todd. *The Real Gaze: Film Theory After Lacan*. Albany: State University of New York Press, 2008.
Maclean, Kate. "Gender, Risk and the Wall Street Alpha Male." *Journal of Gender Studies* 25, No. 4 (January 2015), 427–44.
McManus, Ruth. *Death in a Global Age*. Basingstoke: Palgrave Macmillan, 2013.
Madame Curie. Directed by Mervyn LeRoy. Metro-Goldwyn-Mayer, 1943.
Magnolia. Directed by Paul Thomas Anderson, 1999.

Man on the Moon. Directed by Miloš Forman. Universal Pictures, 1999.

Marie Antoinette. Directed by Sofia Coppola. Sony Pictures Releasing, 2006.

Maron, Marc. "Bret Easton Ellis." *WTF with Marc Maron*. Episode 552. November 20, 2014. Accessed February15, 2017. Available: http://www.wtfpod.com/podcast/episodes/episode_552_-_bret_easton_ellis

Marriott, Hannah. "Margaret Atwood: the unlikely style soothsayer of 2017." *The Guardian*, December 27, 2017. Accessed July 1, 2018. Available: https://www.theguardian.com/fashion/2017/dec/27/margaret-atwood-the-unlikely-style-soothsayer-of-2017

Meehan, Eileen R. and Jackie Bryars. "Telefeminism: How Lifetime Got Its Groove 1984–1987." *Television and New Media* 1, No. 1 (2000), 33–51.

Memento. Directed by Christopher Nolan. Newmarket, 2000.

Messner, Michael A., and James W. Messerschimdt. "Hegemonic, nonhegemonic and 'new' masculinities," in *Gender Reckonings: New social theory and research*. Edited by James W. Messerschmidt, Patricia Yancy Martin, Michael A. Messner, and Raewyn Connell. New York: New York University Press, 2017.

Meyerowitz, Joanne. "Women, Cheesecake, and Borderline Material: Responses to Girlie Pictures in the Mid-Twentieth-Century U.S." *Journal of Women's History* 8, No. 3 (1999), 9–35.

Mijovic, Nikola. "Narrative forms and the rhetoric of fashion in the promotional fashion film." *Film, Fashion & Consumption* 2, No. 2 (2013), 175–86.

Mills, Charles Wright. *White Collar: The American Middle Class*. New York: Oxford University Press, 1956.

Mindhunter. Created by Joe Penhall. Netflix, 2017–present.

Mitford, Jessica. *The American Way of Death*. New York: Simon & Schuster, 1963.

Moore, Booth. "Unfashioning Costume Design," in *Hollywood Costume*. Edited by Deborah Nadoolman Landis. London: V&A Publishing, 2012.

Mui, Sian. "Dead Body Language: Positioning, posture, and representation of the corpse." *Theoretical Archaeology Group Conference* (2016) Southampton, December 19–21, 2016. Accessed March 24, 2018. Available: https://www.southampton.ac.uk/tag2016/sessionsabstracts/session3.page

Mulvey, Laura. *Fetishism and Curiosity*. London: Indiana University Press, 1996.

Mulvey, Laura. "Visual Pleasures and Narrative Cinema," in *Issues in Feminist Film Criticism*. Edited by Patricia Erens. Bloomington: Indiana University Press, 1991.

Mulvey, Laura. "Visual Pleasures and Narrative Cinema." *Screen* 16, No. 3 (1975), 6–18.

Natural Born Killers. Directed by Oliver Stone. Warner Bros., 1994.

Needham, Gary. "The Digital Fashion Film," in *Fashion Cultures Revisited: Theories, Explorations and Analysis*, 2nd Edition. Edited by Stella Bruzzi, and Pamela Church Gibson. London and New York: Routledge, 2013.

Negrin, Llewellyn. *Appearance and Identity: Fashioning the Body in Postmodernity*. New York: Palgrave Macmillan, 2008.

Newman, Michael Z. *Indie: An American Film Culture*. New York: Columbia University Press, 2011.

Night Moves. Directed by Kelly Reichardt. Cinedigm, 2013.

Once Upon a Time In . . . Hollywood. Directed by Quentin Tarantino. Columbia Pictures, 2019.

Orange, B. Alan. "Anna Nicole: Exclusive Interview with Director Mary Harron." *MovieWeb*. Accessed December 6, 2016. Available: http://movieweb.com/anna-nicole-exclusive-interview-with-director-mary-harron/

Ortner, Sherry B. "Against Hollywood: American Independent Film as a Critical Cultural Movement." *HAU: Journal of Ethnographic Theory* 2, No. 2 (2012), 1–21.

Pasadena. Created by Mike White. Fox, 2001.
Paszkiewicz, Katarzyna. *Genre Authorship and Contemporary Women Filmmakers*. Edinburgh: Edinburgh University Press, 2019.
Patterson, Orlando. *Slavery and Social Death: A comparative study*. Cambridge, MA: Harvard University Press, 1985.
Perkins, Claire. "Beyond Indiewood: The Everyday Ethics of Nicole Holofcener." *Camera Obscura*, 85, Vol. 29, No. 1 (2014), 137–59.
Piercy, Gemma. L. *Baristas: The artisan precariat*. PhD Thesis, University of Waikato, Hamilton, New Zealand. Accessed March 8, 2020. Available: https://researchcommons.waikato.ac.nz/handle/10289/12038
Pierson, John. *Spike Mike Reloaded: A Guided Tour Across a Decade of American Independent Cinema*. New York: Miramax Books, 2003.
Plan 9 from Outer Space. Directed by Edward D. Wood, Jr. Valiant Pictures, 1959.
Poison. Directed by Todd Haynes. Zeitgeist Films, 1991.
Pravadelli, Veronica. "US Independent Women's Cinema, Sundance Girls, and Identity Politics," in *Feminisms: Diversity, Difference and Multiplicity in Contemporary Film Cultures*. Edited by Laura Mulvey, and Anna Backman Rogers. Amsterdam: Amsterdam University Press, 2015.
"Production Notes: *The Notorious Bettie Page*." Dendy Films, March 8, 2007.
Psycho. Directed by Alfred Hitchcock. Paramount Pictures, 1960.
Pulp Fiction. Directed by Quentin Tarantino. Miramax Films, 1994.
Punter, Jennie. "The Monday Q&A: Mary Harron." *The Globe and Mail* (2011). Accessed May 24, 2018. Available: https://www.theglobeandmail.com/arts/the-monday-qa-mary harron/article600379/
Queen Christina. Directed by Rouben Mamoulian. Metro-Goldwyn-Mayer, 1933.
Quinnette, Celia. "3 Questions with American Psycho Director Mary Harron." *Sundance TV*. December 31, 2014. Accessed February 15, 2017. Available: http://www.sundance.tv/blog/2014/12/3-questions with-american-psycho-director-mary-harron
Rambo: First Blood. Directed by Ted Kotcheff. Orion Pictures, 1982.
Ramey, Mark. *Studying Fight Club*. Leighton Buzzard: Auteur, 2012.
Redmond, Sean. "The Whiteness of Stars: Looking at Kate Winslet's Unruly White Body," in *Stardom and Celebrity: A Reader*. Edited by Sean Redmond, and Sue Holmes. London: Sage, 2007.
Rembrandt. Directed by Alexander Korda. United Artists, 1936.
Reservoir Dogs. Directed by Quentin Tarantino. Miramax Films, 1992.
Revolutionary Road. Directed by Sam Mendes. Vantage Paramount/Disney Films, 2008.
Risman Barbara J. "Gender as a Social Structure," in *Handbook of the Sociology of Gender*. Edited by Barbara Risman, Carissa Froyum, and William Scarborough. Cham: Springer, 2018.
Robinson, David. "The Unattainable Narrative: Identity, Consumerism and the Slasher Film in Mary Harron's *American Psycho*." *Cineaction* 68 (2006), 26–35.
Rogers, Martin. "Video Nasties and the Monstrous Bodies of *American Psycho*." *Literature Film Quarterly* 39, No. 3 (2011), 231–44.
Rojek, Chris. *Celebrity*. London: Reaktion Books, 2001.
Rose, Jacqueline. "I am a knife." *London Review of Books* Vol. 40, No. 4. Accessed February 22, 2018.
Rose, Sonya O. "Gender at work: Sex, class and industrial capitalism." *History Workshop Journal* 21 (Spring 1986), 113–31.
Rutter, Virginia. E., and Braxton Jones. "The Sexuality of Gender," in *Handbook of the Sociology of Gender*. Edited by Barbara Risman, Carissa Froyum, and William Scarborough. Cham: Springer, 2018.

Saito, Steven. "The Moveable Fest: Interview: Mary Harron and Guinevere Turner on Restoring the Female Voice to History in 'Charlie Says'." Accessed May 4, 2020. http://moveablefest.com/mary-harron-guinevere-turner-charlie-says/

Sarris, Andrew. *The American Cinema: Directors and Directions, 1929–1968*. New York: Dutton, 1968.

Sartre, Jean-Paul. *Being and Nothingness*. Reprinted Edition. New York: Washington Square Press, 1993.

Schatz, Thomas. "Going Mainstream: The Indie Film Movement in 1999," in *A Companion to American Indie Film*. Edited by Geoff King. Chichester: John Wiley & Sons, 2017.

Schatz, Thomas. "Conglomerate Hollywood and American Independent Film," in *American Independent Cinema: Indie, Indiewood and Beyond*. Edited by Geoff King, Claire Molloy, and Yannis Tzioumakis. Abingdon: Routledge, 2013

Schilling, Dave. "*American Psycho*'s Morning Ritual: Would Patrick Bateman's routine work today?" *The Guardian* (2016). Accessed March 14, 2018. Available: https://www.theguardian.com/stage/2016/apr/22/american-psycho-musical-film-morning-routine-patrick-bateman.

Schreiber, Michele. "'I'm Absolutely the Right Person for this Job': Allison Anders and Mary Harron on Lifetime Television," in *Indie Reframed: Women's Filmmaking and Contemporary American Independent Cinema*. Edited by Linda Badley, Claire Perkins, and Michele Schreiber. Edinburgh: Edinburgh University Press, 2016.

Schreiber, Michele. "Their Own Personal Velocity," in *American Independent Cinema: Indie, Indiewood and Beyond*. Edited by Geoff King, Claire Molloy, and Yannis Tzioumakis. Abingdon: Routledge, 2013.

Sconce, Jeffrey. "Irony, nihilism and the new American 'smart' film." *Screen* 43, Vol. 4 (2002), 349–69.

Scream. Directed by Wes Craven. Dimension Films, 1996.

Segal, Lynne. *Slow Motion: Changing Masculinities, Changing Men*. 3rd Edition. Basingstoke: Palgrave Macmillan, 2007.

Seidler, Victor J. "Differences: Feminisms/enemies/equalities," in *Embodying Identities: Culture, differences and social theory*. Bristol: The Policy Press, 2010.

Sellors, Paul C. "Collective Authorship in Film." *Journal of Aesthetics and Art Criticism* 65, No. 3 (2007), 263–71.

Seltzer, Mark. *Serial Killers: Death and Life in America's Wound Culture*. New York: Routledge, 1998.

Se7en. Directed by David Fincher. New Line Cinema, 1995.

Sex and the City. Created by Darren Starr. HBO, 1998–2004.

Sex, lies, and videotape. Directed by Steven Soderbergh. Miramax Films, 1989.

Silence of the Lambs. Directed by Jonathan Demme. Orion Pictures, 1991.

Silverstein, Melissa. "Interview with Mary Harron—Director of *The Moth Diaries*." *IndieWire*, April 18, 2012, Available: http://www.indiewire.com/2012/04/interview-with-mary-harron-director-of-the-moth-diaries-211491/

Simpson, Philip L. *Psycho Paths: Tracking the Serial Killer Through Contemporary American Film and Television*. Carbondale: Southern Illinois University Press, 2000.

Six Feet Under. Created by Alan Ball. HBO, 2001–2005.

Sliding Doors. Directed by Peter Hewitt. Miramax Films, 1998.

Slocum, Joshua, and Lisa Carlson. *Final Rights: Reclaiming the American Way of Death*. Hinesburg, VT: Upper Access Books, 2011.

Smith, Frances, and Timothy Shary. "Introduction," in *ReFocus: The Films of Amy Heckerling*. Edited by Frances Smith, and Timothy Shary. Edinburgh: Edinburgh University Press, 2016.

Solanas, Valeris, *SCUM Manifesto*. Paris: Olympia Press, 1967.
Solanas, Valerie. "A Young Girl's Primer, or How to Attain the Leisure Class." *Cavalier*, July 1966.
Solomon-Godeau, Abigail. "The Other Side of Venus: The Visual Economy of Sexual Display," in *The Sex of Things: Gender and Consumption in Historical Perspective*. Edited by Victoria de Grazia. Berkeley: University of California Press, 1996
Spigel, Lynn. *Welcome to the Dreamhouse: Popular Media and Postwar Suburbs*. Durham, NC: Duke University Press, 2001.
Stabile, Carol A. "Getting What She Deserved: The News Media, Martha Stewart, and Masculine Domination." *Feminist Media Studies* 4, No. 3 (2004), 315–32.
Staiger, Janet. "Independent of What? Sorting out Difference from Hollywood," in *American Independent Cinema: Indie, Indiewood and Beyond*. Edited by Geoff King, Claire Molloy, and Yannis Tzioumakis. Abingdon: Routledge, 2013.
Star Wars. Directed by George Lucas. Twentieth Century Fox, 1977.
Storey, Mark. "'And As Things Fell Apart': The Crisis of Postmodern Masculinity in Bret Easton Ellis' *American Psycho* and Dennis Cooper's *Frisk*." *Critique* 47, No. 1 (2005), 57–72.
Street, Sara. *Costume and Cinema: Dress Codes in Popular Film*. London: Wallflower Press, 2001.
Tabb, William K. "The Criminality of Wall Street." *Monthly Review* 66, No. 4 (2014). Accessed March 1, 2018. Available: https://monthlyreview.org/2014/09/01/thecriminality-of-wall-street/
Taxi Driver. Directed by Martin Scorsese. Columbia Pictures, 1976.
Taylor, Trey. "How *American Psycho* Became a Feminist Statement." *Dazed* (2014). Accessed February 15, 2017. Available: http://www.dazeddigital.com/artsandculture/article/20751/1/how-american-psychobecame-a-feminist-statement
The Anna Nicole Show. Produced by Darren Ewing, Kevin Hayes, and Mark McDermott. E!, 2002–2004.
The Assassination of Richard Nixon. Directed by Niels Mueller. ThinkFilm, 2004.
The Aviator. Directed by Martin Scorsese. Miramax Films, 2004.
The Beach. Directed by Danny Boyle. Twentieth Century Fox, 1999.
The Doors. Directed by Oliver Stone. TriStar Pictures, 1991.
The Exorcist. Directed by William Friedkin. Warner Bros., 1973.
The Graduate. Directed by Mike Nichols. United Artists, 1967.
The Handmaid's Tale. Created by Bruce Miller. Hulu, 2017–present.
The Haunting of Sharon Tate. Directed by Daniel Farrands. Skyline Entertainment, 2019.
The Hurt Locker. Directed by Kathryn Bigelow. Summit Entertainment, 2008.
The L Word. Created by Ilene Chaiken, Michele Abbot, and Kathy Greenberg. Showtime, 2004–2009.
The Lady with a Lamp. Directed by Herbert Wilcox. British Lion Films, 1951.
The Life of Emile Zola. Directed by William Dieterle. Warner Bros., 1937.
The Limey. Directed by Steven Soderbergh. Artisan Entertainment, 1999.
The Office. Created by Ricky Gervais and Stephen Merchant. BBC, 2001–2003.
The People vs. Larry Flynt. Directed by Miloš Forman. Columbia Pictures, 1996.
The Scarlet Empress. Directed by Josef von Sternberg. Paramount Pictures, 1934.
The Sound of Music. Directed by Robert Wise. Twentieth Century Fox, 1965.
The South Bank Show. ITV Studios/Sky Arts, 1978–present.
The Story of Louis Pasteur. Directed by William Dieterle. Warner Bros., 1936.
The Texas Chainsaw Massacre. Directed by Tobe Hooper. Bryanston Pictures, 1974.
The Twilight Saga: Breaking Dawn—Part 2. Directed by Bill Condon. Summit Entertainment, 2012.

This Is 40. Directed by Judd Apatow. Universal Pictures, 2012.

Three Kings. Directed by David O. Russell. Warner Bros., 1999.

Truffaut, François. "A Certain Tendency of the French Cinema," in *Movies and Methods: An Anthology*. Edited by Bill Nichols. Vol. 1. Berkeley: University of California Press, 1975.

Tungate, Mark. *Fashion Brands: Branding Style from Armani to Zara*. London: Kogan Page, 2012.

Turner, Graeme. *Understanding Celebrity*. 2nd Edition. Los Angeles: SAGE, 2014.

Tzioumakis, Yannis. "Between 'indiewood' and 'nowherewood': American independent cinema in the twenty-first century." *International Journal of Media & Cultural Politics* 10, No. 3 (2014), 285–300.

Uhlirova, Marketa. "100 Years of the Fashion Film: Frameworks and Histories." *Fashion Theory* 17, No. 2 (2013), 137–58.

Vineyard, Jennifer. "How a Pink Dress Made It Into Margaret Atwood's Murder Mystery." *Racked.com*, November 30, 2017. Accessed July 1, 2018. Available: https://www.racked.com/2017/11/30/16715278/alias-grace-costumes

Vonnegut, Kurt. *Slaughterhouse-Five, or, The Children's Crusade: A Duty Dance with Death*. London: Vintage, [1969] 1991.

Wagner-Martin, Linda. *Telling Women's Lives: The New Biography*. New Brunswick, NJ: Rutgers University Press, 1994.

Waugh, Patricia. *Metafiction: The Theory and Practice of Self-Conscious Fiction*. London: Routledge, 1984.

Waxman, Sharon. *Rebels on the Backlot: Six Maverick Directors and How They Conquered the Hollywood Studio System*. New York: HarperCollins, 2005.

Wes Craven's New Nightmare. Directed by Wes Craven. New Line Films, 1994.

White, Abbey. "*The Hollywood Reporter: Charlie Says*' Director Mary Harron Talks Depicting the 'Tiny Choices' of the Manson Women." Accessed April 28, 2020. Available: https://www.hollywoodreporter.com/news/charlie-says-director-maryharron-interview-1209251

White, Patricia. "Killer Feminism," in *Indie Reframed: Women's Filmmaking and Contemporary American Independent Cinema*. Edited by Linda Badley, Claire Perkins, and Michelle Schreiber. Edinburgh: Edinburgh University Press, 2016.

White, Patricia. *Women's Cinema, World Cinema: Projecting Contemporary Feminisms*. Durham, NC: Duke University Press, 2015.

Williams, Linda. "When the Woman Looks," in *The Dread of Difference: Gender and the Horror Film*. 2nd Edition. Edited by Barry Keith Grant. Austin: University of Texas Press, 2015, 17–36.

Williams, Raymond. "Dominant, residual and emergent," in *Marxism and Literature*. Oxford: Oxford University Press, 1977.

Willis, Susan. *A Primer for Daily Life*. New York: Routledge, 1991.

Wissinger, Elizabeth A. *This Year's Model: Fashion, Media, and the Making of Glamor*. New York: New York University Press, 2015.

Wissinger, Elizabeth A. "Managing the semiotics of skin tone: Race and aesthetic labor in the fashion modeling industry." *Economic and Industrial Democracy* 33, No. 1 (January 2012), 125–43.

Wonder Woman. Directed by Patty Jenkins. Warner Bros., 2017.

Wonder Woman: 1984. Directed by Patty Jenkins. Warner Bros., 2020.

Young, Elizabeth. "The Beast in the Jungle, the Figure in the Carpet: Bret Easton Ellis' *American Psycho*," in *Shopping in Space: Essays on America's "Blank Generation" Fiction*. Edited by Elizabeth Young, and Graham Caveney. New York: Atlantic Monthly Press/Serpent's Tail, 1993.

Young, Elizabeth, and Graham Caveney. *Shopping in Space: Essays on American "Blank Generation" Fiction*. London: Serpent's Tail, 1992.
Young, Neil. "*The Moth Diaries*: Venice Film Review." *Hollywood Reporter* (2011). Accessed May 23, 2018. Available: https://www.hollywoodreporter.com/review/mothdiariesvenice-film-review-231656
Yuko, Elizabeth. "Rolling Stone: Manson Family Movies: 11 Streaming Films Go Inside Terrifying 1969 Cult." Accessed April 20, 2020. Available: https://www.rollingstone.com/movies/movie-lists/manson-family-movies-streaming-864045/

Index

advertising, 147–8
aesthetics, 4, 9–10, 40, 57, 70, 84, 97
   cinematography, 3, 7, 26, 58, 62, 68–9
   mise en scène, 66, 100, 142
   visual style, 4, 62, 66, 68
Alias Grace (CBC, 2017), 7, 11, 90, 141–4; *see also* Atwood, Margaret
American Beauty (DreamWorks Pictures, Mendes, 1999), 60, 126
American Horror Story (FX, 2011–present), 24
American Psycho (Lions Gate Films, Harron, 2000) 5–6, 9–11, 26, 57, 63–4, 66, 70, 74–87, 89, 114, 119, 123–37, 141, 144–5, 153
   adaptation, 5, 10, 63–4, 67, 74–87, 125–6, 128, 137
   music, 83–4
   yuppie, 5, 63, 75–7, 85, 126, 141; *see also* horror genre
American Splendor (Fine Line Features & HBO Films, Berman & Pulcini, 2003), 22

Anderson, Paul Thomas, 5, 56
Anderson, Wes, 56, 147
Anna Nicole (Lifetime, Harron, 2013), 3, 8–10, 17–18, 22, 24–6, 28–31, 34–49, 89–90, 97, 103, 106, 114
   glamor, 25, 38, 40, 43, 47
   Lifetime, 3, 9–10, 17, 29–30, 37, 40
   Marshall II, J. Howard, 9, 35
   Monroe, Marilyn, 25, 40, 42–5, 48
   Smith, Anna Nicole, 9, 17, 22, 24–6, 28–31, 35–49
The Anna Nicole Show (E! Entertainment Network, 2002–4), 9, 48;
   see also celebrity; fame
Armani (Harron, 2012), 11, 140–58
   Armani, Georgio, 11, 141–2, 148–53
   fashion, 140–58
   short film, 10–11, 149, 152–3
Atwood, Margaret, 90, 142, 143
authorship, 1, 11, 58, 60, 141, 143–4, 146, 148
auteur theory, 146–8

Basquiat (Miramax Films, Schnabel, 1996), 10, 57, 61, 62–3, 70
Bale, Christian, 5, 64, 66, 75, 80, 83, 118, 126, 145
Bateman, Patrick (character), 5, 11, 63–6, 75–6, 79–87, 125–35, 137, 145–6
BBC, 2, 63, 108, 134
Bingham, Dennis, 19, 20–2, 30
Bonnie and Clyde (Warner Bros., Penn, 1967), 4, 58
Bruzzi, Stella, 140, 142, 151–2

CBC (Canadian Broadcast Corporation), 2, 7
celebrity, 3, 9–10, 18, 20, 22–3, 29–31, 34–6, 38–9, 40–1, 43–6, 48–9, 62, 64, 147
  fame, 3, 9, 10, 17–19, 20–5, 27–8, 30–1, 43, 62–3, 69
Chaplin (TriStar Pictures, Attenborough, 1992), 23–4
Charlie Says (IFC Films, Harron, 2018), 9, 11, 26, 105–20
class, 2, 25, 38–9, 41, 43, 65, 68, 112, 140, 142–3, 145
Coppola, Francis Ford, 55
Coppola, Sofia, 1, 10, 57, 67–8

Dyer, Richard, 34, 40, 44

Easy Rider (Columbia Pictures, Hopper, 1969), 4, 58–9
Ebert, Roger, 5
Ed Wood (Touchstone Pictures, Burton, 1994), 18–19, 22, 31
Ellis, Brett Easton, 5, 63, 74, 76, 78–80, 83, 87, 125, 131
  American Psycho (novel, 1991) 5, 63–4, 66, 74, 77, 78–80, 81–7, 125

Fear Itself (NBC, 2008), 89
  "Community" (episode), 89
femininity, 10, 35–7, 40–1, 44, 46, 67, 75, 77, 106–8, 108, 111–12, 114, 117, 119–20
feminism, 2, 5, 34, 37, 39, 63, 84, 86–7, 106–7
  feminist, 2–3, 5, 17–18, 34–5, 37, 39, 40, 76, 80, 86–7, 90, 107, 136, 153
Fight Club (Twentieth Century Fox, Fincher, 1999), 10, 57, 63–7, 70; see also masculinity
Fincher, David, 7, 10, 57, 64–6, 75, 79
First Blood (Orion Pictures, Kotcheff, 1982), 75–6
Foucault, Michel, 11, 91–3
French New Wave, 58

gaze, 28, 57, 67–9, 70, 80, 82, 86, 92–4, 116, 128, 149–50
  female, 81, 93, 142
  male, 7–8, 67, 81, 93, 108
  social, 28–9
gender, 2, 11, 21, 35, 39, 41, 76, 78, 82, 93, 103, 111–14, 117, 119–20, 140, 142, 144
  gendered metafiction, 10, 74–87
  performance, 107–8, 110, 113
  power relations, 105–20
  social construction, 77;
  see also feminism and masculinity
genre, 1–3, 6, 9, 37, 39–41, 57–8, 60, 63, 70, 76, 81, 95, 144, 146, 148, 153
  anti-biopic, 10, 17–31
  biopic, 3, 7–9, 10, 17–31, 35, 38, 57, 62, 67, 90, 105
  crime, 4, 60
  horror, 5–6, 8, 24, 66, 70, 76, 81, 84, 89, 95–6, 99, 101, 146, 153
  thriller, 60

174 INDEX

Gladiator (DreamWorks Pictures, Scott, 2000), 75–6
Go Fish (Samuel Goldwyn Company, Troche, 1994), 3, 5, 61, 63, 125

Harris, Jared, 3, 61, 69
Harris, Mark, 129, 131
Harron, Dan, 2
Haynes, Todd, 60–1
Heaven's Gate (United Artists, Cimino, 1980), 4, 59
Hollywood cinema, 1–2, 4, 38, 40, 55, 57–8, 60, 64, 80, 105
  big budget, 57
  blockbuster, 1, 59, 60
  classical, 19, 21, 25, 142
  independent, 1–7, 5, 7, 34, 55–61, 71, 76
  Indiewood, 5–6, 10, 55, 56–61, 63–4, 70–1
  New Hollywood, 4–5, 55–6, 58–9
  system, 4, 55, 58–9
Hopper, Dennis, 4, 58

I Shot Andy Warhol (Samuel Goldwyn Company, Harron, 1996), 3, 5, 7, 10, 17–31, 57, 61–2, 67–70, 76, 89–90, 93, 97, 103, 106, 108, 136, 141
  assassination, 2, 62
  mental illness, 23, 27;
  see also Warhol, Andy; Solanas, Valerie

Jaws (Universal Pictures, Spielberg, 1975), 4, 55, 59
Jonze, Spike, 5, 56
Juarez (Warner Bros., Dieterle, 1939), 19

King, Geoff, 5, 55
Klein, Rachel, 8, 89, 91, 102–3
Koffler, Pamela, 3, 61

Lee, Spike, 147
LGBTQ+, 3, 29, 61, 91, 95, 99–100, 102–3, 111–12
  New Queer Cinema, 3, 57, 61
  same-sex desire, 89, 91, 95–6, 98–9, 101–3

Man on the Moon (Universal Pictures, Forman, 1999), 18, 20
Manson, Charles, 22, 26, 105–20;
  see also masculinity; alpha and beta males; *Charlie Says*
Marie Antoinette (Sony Pictures, Coppola, 2005), 10, 57, 67–70
masculinity, 10, 31, 43, 63–5, 70, 74–87, 105–12, 114–15, 119–20, 151
  alpha male, 105–6, 114–15, 117–20
  beta male, 105–6, 114–15, 117–20
  crisis of, 10, 65, 67, 74–5, 77
  hyper-, 5, 11, 43, 77, 114–15
  patriarchy, 2, 5, 7, 9, 11, 17, 68–9, 106–9, 136, 142
  violent, 10, 66, 74, 75–9, 81, 82–7, 119
May, Elaine, 4, 55
Minahan, Dan, 3
Mol, Gretchen, 7, 26, 67, 70
Monroe, Marilyn, 25, 40, 42–5, 48
Mulvey, Laura, 67, 80, 93, 99

neoliberal, 76, 82
Netflix, 7, 90, 105

Once Upon a Time In . . . Hollywood (Sony Pictures Releasing, Tarantino, 2019), 9, 105, 109

Payne, Alexander, 5, 56
Penn, Arthur, 4, 55, 58
performativity, 36
Poison (Zeitgeist Films, Haynes, 1991), 61
postmodern, 6, 58, 60–1, 63–4, 70, 146
Psycho (Paramount Pictures, Hitchcock, 1960), 84, 99
Pulp Fiction (Miramax Films, Tarantino, 1994), 10, 56, 60, 75

Reservoir Dogs (Miramax Films, Tarantino, 1992), 4, 75–6, 83, 86
Rojek, Chris, 23–4
Russell, David O., 56, 64

Schrader, Paul, 55
Schreiber, Michelle, 7, 26, 57, 68–9
Scorsese, Martin, 4, 24, 55, 58
Se7en (Fincher, 1995), 75, 79
sex, lies, and videotape (Miramax Films, Soderbergh, 1989), 4, 56
Silence of the Lambs (Orion Pictures, Demme, 1991), 10, 75, 78–9, 81, 86
Six Feet Under (HBO, 2001–5), 11, 125–7
  death, 11, 125–7, 129–30, 132, 137
  funeral, 11, 126, 129
  funeral director, 126–9, 132, 137
  funeral industry, 131
  funeral service, 126, 130
  social death, 133
  "The Rainbow of Her Reasons" (episode) 125–37
Soderbergh, Steven, 4, 56, 60

Solanas, Valerie, 2–3, 17–18, 20–31, 61–3, 67, 76, 90, 93, 135–6
  SCUM Manifesto (Solanas, 1967), 2, 17–20, 23, 25, 27, 61–2, 90, 135–6
  Up Your Ass (Solanas, unpublished), 23, 25, 62
Star Wars (Twentieth Century Fox, Lucas, 1977), 4, 59
Stone, Oliver, 62, 64

Tarantino, Quentin, 4, 9, 10, 56, 60, 75, 82–3, 105, 109
Taylor, Lili, 3, 17, 21, 26, 61, 69
television, 6, 8, 37, 55, 89–90, 125–37
  made-for-television movie, 10, 29, 35–7
  reality TV, 9, 35, 40, 48–9
The Aviator (Miramax Films, Scorsese, 2004), 24
The Doors (TriStar Pictures, Stone, 1991), 62
The Exorcist (Warner Bros., Friedkin, 1973), 55, 59
The Graduate (United Artists, Nichols, 1967), 58
The Life of Emile Zola (Warner Bros., Dieterle, 1937), 19
The Moth Diaries (IFC Films, Harron, 2011) 8, 10–11, 89–103
  adaptation, 8, 89, 91
  boarding school, 8, 11, 90, 93, 95
  surveillance, 10–11, 90, 92–5;
  see also same-sex desire
The Notorious Bettie Page (Picturehouse, Harron, 2005), 3, 6–7, 10–11, 17–18, 22, 24–6, 28, 30–1, 40, 57, 67–8, 70, 89–90, 93, 97, 103, 106, 108, 141, 146
  conservative, 7, 29, 69, 90
  pin-up, 7, 26, 30, 67, 69, 90, 153
  pornography, 26, 29, 67, 69;
  see also gaze

The People vs. Larry Flynt (Columbia Pictures, Forman, 1996), 20, 31
The Story of Louis Pasteur (Warner Bros., Dieterle, 1936), 19
The Texas Chainsaw Massacre (Bryanston Distribution Company, Hooper, 1974), 6, 66, 85
The Velvet Underground, 19
Troche, Rose, 3, 61, 125
Turner, Graeme, 22, 31
Turner, Guinevere, 5, 7, 26, 31, 57, 63–4, 76, 81, 84, 90, 108, 116, 119, 125

Twilight franchise (Summit Entertainment, 2008–12), 8

Vachon, Christine, 3–4, 7, 57, 60–1, 63
  Killer Films, 3, 61
Warhol, Andy, 2, 17, 19–20, 23, 26–8, 31, 57, 61–3, 69–70, 90, 136
  The Factory, 3, 19, 26–7, 61–2, 69
White, Patricia, 3, 61

EU representative:
Easy Access System Europe
Mustamäe tee 50, 10621 Tallinn, Estonia
Gpsr.requests@easproject.com

www.ingramcontent.com/pod-product-compliance
Lightning Source LLC
Chambersburg PA
CBHW070358240426
43671CB00013BA/2553